W9-BGP-708

Teaching Reading and Writing in Spanish in the Bilingual Classroom

Teaching
Reading and Writing
in Spanish
in the Bilingual Classroom

Yvonne S. Freeman and David E. Freeman

HEINEMANN
Portsmouth, NH

HEINEMANN
A division of Reed Elsevier Inc.
361 Hanover Street
Portsmouth, NH 03801-3912
Offices and agents throughout the world

© 1996 by Yvonne S. Freeman and David E. Freeman
All rights reserved. No part of this book may be reproduced in any form or by any
electronic or mechanical means, including information storage and retrieval systems,
without permission in writing from the publisher, except by a reviewer, who may quote brief
passages in a review.

Library of Congress Cataloging-in-Publication Data
Freeman, Yvonne S.
      Teaching reading and writing in Spanish in the bilingual classroom
   / Yvonne and David Freeman.
          p.   cm.
      Includes bibliographical references and index.
      ISBN 0–435–07231–5
      1. Spanish language—Study and teaching—United States.
   2. Language arts—United States.   3. Bilingual education—United
   States.   4. Literacy—United States.   I. Freeman, David E.
   II. Title.
   LB1577.S7F74   1997
   372.6′044—dc20   96-30430
                                               CIP

Editor: Scott Mahler
Production: J.B. Tranchemontagne
Manufacturing: Louise Richardson
Cover Design: Mary C. Cronin

Printed in the United States of America on acid-free paper
03 02 01 EB   8 9

We dedicate this book to all those bilingual teachers
who are providing the essential primary language literacy instruction
Spanish-speaking children need to succeed in school and in life.
We hope that the ideas and examples we share here
will help spark their teaching.

We want to extend this dedication especially to our daughters,
Mary and Ann, who have now joined the ranks
of bilingual teachers.

CONTENTS

ACKNOWLEDGMENTS

We wish to acknowledge the support of Dr. Alan Crawford on the writing of this book. He has provided encouragement, resources, and valuable feedback on all parts of the manuscript. In addition, we would like to thank two special Venezuelan friends and colleagues: Profesora Marisela Serra and Profesor Jesús Serra. Marisela has carefully read the Spanish portions of this book and offered valuable suggestions for both the Spanish and the English text. Jesús is a poet whose faith in us and reflections about our work have continually encouraged us.

Other colleagues have also been central to this work in progress. Dr. Sabrina Mimms read the entire manuscript and offered us valuable comments and support. Jim Chapman and Della Verdugo also have read the manuscript, and encouraged us as we struggled to make complex theory comprehensible. Responses to the sections of the manuscript from graduate student Margarita Fuentes and students in Yvonne's Bilingual Theory, Methods, and Materials class have helped us fine tune sections. Finally, Dr. Jean Fennacy deserves the credit for planting the seed for the book. She stopped Yvonne one day in the hall of our university several years ago and told her, "You need to write a book about reading in Spanish. Bilingual teachers need it!"

We want to acknowledge the contributions of all the talented teachers who have shared their classroom practices and samples of their students' work with us for this book. They include: Jeff Morris, Sue Piper, Blanca Aguirre, Sue Scott, Carolina Cervantes-Ruiz, Rhonda Dutton, and Carol Fincham. In addition, we want to acknowledge the new bilingual teachers who have shared their stories with us: Francisco Soto, Janie Aranda, and Ann Freeman. All these people have inspired us through their commitment to helping their bilingual students.

We also thank the students whose work we have used to show how writing develops naturally in both Spanish and English in classrooms where teachers follow effective literacy practices.

Finally, a special thanks to our editor, Scott Mahler, whose encouragement and practical suggestions have helped shape this work. We are especially grateful to have an editor who appreciates the richness of the Spanish language and culture and who could give us the kinds of advice that no monolingual editor could have provided.

1

How Do I Teach
Reading and Writing
in Spanish?

How do I teach reading and writing in Spanish? This question is one that both beginning and experienced Spanish/English bilingual teachers often ask themselves. The answer is not an easy one. Many factors influence the kinds of reading and writing programs teachers develop. These factors might include the teacher's own experiences in teaching and in being taught to read and write, the students' literacy backgrounds, state, district, or school requirements, and the materials that are available. Because literacy is so critical for students' academic success, it is important for educators to make informed decisions about their Spanish literacy programs.

In this book we provide teachers, program directors, administrators, and parents with concrete ideas that will support the development of reading and writing programs in Spanish. Through the many scenarios in the book we attempt to bring to life literacy approaches that are effective and empowering for Spanish-speaking children in our schools. We provide descriptions of classroom activities and many references to Spanish children's literature that supports the curriculum we advocate. In addition, we include ideas and checklists to help teachers organize and evaluate their literacy programs.

Research and theory call for strong primary language literacy programs for bilingual students. First language support is essential for first and second language literacy development, as well as for academic and cognitive development. The purpose of this book is not to argue this point of view: The theory and research that support primary language development can be found elsewhere. For further reading in this area, we have provided a short bibliography of key studies that describe in more detail the rationale and theoretical support for teaching English learners in their mother tongue (see Table 1–1).

Our concern in this book is with how theories of literacy development for

Berman, Paul. *Meeting the challenge of language diversity: An evaluation of programs for pupils with limited proficiency in English.* BW Associates (1992).

Collier, Virginia. How long? A synthesis of research on academic achievement in a second language. *TESOL Quarterly, 23,* (3) 509–532 (1989).

Collier, Virginia. A synthesis of studies examining long-term language-minority student data on academic achievement. *Bilingual Research Journal, 16,* (1,2) 87–212 (1992).

Collier, V. Acquiring a second language for school. *Directions in Language and Education.* Washington, D.C.: National Clearinghouse for Bilingual Education, 1.4 (1995).

Crawford, James. *Bilingual education: History, politics, theory and practice.* Los Angeles: Bilingual Education Services (1995).

Cummins, Jim. The acquisition of English as a second language. *Kids come in all languages: Reading instruction for ESL students.* (Spangenberg-Urbschat, K., and Pritchard, R., eds.) Newark: International Reading Association, 36–62 (1994).

Cummins, Jim. *Negotiating identities: Education for empowerment in a diverse society.* Sacramento: CABE (1996).

Daniels, Harvey, (ed.). *Not only English: Affirming America's multilingual heritage.* Urbana, IL: National Council of Teachers of English (1990).

TABLE 1–1, Part 1: References for Bilingual Support

Spanish readers and writers translate into practice in bilingual Spanish/English classes. To help teachers evaluate their language arts programs, we introduce three checklists in this chapter. These checklists will be referred to throughout the book, because they provide a base for evaluating all the literacy lessons that we describe. In order to help readers visualize from the beginning how these checklists relate to classroom practice, we also include in this chapter examples of language arts lessons in bilingual classrooms.

In Chapter Two we explain two different views of the reading process and present evidence that supports a socio-psycholinguistic view. In Chapters Three and Four we describe the different reading methods that have been used to teach Spanish reading. We evaluate them using the checklists and provide positive alternatives to methods that do not reflect effective practices. In Chapters Five and Six we discuss spelling development, making a comparison between English and Spanish spelling. When teachers understand how writing develops, they can better evaluate their students' writing progress.

Dolson, David, and Mayer, Jan. Longitudinal study of three program models for language-minority students. *Bilingual Research Journal, 16,* (1,2) 105–157 (1992).

Freeman, David, and Freeman, Yvonne. *Between worlds: Access to second language acquisition.* Portsmouth: Heinemann (1994).

Freeman, David, and Freeman, Yvonne. Strategies for promoting the primary languages of all students. *The Reading Teacher, 46,* (7) 552–558 (1993).

Freeman, Yvonne, and Freeman, David. *Whole language for second language learners.* Portsmouth: Heinemann (1992).

Krashen, Stephen D. *Under attack: The case against bilingual education.* Culver City: Language Education Associates (1996).

Krashen, Stephen D., and Biber, Douglas. *On course: Bilingual education's success in California.* Sacramento: California Association of Bilingual Education (1988).

Ramírez, David. *Final report: Longitudinal study of structured English immersion strategy, early-exit and late-exit bilingual education programs.* United States Department of Education (1991).

Skutnabb-Kangas, Tove. *Bilingualism or not: The education of minorities.* Clevedon, England: Multilingual Matters (1983).

TABLE 1–1, Part 2

Although we provide examples of classroom practice throughout the book, Chapter Seven brings the theory and methodologies discussed in the previous chapters together by describing positive practices, including the use of literature studies and thematic units. In addition, we suggest materials that can support an enriched Spanish literacy program. The examples we provide in this final chapter also include ideas for helping students move back and forth naturally between reading and writing in Spanish and in English as they become both bilingual and biliterate.

Reading Instruction

We begin our discussion of reading by describing how two teachers introduced thematic units that centered on animals. The first unit was developed by a kindergarten teacher and the second by a fourth-grade teacher. Both teachers have Spanish/ English bilingual classrooms that include native Spanish speakers and native English speakers. Although reading and

CHECKLIST FOR EFFECTIVE READING INSTRUCTION

1. Do students value themselves as readers and do they value reading?
2. Do teachers read frequently to students from a wide variety of genres?
3. Do students see teachers engaged in reading for pleasure as well as for information?
4. Do students have a wide variety of reading materials to choose from and time to read?
5. Do students make good choices and read a variety of genres for authentic purposes?
6. Do students regard reading as meaning making at all times?
7. Are students effective readers? That is, do they make a balanced use of all three cueing systems?
8. Are students efficient readers? That is, do they make a minimal use of cues to construct meaning?
9. Do students have opportunities to talk about what they have read, making connections between the reading and their own experiences?
10. Do students revise their individual understandings of texts in response to the comments of classmates?
11. Is there evidence that students' writing is influenced by what they read?
12. Are students provided with appropriate strategy lessons if they experience difficulties in their reading?

FIGURE 1–1, Part 1: Reading Checklist (English)

writing are never separated in these two classes, in the first examples, we emphasize reading.

To evaluate reading instruction, we offer two checklists: one for effective reading instruction and one for effective materials selection. The teachers whose units we describe below use these checklists all through the year. They know that literacy development takes time. They review their reading curriculum and also monitor their students' progress in reading by asking the questions from the checklist (see Figure 1–1). We invite you to use these checklists for that same purpose.

Developing an effective literacy program depends on having a variety of stories and content texts that are written at appropriate levels for the different students in a class. The fourth question on the checklist focuses on this need for providing the right reading materials. The right materials are those that have characteristics that make reading and learning to read easier for all students.

LISTA DE PREGUNTAS PARA VERIFICAR SI LA ENSEÑANZA DE LA LECTURA ES EFECTIVA.

1. ¿Valoran los estudiantes la lectura y se valoran a sí mismos como lectores?
2. ¿Leen frecuentemente los maestros a sus estudiantes materiales de diversos géneros literarios?
3. ¿Observan los estudiantes a sus maestros leyendo bien sea por placer o también para buscar y obtener información?
4. ¿Disponen los estudiantes de una amplia variedad de materiales de lectura para escoger lo que quieren leer? ¿Disponen de tiempo para leer?
5. ¿Se les ofrecen a los estudiantes oportunidades para escoger los materiales? ¿Leen ellos con fines verdaderamente auténticos diversos materiales de lectura correspondientes a diversos géneros literarios?
6. ¿Al leer, consideran los estudiantes que la lectura es en todo momento una construcción de significados?
7. ¿Se considera que los estudiantes son lectores efectivos? Es decir, ¿utilizan en forma balanceada los tres sistemas de claves (grafofónico, sintáctico y semántico)?
8. ¿Se considera que los estudiantes son lectores eficientes? Es decir, ¿hacen uso mínimo de las claves para la construcción del significado?
9. ¿Se les proporcionan oportunidades para hablar acerca de lo que han leído, pudiendo de esta manera relacionar la lectura con sus propias experiencias?
10. ¿Revisan y comparan su propia comprensión de los textos en atención a los comentarios de sus compañeros de clase?
11. ¿Se observa en la escritura de los estudiantes la influencia de lo que leen?
12. ¿Les ofrecen los maestros ayuda mediante estrategias apropiadas cuando confrontan problemas con la lectura?

FIGURE 1–1, Part 2: Reading Checklist (Spanish)

The following checklist (see Figure 1–2) can help teachers determine whether or not they are providing their students with good reading materials.

When teachers engage children with a variety of texts that support reading, students come to value reading and to value themselves as readers (Goodman, 1986b). The best reading instruction occurs naturally in the context of thematic instruction. The two teachers described below involved their students in reading and writing as they explored a theme based on animals. We describe how each teacher introduced the theme and list the materials they used. We use the questions from the checklist to evaluate each unit.

CHARACTERISTICS OF TEXTS THAT SUPPORT READING

1. Are the materials predictable? Prediction is based on the use of repetitive patterns, cumulative patterns, rhyme, alliteration, and rhythm. Books are also predictable if students have background knowledge about the concepts presented.
2. For picture books, do the visuals provide support for the text? Is the placement of the text and pictures predictable and easy to follow?
3. Are the materials interesting and/or imaginative?
4. Is the language in the texts natural? For Spanish materials, was the book originally written in Spanish or translated from English? If the book was translated, how good is the translation?
5. Do the situations and characters in the book represent the experiences and backgrounds of the students in the class?

CARACTERISTICAS DE LOS TEXTOS QUE APOYAN LA LECTURA

1. ¿Permiten la predicción los materiales de lectura que se utilizan? Los materiales que permiten la predicción son aquellos que contienen patrones repetitivos, acumulativos, rima, aliteración, y ritmo. También son predecibles aquellos libros que presentan conceptos sobre los cuales los estudiantes ya tienen conocimientos previos.
2. En el caso de los libros ilustrados, ¿Proporcionan las ilustraciones apoyo al texto? ¿Están el texto y las ilustraciones colocados de una manera predecible y fácil de seguir?
3. ¿Son los materiales de lectura interesantes y/o imaginativos?
4. ¿Está provisto de naturalidad el lenguaje que contienen los textos? En el caso de aquellos materiales escritos en español, ¿fueron los textos escritos originalmente en este idioma, o fueron traducidos del inglés? Si fueron traducidos, ¿está bien hecha la traducción?
5. ¿Representan las situaciones y los personajes que aparecen en el libro las experiencias de los estudiantes de la clase?

FIGURE 1–2: Characteristics of Texts that Support Reading

Animal Unit with Reading Focus—Kindergarten

<Todas las cosas cambian al crecer.> (Allen & Rotner, 1991, pp. 4–5) (All things change as they grow.). This is the text for the first two pages of the big book, *Cambios* (*Change*), which Teresa reads to begin her unit on animals for the kindergarten students in her bilingual classroom. She then brainstorms with her students a list of all the things they know that

change and grow. Once the children have listed many things including *las flores* (flowers), *mi perro* (my dog), and *mi hermanito* (my little brother), Teresa reads the rest of the big book to the children so that they can see how many of the things they thought of are also included in the book. The book ends with several examples of baby animals and a human baby growing up. Teresa then moves to another big book and reads the first page:

> ¿Has visto alguna vez perritos chiquititos? Son preciosos, ¿no es verdad? Los animales nacen chiquitos. Pero todos crecen hasta llegar a ser igualitos a sus padres (Kratky, 1991, p. 3).

Translation:

> Have you ever seen little puppies? They are precious, aren't they? Animals are born small. But they all grow up to be like their parents.

For Teresa this book, *Los animales y sus crías* (*Animals and Their Young*), is important because it introduces topics such as how mothers care for their young, which animals are hatched from eggs and which are born alive. The topics in this book fascinate Teresa's young students, and the colorful pictures attract them. As they listen to their teacher read the first page, they watch her track the words by drawing her hand under them as she reads. Several of the children focus on the words. Others attend more to the pictures.

Many hands go up. The kindergartners are anxious to tell their teacher and classmates about their experiences with puppies, kittens, and baby bunnies. Teresa's choice of topic has engaged her young learners. To complement this content book, Teresa will later read the delightful story *Oli, el pequeño elefante* (*Oli, the Baby Elephant*) (Bos and De Beer, 1989) which reinforces the key concepts about animals her young learners will investigate during the unit.

Teresa has other small books in her classroom to read to the children. She also encourages her students to read these books alone or with a partner. The small books reinforce the concepts introduced by the big books and the story book. These include the series *Libros del Rincón* (1993), four colorful, hardback books that explain how mothers care for their babies, *Un cariñito, mi bebé* (*A Caress, My Baby*) (Paqueforet, 1993), how and where animals move, *A pasear, mi bebé* (*About Moving Around, My Baby*) (Paqueforet, 1993), where and how animals sleep, *A dormir, mi bebé* (*About Sleeping, My Baby*) (Paqueforet, 1993), and what animals eat and where they get their food, *A comer, mi bebé* (*About Eating, My Baby*) (Paqueforet, 1993).

Another book, *¿Cómo son los animales bebés?* (*What Are Animal Babies Like?*) (Kuchalla, 1987), from the *¿Cómo son?* (*What Are They Like?*) series, is particularly good for emergent readers. Working alone or in pairs, students can construct meaning as they read because the pictures support the text so well. Teresa's students love identifying different animal body parts, so the class reads together *¿De quién es este rabo?* (*Whose Tail is This?*) (Barberis, 1974). The children then read together in small groups with the teacher or the teacher's aide books like *Pistas de animales* (*Animal Tracks*) (Drew, 1993), *Veo, veo colas* (*I See, I See Tails*) (Kratky, 1995), *Orejas* (*Ears*) (Kratky, 1995), *Patas* (*Feet*) (Beck, 1994), and *¿Quién está en la choza?* (*Who's in the Hut?*) (Parkes, 1990). These limited text picture books are very predictable. The patterns help students begin to build meaning as they make connections between the text and the illustrations.

Teresa includes both reading and writing in other activities she uses to introduce her unit. For example, she brainstorms with the children what they know about different animals. For this activity, she puts pictures on the bulletin board, and the children tell her what they notice about the animals in the pictures. They use their background experiences and ideas they have picked up during reading. Teresa prints what the children say under the pictures so that they can later read what they have dictated and can also go back to their own words during writing time.

Teresa's unit introduction involves her students with a number of texts whose characteristics support reading. Teresa reads to her students every day, and she helps students make good choices for their own reading as they become independent readers. She is sure to include a variety of genres when she reads so that her students will become familiar with both fiction and nonfiction texts in their study of animals. Teresa's students focus on meaning. She observes how they use the three cueing systems as they read. Since Teresa's students are emergent readers, she is more concerned with keeping them engaged in reading than in giving them specific strategy lessons. She realizes that some of her students simply need more time, not more instruction. Teresa's students love to talk about what she reads and what they read. In Teresa's classroom this talk is essential for building and developing the concepts introduced in the reading. Teresa's students are surrounded by interesting and imaginative texts written in language that is natural and engaging. All these elements are key to these children's early literacy development. Table 1–2 lists the books from the kindergarten animal units (both reading and writing).

Allen, Majorie, and Rotner, S. *Cambios*. Carmel, CA: Hampton Brown (1991).

Barberis. *¿De quién es este rabo?*, *Colección Duende*. Valladolid, Spain: Miñon (1974).

Beck, Jennifer. *Patas*, *Literacy 2000*, *Nivel 3*. Crystal Lake: Ribgy (1994).

Bos, Burny, and De Beer, Hans. *Oli, el pequeño elefante*. Barcelona, Spain: Editorial Lumen (1989).

Drew, David. *Pistas de animales*. Crystal Lake: Rigby (1993).

Ediciones Litexsa Venezolana, (ed.). *Aprender a contar*. Caracas, Venezuela: Cromotip (1987).

Kratky, Lada Josefa. *Los animales y sus crías*, *¡Qué maravilla!* Carmel: Hampton-Brown (1991).

Kratky, Lada Josefa. *Orejas*, *Pan y Canela*, *Colección B*. Carmel: Hampton-Brown (1995).

Kuchalla, Susan. *¿Cómo son los animales bebés?*, *¿Cómo son?* México, D.F.: SITESA (1987).

Paqueforet, Marcus. *A comer, mi bebé*, *Libros del Rincón*. México, D.F.: Hachette Latinoamérica/SEP (1993).

Paqueforet, Marcus. *A dormir, mi bebé*, *Libros del Rincón*. México, D.F.: Hachette Latinoamérica/SEP (1993).

Paqueforet, Marcus. *A pasear, mi bebé*, *Libros del Rincón*. México, D.F.: Hachette Latinoamérica/SEP (1993).

Paqueforet, Marcus. *Un cariñito, mi bebé*, *Libros del Rincón*. México, D.F.: Hachette Latinoamérica/SEP (1993).

Parkes, Brenda. *¿Quién está en la choza?* (Flores, B., Trans.) Crystal Lake: Rigby (1990).

Sempere, Vicky. *ABC*. Caracas, Venezuela: Ediciones Ekaré-Banco del Libro (1987).

TABLE 1–2: Literature for Kindergarten Animal Unit

Animal Unit with Reading Focus—Fourth Grade

At the beginning of the school year, Roberto, a fourth-grade Spanish/ English bilingual teacher brainstorms with his students questions they have about their world. One main overarching concern his students have is how to care for our earth. Roberto reads them the book, *Conservación* (*Conservation*) (Ingpen and Dunkle, 1991), a Spanish translation of a

Animals of the World) (Granowsky, 1986), *El bosque tropical* (*The Tropical Forest*) (Cowcher, 1992), *Podría ser un mamífero* (*It Could Be a Mammal*) (Fowler, 1991), and *La culebra verde* (*The Green Snake*) (Urbina).

To culminate this unit of study, Roberto and his students decide to make a class big book. Students work in groups, and each group creates a page that includes a picture of an endangered animal and information about the animal. They plan a day when they can present their findings to other classes in the school. They decorate the room with pictures of animals in their natural habitats. They also find recordings of wild animal cries. Each group creates a large scale model of the animal they have studied. Then they design centers where they group the models of animals that live in similar environments. They put up butcher-paper backgrounds to represent the habitats.

As other classes come in, the students are divided into small groups and directed to one of the centers. There they examine the models as they listen to the expert groups tell about the different animals. The groups rotate through the centers so they can learn about all the animals Roberto's class has studied. This culminating event provides a natural way for Roberto's students to present the knowledge they have developed. At the same time, students from other classes, particularly the third graders, get excited about what they will be doing when they are in Roberto's fourth-grade class.

Roberto drew on his students' background knowledge and interests as he introduced the important topic of animals in danger of extinction. Students in his classroom were immersed in reading meaningful texts to answer their own questions. They increased their vocabulary and developed important concepts as they read and discussed a variety of engaging books. Since Roberto's students are older readers, he carefully observed their reading to determine how they used the different cueing systems. For students who were not making a balanced use of graphophonic, syntactic, and semantic cues, Roberto planned specific reading strategy lessons. We will say more about these lessons in Chapter Two. (Table 1–3 lists the books from the units for fourth grade.)

Writing Instruction

Students need to become proficient writers as well as proficient readers. Roberto and Teresa, like other good teachers, always combine reading and writing activities. Below, we present two more examples of teachers introducing animal themes. These teachers also combine reading with writing. In our description of these units we focus on the writing. In order to contrast younger, emergent writers with more proficient writers, we again pro-

Barrett, Norman. *Cocodrilos y caimanes, Biblioteca Gráfica.* New York: Franklin Watts (1991).

Barrett, Norman. *Monos y simios, Biblioteca Gráfica.* New York: Franklin Watts (1991).

Browne, Anthony. *Gorila.* (Esteva, C., Trans., *A la orilla del viento.*) México, D.F.: Fondo de Cultura Económica (1991).

Browne, Anthony. *Zoológico.* (Esteva, C., Trans., *A la orilla del viento.*) Méxcio, D.F.: Fondo de Cultura Económica (1993).

Cherry, Lynne. *La ceiba majestuosa: Un cuento del bosque lluvioso.* Boston: Houghton Mifflin (1996).

Comerlati, Mara. *Conoce nuestros mamíferos.* Caracas, Venezuela: Ediciones Ekaré Banco del Libro (1983).

Cowcher, Helen. *El bosque tropical.* New York: Scholastic (1992).

Fowler, Allan. *Podría ser un mamífero.* (Marcuse, A.E., Trans., *Mis primeros libros de ciencia.*) Chicago: Childrens Press (1991).

Goodall, Jane. *La familia del chimpancé.* México, D.F.: SITESA (1991).

Granowsky, Alvin. *Los animales del mundo.* (Johnson, C., ed., *Especies del mundo en peligro de extinción.*) Lexington: Schoolhouse Press (1986).

Hofer, Angelika, and Ziesler, Günter. *La familia del león.* México, D.F.: SITESA (1992).

Ingpen, Robert, and Dunkle, Margaret. *Conservación.* México, D.F.: Editorial Origen S.A. (1991).

Pratt, Kristin Joy. *Un paseo por el bosque lluvioso.* Nevada City: Dawn Publications (1993).

Urbina, Joaquín. *La culebra verde.* Caracas, Venezuela: Gráficas Armitano.

Wexo, John Bonnett. *Los animales en extinción.* Zoobooks (1981).

Willow, Diane, and Jacques, Laura. *Dentro de la selva tropical.* Watertown: Charlesbridge Publishing (1993).

Wright, Alexandra. *¿Les echaremos de menos?* Watertown: Charlesbridge Publishing (1993).

Zak, Monica. *Salven mi selva.* México, D.F.: Sistemas Técnicos de Edición (1989).

Zawisza, Tita. *Conoce a nuestros insectos.* Caracas, Venezuela: Ediciones Ekaré-Banco del Libro (1982).

TABLE 1–3: Literature for Grade 4 Units

CHECKLIST FOR EFFECTIVE WRITING INSTRUCTION

1. Do teachers model the steps they go through to choose topics? Do they help students to go through these same steps as they choose topics to write about?
2. Are students encouraged to draw upon their own experiences when they choose topics? Do they write for authentic purposes?
3. Do students make connections between their reading and writing? Do they see that reading provides ideas for writing?
4. Do students keep and update a list of topics that they have written about and that they plan to write about?
5. Do students see writing as a process, and do they understand the various activities they should engage in as they move a piece of writing toward its final form?
6. Does the classroom have ample accessible literature, content, and resource books for students to reference as they write?
7. Are students allowed to invent spelling, drawing on their internal phonics hypotheses and their pictures of words derived from their reading experiences as they write?
8. Do students have opportunities to share their writing with others? Is there authentic response which is both critical and sensitive to the writer's needs?

FIGURE 1–4, Part 1: Writing Checklist (English)

vide an example from kindergarten and one from fourth grade. To evaluate their writing programs the teachers in these classes use the Checklist for Effective Writing Instruction (see Figure 1–4). We invite you to use this checklist to evaluate your own lessons.

Writers go through a series of stages as they write. These include choosing a topic, gathering information, writing a draft, revising the draft, editing, and presenting their writing to classmates for discussion. This may lead to further revision. Younger writers may do less revision, but they follow the same general pattern. The books teachers read to students or that students read by themselves serve as sources of ideas for writing and models of the finished product. As students write, they read and reread what they have written. The lessons described below demonstrate the important role teachers play as catalysts in the writing process.

Animal Lessons with Writing—Kindergarten

Jeff teaches kindergarten in a rural community with a high Hispanic population. In his classroom he has both native Spanish and native English speakers. In his bilingual program, he teaches content in both Spanish and

LISTA DE PREGUNTAS PARA VERIFICAR SI LA ENSEÑANZA DE LA ESCRITURA ES EFECTIVA

1. ¿Ejemplifican los maestros los pasos que ellos siguen para escoger los tópicos? ¿Ayudan ellos a sus estudiantes a seguir estos mismos pasos cuando escogen los tópicos sobre los que quieren escribir?
2. ¿Se estimula a los estudiantes que escriben a tomar en cuenta sus propias experiencias cuando escogen los tópicos acerca de los cuales van a escribir? ¿Escriben ellos con fines verdaderamente auténticos y comunicativos?
3. ¿Establecen ellos relaciones entre lo que leen y lo que escriben? ¿Pueden percibir que la lectura les proporciona ideas para la escritura?
4. ¿Mantienen permanentemente los estudiantes una lista de los tópicos sobre los cuales ya han escrito y de aquellos otros sobre los que están planificando escribir?
5. ¿Perciben ellos que la escritura es un proceso? ¿Entienden ellos que deben desarrollar una serie de actividades antes de poder llegar a la escritura final de un texto?
6. ¿Disponen ellos en el aula de una amplia variedad de libros de literatura y otros materiales de consulta que les puedan servir de referencia cuando van a escribir?
7. Cuando ellos escriben, ¿se les permite inventar su propia ortografía partiendo de sus hipótesis fónicas internas y de las imágenes que se han formado de las palabras a partir de sus experiencias previas con la lectura?
8. ¿Tienen ellos oportunidades de compartir con otras personas lo que escriben? ¿Reciben de estas personas respuestas auténticas que les servirán de apoyo a su sensibilidad y necesidades como escritores?

FIGURE 1–4, Part 2: Writing Checklist (Spanish)

English. Jeff involves his students in a number of activities that gradually move them into writing.

Early in their kindergarten year, Jeff's students study animals. Although they are interested in all kinds of animals, the children are especially intrigued by wild African animals. One way that Jeff introduces concepts and print about wild animals is through a lion hunt chant. Jeff uses pictures of the animals in the chant including the lion, the elephant, the monkey, the zebra, and the giraffe. He tracks the words on a chart as the children chant with him:

> ¿Dónde está el león?
> ¿Está bañándose en el río?
> No, el elefante está bañándose en el río.
>
> ¿Está jugando en el árbol?
> No, el mono está jugando en el árbol.

¿Está pastando en el prado?
No, la cebra está pastando en el prado.

¿Está comiendo hojas de los árboles?
No, la jirafa está comiendo hojas de los árboles.

¿Está deslizándose hacia arriba en el árbol?
No, la boa constrictora está deslizándose hacia arriba en el árbol.

¿Está cazando animales para comer?
Sí, está cazando animales para comer. Sh . . . Sh . . . Sh . . . .

Translation:

Where is the lion?
Is he taking a bath in the river?
No, the elephant is bathing in the river.

Is he playing in the tree?
No, the monkey is playing in the tree.

Is he grazing in the meadow?
No, the zebra is grazing in the meadow.

Is he eating the leaves of the trees?
No, the giraffe is eating the leaves of the trees.

Is he wiggling up in the tree?
No, the boa constrictor is wiggling up in the tree.

Is he hunting animals to eat?
Yes, he is hunting animals to eat . . . Sh . . . Sh . . . Sh. . . .

In addition to having students chant the words, Jeff writes the basic expressions of the chant on strips for two pocket charts. For example, a strip might read <un elefante bañándose> (an elephant bathing) or <un león cazando> (a lion hunting). In one chart the words are in order. In the other chart the words are mixed up. Working in pairs or small groups, the students put the words in the second chart in the same order as the model.

Jeff also uses the lion chant as a model for small books the students take home to read to their families. He makes and illustrates his own book based on the chant. The first page asks, <¿Dónde está el léon?> (Where is the lion?). Under the words is the picture of a lion. Each of the following pages focuses on one of the other animals in the chant. The pages have a repetitive pattern. For example the second page (see Figure 1–5) has a picture of an elephant and the words, <¿Está bañándose en el río? No, el elefante está bañándose en el río.>.

The student books are exactly like the teacher's model. Jeff collates and staples the student books ahead of time since his kindergarten students have difficulty doing this task on their own without considerable adult supervision.

As Jeff creates these books, he models the writing and sometimes does a directed drawing on each page with the children. To create each page, Jeff works with small groups of six to nine students. For example, when working on the page that says, <¿Está bañándose en el río?> (Is he bathing in the river?) <No, el elefante está bañándose en el río.> (No, the elephant is bathing in the river.), Jeff clips a copy of *¿Donde está el león? (Where is the Lion?)* on an easel so that all of the students in the group can see it easily. Jeff and the children write the word *elefante (elephant)* at the bottom of the page. Jeff models the correct letter formation, says the name of the letter and helps the students to hear the letter sound as each letter of the word *elefante* is written. In this way he can teach the mechanics of letter formation and letter sounds and names in meaningful context.

The students then read the elephant page chorally with Jeff as they

FIGURE 1–5: Elephant Page from the *Lion Hunt Chant* book

¿Está bañandose en el río?
No, el elefante está bañandose en el río.

track the words from left to right and from top to bottom with their finger. Although Jeff is modeling the tracking of the words exactly, the kindergarten students often just make sweeping motions, especially at the beginning of the year. This is fine because they are getting the general idea. Their tracking becomes more accurate as the year progresses.

Jeff also works with the students to make a second kind of take-home book. This is created at an independent writing center. At this center the students can make their own original books from sheets of photocopy paper that are sandwiched and stapled between colored construction paper. Students use felt pens, regular pens, colored pencils, and crayons to write and illustrate their books, which they will later read to their peers during author's chair. Hanging on the wall next to the writing center is a word bank that reflects the theme that the class is currently working on. The word bank is a pocket chart that has pictures of things that students might want to write about. Next to the pictures are the words for the pictures, which are color coded in Spanish and English. For example, next to a picture of a lion is the word *lion* written in orange and *león* written in green. The children know that the orange words are English and the green words are Spanish. As they write their books, the children can choose to copy words from the word bank, or they can use scribble writing, random letters, initial letters, or invented spelling, depending on their developmental stage.

The students spend much class time talking and reading about animals. Books such as *ABC* (Sempere, 1987), which is an alphabet book about animals, help the students focus on sounds and letters with silly rhymes. For example, the letter *c* is emphasized with a picture of five pigs eating cherries, squash, fish, coconuts, and beans. The rhyme reads:

Cuatro cochinos comían
cinco ciruelas grandotas,
con coco, cazón y casabe
y cuarenta caraotas. (pp. 8–9)

Translation:

Four pigs were eating
five huge cherries
with coconut, shark and squash
and forty beans.

The counting book, *Aprender a contar* (*Learning to Count*) (Lavie, 1987) also reinforces both the numbers one to ten and the names of different animals. In this book a little boy left alone invites many animals into his house. When his mother comes home, he renames all the animals as he explains what occurred:

> Nos estábamos divirtiendo mucho
> riendo y alborotando todos juntos,
> cuando mi mamá regresó y encontró
> la ranita, el conejo, el tucán, el gato,
> el mono, el perro, el cocodrilo,
> el tigrito, el burrito y el elefantito.
> Al ver que habíamos revuelto toda la casa,
> echó a todos los animales.
> Ahora tengo cero animales y vuelvo a estar aburrido.
> Otro día habrá que portarse mejor.

Translation:

> We were enjoying ourselves very much
> laughing and making a racket all together,
> when my mother returned and found
> the little frog, the rabbit, the toucan, the cat,
> the monkey, the dog, the crocodile,
> the little tiger, the little donkey, and the little elephant.
> When she saw that we had messed up all the house,
> she threw out all the animals.
> Now I have zero animals and I'm bored again.
> Another day we will have to behave better.

During these activities, Jeff's students are developing academic concepts as well as literacy. Using an opaque projector, Jeff shines pictures of animals such as elephants and lions onto large pieces of butcher paper. The projector allows Jeff to blow up the pictures to large sizes. He then uses the pictures to draw outlines of the animals. The children paint the animals and draw in the proper background settings. These murals are kept up on the walls throughout the unit. When students are working on projects, a cassette tape of wild animal sounds plays in the background to develop that sense and stimulate further discussion among the children.

As an additional activity, students in small groups sort pictures of animals into different categories such as <los que viven en la selva> (those who live in the jungle), <los que viven en el prado> (those that live in the meadow), <los que comen prado> (those that eat grass), or <los que comen carne> (those that eat meat). Together the class makes charts to record what they have learned. For example, after students sort pictures of animals by their outer covering, Jeff puts up a chart with several columns. At the top of each column is a piece of material that resembles one kind of covering—fur, scales, leather, or feathers. Students put their animal pictures up on the chart under the appropriate heading and then label each picture.

Some teachers might not consider any of the activities we've described so far as *writing* in the usual sense, but the activities do represent early stages of writing. Students are associating words with pictures. The alphabet books help them recognize the letters in the words. They are putting words together into patterns. They are learning how pages are assembled into a book. In all of these activities, students are actively constructing meaning using print. These experiences are the important first steps toward independent writing.

As a final activity, the children work in small groups to create a class big book of *Animales salvajes* (*Wild Animals*). This book is also modeled on the lion chant. It features the same animals and focuses on where they live. Each page has one of two pattern sentences with a blank space <_____ viven en la selva> (_____ live in the jungle), or <_____ viven en prados> (_____ live in the meadows). Using animal stencils, the students trace and then cut out the animals from the chant and decide on their setting. If their animal is a grasslands animal like an elephant, it is pasted on yellow paper. If it is a jungle animal like a monkey, it is pasted on light green paper. (Jeff has the students use light green because the trees and grass will be dark green.) The illustrations are particularly striking if they are done entirely from colored construction paper. The students cut the animals, trees, grass, rivers, sun, and so on, from the construction paper and glue the items onto the large twelve-by-eighteen-inch construction paper (yellow or green depending on the animal's habitat). This becomes the actual page of the book. It is the same sheet that has the pattern sentence written on it.

After their pages are assembled, the children write the name of the animal on the page. They use the books, charts, and labeled pictures around the room to help them spell the animal names. Each student in a group that creates a page signs it. Once the book is finished, it is laminated and stays in the classroom for students to look at and read together (see Figure 1–6).

These activities are the beginning of writing development for the children. The students in Jeff's class continue to develop their writing as the year progresses. They share their writing with their classmates and are encouraged at all stages to express their ideas using drawings and invented spellings. Because the words they want to write are available on the classroom walls and in big and little books, Jeff's kindergartners can begin to write from early in the year, and they start to make the important connection between reading and writing.

tucanes _____ viven en selvas.

FIGURE 1–6: Page from *Animales Salvajes*

Animal Lessons with Writing—Fourth Grade

la bosque es verde con muchos animales bien bonitos ai serpientes con muchos flores en los arboles los arboles son verdes unos son grandes y unos pequeños ai unos rios con muchos pescados pirañas muchos pajaros volan por los arboles porque los arboles son bien bonitos

Translation:

the forest is green with many animals very beautiful there are snakes with many flowers in the trees the trees are green some are big and some are small there are rivers with many piranha fish many birds fly through the trees because the trees are very beautiful

This journal entry comes from Ricardo, a fourth-grade Hispanic student in a rural community in the central valley of California. Although his spelling and punctuation are not conventional, his writing shows that he has started to develop images of the tropical rain forest through the study he and his classmates have been doing in Susan's bilingual class.

Susan involves her students in many different activities during their thematic study of *el bosque lluvioso* (the rain forest). She begins by brainstorming with the students to answer <¿Qué sabemos acerca del bosque

For their final project students working in pairs choose a rain forest animal or plant. They conduct research on their animal or plant and use this information as they plan an unusual presentation. They write up their information in interview format. Then, they make a mask that represents their plant or animal. One student wears the mask and the other student conducts the interview. As their classmates watch, they pose and answer questions that reflect what they have discovered. Through this process, they learn that different genres of writing can be used to present different kinds of information.

This unit not only involves students in reading and writing and learning about the rain forest, but it also helps them begin to think about important environmental issues. In his last journal entry Felipe explained what he learned during the unit:

> yo aprendi que la gente vive en la selva tambien que cuando los ombres cortan los arboles estan destruyendo las casas de los pajaros y que unas veces cuando cortan los arboles los animales se pueden murir y que en la selva no ay tods los tipos de animales

Translation:

> I learned that people live in the jungle too and that when men cut the trees they are destroying the homes of the birds and that sometimes when they cut the trees the animals can die and that in the jungle there are all kinds of animals

In Susan's classroom students are encouraged to write informally to express their ideas and feelings without the fear that their invented spellings will be criticized. At the same time, when they write to *publish* as the students did with their poetry, their work is revised after conferencing and carefully edited by peers and the teacher.

The readings and activities Susan's students engage in are interesting and relevant and lead to authentic writing. Susan makes a point of demonstrating the steps she goes through to choose a topic and then helps students move through those same steps. She encourages her students to draw on their backgrounds and interests as they write. She ensures that ample class time is available for the talking and reading that leads to effective writing. Susan's students see writing as a process. They understand that different kinds of writing are treated differently. The poems are carefully edited, but much of the informal writing is left in rough draft form. Because her students read every day and because the classroom is filled with interesting books, Susan's students have access to the resources they need as models and sources of information for their writing. Susan also provides time and encouragement for students to share their writing with one another on a regular basis. Susan's class has all the elements students need to grow as writers.

In the chapters that follow we will offer many other examples of literacy practices in bilingual classrooms. In addition, we will present the theory and research that support the kind of teaching we have described in these four scenarios. Through literature, thematic study, interactive activities, opportunities for choice, and meaningful reading and writing experiences, all students can become competent readers and writers of both Spanish and English.

2
Two Approaches to Teaching Reading

Reading instruction can look very different in different classrooms, even in the same school. If we could peek into Alicia's bilingual second-grade class during reading time, this is what we'd see. A poster of various sized eggs and the animals that come from them is tacked up on the bulletin board with the words, "Animals that lay eggs" <Los animales que ponen huevos>, neatly printed below. On one of the walls there are construction paper eggs that have been decorated with bits of colored paper. Another wall has drawings of the inside of an egg that the children have neatly colored and labeled. In one corner of the room there are several computer stations, and in another corner there is a neat shelf of basal anthologies, along with some trade books.

The twenty-seven children in the class have been divided into five groups, three for Spanish reading and two for English. Right now, four of the groups are busy at centers doing various activities. At one center students are finishing pages in a take-home book which consists of pictures of animals that come from eggs with the name of the animal labeled beneath it. The students are coloring the picture of each animal and copying the text label in their own handwriting on the line underneath the printed text. One group at this center is working with the English version of the book and another group is working in Spanish with the bilingual aide. Other children are at the computers working on a program that helps them practice basic vocabulary words in Spanish and English using the CD-ROM program, *Lyric Language* (Knowles and Morse, 1992). Still others are working on an art project with plastic eggs that nylon stockings come in. They are following a model provided and making a clay duck to go into the egg.

Meanwhile, Alicia is sitting in a small circle with the four children who comprise her middle Spanish reading group. First, Alicia shows the children a list of words that she has printed on a paper: *pato* (duck), *huevo* (egg), *tiempo* (time), *pronto* (soon), *cinco* (five), *nido* (nest), and *dijo* (said).

She begins by reading the words to the students and then asking them some questions about the words:

ALICIA: ¿Qué notan ustedes en estas palabras?

ALICIA: What did you notice about these words?

FELICIANA: Un pato pone huevos.

FELICIANA: A duck lays eggs.

ALICIA: Sí, pero no estamos hablando de las palabras. Estamos viendo las letras de las palabras. ¿Tienen algo en común las letras dentro de las palabras?

ALICIA: Yes, but we are not talking about the words. We are looking at the letters of the words. Do the letters in the words have anything in common?

MARCO: Todas las palabras terminan en la letra o.

MARCO: All of the words end with the letter o.

ALICIA: Muy bien, Marco. ¿Cuántas sílabas hay en cada palabra?

ALICIA: Very good, Marco. How many syllables are there in each word?

TODOS: Dos.

ALL: Two.

ALICIA: Muy bien. Ahora, ¿Quién me puede decir lo que quieren decir las palabras? ¿Qué es un pato?

ALICIA: Very good. Now, who can tell me what the words mean? What is a duck?

After the children have identified the words, Alicia takes the big book, *El patito feo* (*The Ugly Duckling*) (Parkes and Smith, 1989, Spanish translation) and reads it to them tracking the words with her hand. Then she gives the children little book versions, and they take turns reading the story aloud. If the reader has difficulty with a word, Alicia encourages the student to sound it out. If this strategy fails, Alicia or one of the other children says the word for the reader. After they have read the story again, Alicia asks questions about the story:

ALICIA: Estamos estudiando los animales que nacen de huevos. ¿Cuáles animales nacen de huevos en este cuento?

ALICIA: We are studying animals that come from eggs. Which animals come from eggs in this story?

PEPE: Los patos.

PEPE: The ducks.

ALICIA: Sí, y ¿cuál otro animal?

ALICIA: Yes, and which other animal?

RENÉ: El patito feo.

RENÉ: The ugly duckling.

ALICIA: Y ¿qué otro nombre tiene este animal?

ALICIA: And what is the other name of this animal?

Alicia has organized her curriculum around themes. She has good classroom management, and all her students are engaged in reading, writing, and talking about ducks and other oviparous animals. The children like their teacher, and it is obvious that she likes them. The students stay on task. While one group reads, children in the other groups exhibit excellent self-discipline, especially for second graders. Many of Alicia's students will become successful readers and writers as a result of the experiences they have in this class.

Down the hall in Celia's bilingual second-grade class, students are also reading and writing. But if we could peer into that classroom, we would note some significant differences. Celia's class must also be studying oviparous animals. Student drawings of eggs with the parts labeled cover most of the bulletin board, science journal entries hang above a small incubator, and both the student-made books and trade books that are lying around reflect this theme. Although both Alicia and Celia's classes are studying the same theme, the approach is different. In Celia's class, more student work is visible. The egg drawings reveal more individuality; they don't strictly follow a model. The science journal entries include a variety of observations rather than following a uniform pattern. One bulletin board, labeled "What we know about animals that lay eggs" <¿Qué sabemos de los animales ovíparos?> and "What do we wonder about them?" <¿Qué nos preguntamos sobre los animales ovíparos?> features a list of questions students have generated and written out themselves. The books around the room include trade books in Spanish and English that deal with the theme as well as large class-made books about oviparous animals created by children from previous classes.

Like Alicia, Celia is sitting with a small group of students while the other children work independently. However, while Alicia's children were working on specifically assigned projects at centers or the computer, some of Celia's second graders have paired up and are reading and talking about the books in the reading corner. The story books and content books laid out for them all center on the theme of animals and insects that lay eggs, including, among others, *El patito feo* (*The Ugly Duckling*) (Parkes and Smith, 1989, Spanish translation), the book the children in Alicia's room were reading. Other books include *Los animales y sus crías* (*Animals and Their Babies*) (Kratky, 1991), *¿Cuál es el mío?* (*Which One is Mine?*) (Long, 1995), *Duck* (Watts, 1991), *Patitos* (Watts, 1992), *Ranitas* (Taylor and Burton, 1992), *Frog* (Taylor and Burton, 1991), *The Egg* (Jeunesse and de Bourgoing, 1992), *The Very Hungry Caterpillar* (Carl, 1969), *La oruga muy hambrienta* (Carl, 1989), *La familia del pingüino* (*The Penguin Family*)

(Somme and Kalas, 1991), *Serpientes* (*Snakes*) (Barrett, 1990), and *Cocodrilos y caimanes* (*Crocodiles and Alligators*) (Barrett, 1991).

Other students in Celia's class are at a listening station with their headsets on, following along in books as their story is read on a tape. Some are writing stories, either independently or in pairs. A few students are at the computers typing their stories. Still others are at the incubator making observations and writing them in their science journals.

The students with Celia are discussing a book she has just read to them, *Las gallinas no son las únicas* (Heller, 1990), a translation of *Chickens Aren't the Only Ones* (Heller, 1981). The following is excerpted from the dialogue of their group discussion:

CELIA: ¿Qué recuerdan?

CELIA: What do you remember?

FELICIA: Muchos pájaros diferentes vienen de huevos.

FELICIA: Many birds come from eggs.

SUSANA: Como *El patito feo*. . . .

SUSANA: Like *The Ugly Duckling*. . . .

CELIA: ¿*El patito feo*?

CELIA: *The Ugly Duckling*?

SUSANA: Sí, en *El patito feo* habían huevos de patos y uno de un cisne . . . La mamá se confundió . . . Hablamos de cómo se confundió la semana pasada cuando estábamos discutiendo el libro.

SUSANA: Yes, in *The Ugly Duckling* there were duck eggs and one swan egg. . . The mother got mixed up. . . We talked about how the mother got mixed up when we were talking about the book last week.

CELIA: Sí, muy bien, Susana. Hiciste una comparación muy interesante entre los dos libros. ¿Qué más recuerdan de *Las gallinas no son las únicas*?

CELIA: Yes, very good, Susana. You made an interesting comparison between the two books. What else do you remember from *Chickens Aren't the Only Ones*?

FRANCISCO: Muchos animales nacen de los huevos.

FRANCISCO: Many animals are born from eggs.

FELICIA: Las culebras vienen de huevos . . . No me gustan.

FELICIA: Snakes come from eggs. . . I don't like them.

MARIANA: Hay un libro allá que se llama *Serpientes*. Hay fotos de muchas culebras en el libro y sus huevos también.

MARIANA: There is a book over there called *Snakes*. There are pictures of lots of snakes in the book and their eggs too.

ESTÉBAN: . . . y los insectos también vienen de los huevos.	ESTÉBAN: . . . And insects also come from eggs.
ROBERTO: El colibrí tiene un huevito muy pequeño . . . Tenemos miel para los colibris en nuestra casa. Vienen a chupar. . . .	ROBERTO: The hummingbird has a very tiny egg . . . We have nectar for hummingbirds at our house. They come to drink. . . .

After a few minutes, Celia reminds the children of the questions about animals that lay eggs that the class had brainstormed after their literature study on *El patito feo* (*The Ugly Duckling*). The children read those questions with her. Two questions were <¿Cuáles animales ponen huevos?> (Which animals lay eggs?) and <¿En qué se parecen y en qué se diferencian los huevos?> (How are the eggs the same and how are they different?). Celia suggests that the children might list some possible answers from the book they just read. She also encourages the students to keep these questions in mind as they read other books. Some of the children start writing down their ideas to put on the bulletin board where it says, "What we have learned" <Lo que hemos aprendido>, while others choose books to read. For a complete list of books used for this unit, see Table 2–1.

An observer would find that Celia's class, like Alicia's, is well-organized. The children in both classrooms are engaged in reading, writing, and talking in Spanish and English. Both teachers have developed positive relationships with their students. Alicia and Celia are both good teachers, and most of the children in their classes will become good readers and writers. Despite these similarities, obvious differences between the two classrooms exist. Alicia and Celia hold different views of how children develop literacy, so they have adopted different methods of teaching reading and writing. In this chapter, we will examine the differences in their approaches to reading instruction. In Chapters Five and Six we will focus on writing.

We have pointed out that many of the children in both these classes will become successful readers and writers even though their teachers take different approaches. That might lead readers to believe that we think the two approaches are equally good. But that is not our position. Many students become good readers in spite of the way they are taught. Others, like Bobby, whose writing sample (see Figure 2–1) clearly shows how he feels about reading and school, do not. Bobby was designated to a special day class in the fourth grade. In his school experiences, Bobby continually failed and was continually given remedial work, sounding out words in

Barrett, Norman. *Cocodrilos y caimanes, Biblioteca Gráfica*. New York: Franklin Watts (1991).

Barrett, Norman. *Serpientes, Biblioteca Gráfica*. New York: Franklin Watts (1990).

Carl, Eric. *The very hungry caterpillar*. Cleveland: The World Publishing Company (1969).

Heller, Ruth. *Chickens aren't the only ones*. New York: Scholastic (1981).

Heller, Ruth. *Las gallinas no son las únicas*. México, D.F.: Grijalbo (1990).

Jeunesse, Gallimard, and de Bourgoing, Pascale. *The egg*. First Discovery Books. New York: Scholastic (1992).

Kratky, Lada Josefa. *Animals and their babies*. Carmel: Hampton-Brown (1991).

Kratky, Lada Josefa. *Los animales y sus crías, ¡Qué maravilla!* Carmel: Hampton-Brown (1991).

Long, Sheron. *¿Cuál es el mío?, Pan y Canela, Colección B*. Carmel: Hampton-Brown (1995).

Parkes, Brenda, and Smith, Judith. *El patito feo* (Spanish translation). Crystal Lake: Rigby (1989).

Somme, Lauritz, and Kalas, Sybille. *La familia del pingüino*. México, D.F.: SITESA (1991).

Taylor, Kim, and Burton, Jane. *Frog. See how they grow!* London: Dorling Kindersley (1991).

Taylor, Kim, and Burton, Jane. *Ranitas, Mira cómo crecen*. México, D.F.: SITESA (1992).

Watts, Barrie. *Duck. See how they grow!* London: Dorling Kindersley (1991).

Watts, Barrie. *Patitos, Mira cómo crecen*. México, D.F.: SITESA (1992).

TABLE 2–1: Unit on Animals that Lay Eggs

drills and filling in worksheets. When students are not given opportunities to engage in meaningful activities with *reading*, they may not develop high levels of literacy.

Bobby was fortunate. He participated in a special program where teachers worked with reluctant readers and writers in small groups after school. In this program he read quality literature, wrote in a journal, published his own books, and within six months showed enthusiasm for both

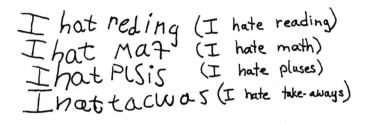

I hat reding (I hate reading)
I hat Maf (I hate math)
I hat PLSis (I hate pluses)
I hat tacwas (I hate take-aways)

I narre ret (I never read.)
I narre domar (I never do math.)

FIGURE 2–1: Bobby's Writing Sample

books and writing. Other students, however, do not overcome ineffective instructional practices. They become what Goodman (1986b) has termed "instructionally handicapped." They don't come to value reading and writing, and they don't come to value themselves as readers and writers. For these children, the teacher's approach makes a significant difference.

In this chapter, we will examine two views of reading: One view is exemplified by Alicia and the other by Celia. Both teachers have some students who are learning to read in English and some who are learning to read in Spanish. The view of reading and reading instruction we advocate here applies equally to English and Spanish. In Chapters Three and Four we will consider in more detail specific methods and programs that have been used to teach reading in Spanish. Those methods reflect the beliefs that Alicia holds, and for each method we will present alternative possibilities that are more consistent with the second view, the one we see in action in Celia's classroom.

Scientific evidence supports the view of the reading process that we hold. We want teachers to be firmly grounded in theory so that when asked why they are teaching a certain way, they can explain. We encourage you, as you read this chapter, to keep thinking about different classrooms you have seen and asking what view of reading the teachers in those classrooms are operating on. We also want you to keep in mind the kind of literacy experiences you would like to create for your students. We believe that the best way to improve your own teaching practice is to reflect critically on what you and other teachers do each day. For critical reflection, a solid theoretical base is essential.

One View of the Reading Process

In Alicia's class, the children identify vocabulary words before they read a story. They do this by repeating the words and breaking them down into parts. Then the students read aloud, and the teacher encourages them to sound out any words they don't know. If children can't sound the words out, Alicia or one of their classmates supplies the word for them. Alicia also reads to her class, and children have time for silent reading. But for Alicia, reading instruction is what goes on in the small group setting.

By observing how Alicia teaches reading, we can make a good guess about the theory of reading she operates on. We call it a *good guess* because, like many teachers, Alicia has not consciously thought out her theory. We can only guess about her theory because she couldn't articulate it.

Her beliefs about reading are what Watson (1994) calls "unexamined" (p. 601). Alicia is probably teaching reading the way she was taught, and the way she was taught to teach. As long as her beliefs about reading are unexamined, Alicia can't reflect critically on them. Nevertheless, it appears that Alicia believes that reading is a process of recognizing words.

A Word Recognition View

The word recognition view of reading is probably the most commonly held and most thoroughly researched view there is. The work of Thonis (1976), Braslavsky (1962), or Goldenberg and Gallimore (1991) in Spanish reading, and Adams (1990), Anderson, et al. (1985), or Chall (1967) in English reading, are good examples of this research base. This approach is quite logical. After all, written language consists of words, so reading must have something to do with making sense out of text by recognizing words.

Much of the research that supports a word recognition view begins by assuming that reading involves recognizing individual words. While the end product of reading is comprehension, the path to comprehension must be through the words. Since the researchers begin with that assumption, many of the studies examine just how good people are at recognizing words. For oral language, it turns out that people are extremely good at this task. Pinker (1994), for example, comments that "human speech perception is, in fact, driven quite strongly by acoustics" (p. 185). For reading, visual factors also come into play, and techniques for accurately measuring visual perception, eye movements, and so on, have become much more sophisticated. However, because people can be shown to be good at recognizing words, it doesn't follow that reading consists of only recognizing words.

If a teacher takes a word recognition view of reading, he or she still has two choices to make. Children can learn to recognize words by using one of two kinds of information: visual information or auditory information. As a result, some methods of reading stress the visual. Children are helped to build up a store of sight words. These are often taken from a list of the words that occur most commonly, such as the Dolch list, a list of high frequency words for English. At times, this approach has led to methods like *look/say* in which students look at words, often on flash cards, and then say them. Since this approach uses complete words, it is often called a whole word method. Because of this name, people have often confused whole word with whole language.

The second option for teachers who take a word recognition approach is to focus on sounds. Like Alicia, these teachers encourage students to "sound it out" when they come to a word they don't know. This phonics approach assumes that reading consists of turning written language into oral language and then using the reader's knowledge of oral language to make sense of the text. A number of different phonics methods, including *Hooked on Phonics* and *Zoo-phonics*, have been developed and marketed. What they all have in common is the idea that children can read if they can decode the written language and pronounce the words the letters represent.

Most of the debates about *Why Johnny Can't Read* (Flesch, 1955; 1981) are really debates between these two ways of recognizing words. If a sight word approach doesn't work, phonics must be the answer. And if phonics fails, students must need a whole word approach instead. A logical solution, of course, is to combine phonics and sight words. This is what most basal reading programs do. Students are encouraged to build up a bank of sight words, but if they don't recognize a word, then they are expected to sound it out.

When we work with teachers, we often explain that the word recognition view of reading seems logical, but it's not supported by research in psycholinguistics. When it comes to processing language, our brains don't work one letter or one word at a time. That would be too inefficient. There is good evidence that reading isn't simply a process of recognizing words. Instead, we comprehend written language the same way we understand oral language. We keep our focus on meaning, and we use a number of different clues to make meaning. The real reason some Johnnys (or Juanitas) can't read is that they are trying so hard to get the words that they miss the meaning. The solution to the debate between phonics and sight words isn't phonics, sight words, or some combination of the two. Rather, it is a whole different approach to reading, one that views reading, like oral language, as a naturally acquired socio-psycholinguistic process.

In the following sections, we discuss in detail this second view of teaching reading. Figure 2–2 summarizes some of the key differences

Word Recognition View	Socio-psycholinguistic View
Goal—identify words to get to the meaning of text.	Goal—use cues from three systems to construct meaning from text.
Learn vocabulary through preteaching activities.	Acquire vocabulary by encountering words in context.
Learn to break words into parts to identify them.	Only study word parts during linguistics investigations.
Build a bank of sight words and use phonics rules to sound out words to identify them.	Use graphophonics as just one of three cueing systems.
Read orally so the teacher can help students learn to identify words and can supply words students don't know.	Read silently using the strategies the teacher has helped students internalize to construct meaning from a text.

FIGURE 2–2, Part 1: Two Views of Teaching Reading (English)

between a word recognition view and the socio-psycholinguistic view that we want to encourage teachers to consider adopting.

A Second View of the Reading Process

In Celia's class, children read on their own and then come together to discuss what they have read. In these discussions, Celia assumes that if students have read a text, they have comprehended it. Her questions are open ended. In the discussion recorded above, she simply asked, <¿Qué recuerdan?> (What do you remember?). On other days, she might begin with <¿Qué más quieren saber?> (What else do you want to know?) or <¿A qué te recuerda lo que leimos?> (What did what we read remind you of?) (Hansen, 1989). Her goal is to create a safe setting where students can talk and think about what they have read.

One reason that Celia can assume that her children comprehend what they read is that they have choice in their reading. She teaches them to make good choices and to develop a sense of their own level of reading proficiency. As the year progresses, she will continue to help students make good choices about what they read. She will also observe her students carefully and present strategy lessons for students who need them. We will dis-

Concepción que considera a la lectura como un reconocimiento de palabras	Concepción Socio-psicolingüística
Objetivo—identificación de palabras para obtener el significado del texto.	Objetivo—uso de los tres sistemas de claves (grafofónico, sintáctico y semántico) para la construcción del significado.
Aprendizaje del vocabulario por medio de la enseñanza directa antes de realizar la lectura.	Adquisición de vocabulario por medio de la lectura de las palabras dentro de un contexto.
Aprendizaje de la división de las palabras en partes para poder llegar a identificarlas.	Estudio de las partes de las palabras sólo cuando se hacen investigaciones lingüísticas
Construcción de un banco de palabras con aquellas que se reconocen a la vista y utilzación de las reglas fónicas para identificarlas.	Uso del el sistema grafofónico sólo como una parte de los tres sistemas de claves.
Lectura en voz alta a fin de que el docente pueda ayudar a los estudiantes a identificar las palabras y a propocionarles aquéllas que no conocen.	Lectura silenciosa para construir el significado del texto utilizando las estrategias que el estudiante had internalizado con la ayuda del docente.

FIGURE 2–2, Part 2: Two Views of Teaching Reading (Spanish)

cuss this approach to instruction below. But Celia's main goal is to get her students to read because, like Smith (1985), she believes that we learn to read by reading. As long as the focus is on meaning, we acquire written language in the same way that we acquire oral language.

However, even though Celia believes children learn to read by reading, she knows that the role she plays is still crucial. Celia has taken classes in reading that have led her to adopt a socio-psycholinguistic view of the reading process. She is able to reflect critically on her teaching because she has examined her beliefs about reading. Celia realizes that she doesn't have all the answers. However, she consciously tries to put the theory she has studied into practice with her second graders every day.

A Socio-psycholinguistic View

Celia holds a socio-psycholinguistic view of the reading process. This view differs from a word recognition view in several ways, but the most important difference is that in this view reading is seen as just one example of a general human ability to use language to make and get meaning. This process involves psychological, linguistic, and social factors. As Goodman (1993) puts it:

> Reading is a psycholinguistic process because readers rely on the same general psychological and linguistic processes to make sense of text that they use to make sense of speech. Reading is a social process because meaning can only be constructed within a particular social context (p. 89).

Much of the research that supports a word recognition view has been carried on in laboratories. Researchers can measure eye movements and reaction times precisely under controlled lab conditions. Sometimes these investigations involve the reading of nonsense words to eliminate meaning altogether from the equation and to get a more objective physical measure of human abilities.

In contrast, the research that supports a socio-psycholinguistic view has been carried on in schools and other settings where teacher researchers can sit down and listen as students read. In an early experiment, Goodman (1965) had children at different grade levels read a list of words and then read a story containing those words. He found that even first graders could read about $2/3$ of the words within the story that they missed on the list. Goodman's study has been replicated in both English and Spanish. The results highlight the fact that reading does not concern itself primarily with words. As Goodman says, "Eventually I believe we must abandon our concentration on words in teaching reading and develop a theory of reading and a methodology that puts the focus where it belongs: on language" (p. 642).

If reading is not a precise process of identifying words, then what is it? Goodman (1967) calls it a "psycholinguistic guessing game." Rather than being exact, reading involves tentative information processing. Guessing is not completely random. We only call something guessing if we have some information but not all the information we need. Readers try to make sense of texts by using different cues as they read. Sometimes readers miss a cue or are misled by a cue, and then they produce responses that Goodman calls miscues instead of errors "in order to avoid value implications" (p. 34).

Miscue Analysis   Miscue analysis was first developed by Kenneth Goodman in the early sixties. Goodman noted that most measures of reading are indirect. They often compare what students knew before reading with what they know after reading. For example, a test on a particular passage might first assess students' background knowledge on the topic, their knowledge of the vocabulary, or their phonics skills. After reading, students could be tested on what they understand and remember. This is a measure of their comprehension. However, these comprehension tests are always indirect. Goodman wanted to develop a more direct measure of reading that would reveal how children are comprehending as they read rather than just measuring what they have comprehended after reading. He reasoned that if we want to develop lessons to help students become more proficient readers, then we must find a way to assess the actual processes they use as they read. Miscue analysis is the tool he developed.

In miscue analysis, readers are given a complete story or article to read, and this reading is recorded and analyzed. Afterward, the reader retells the story or article. Miscue analysis data constitutes the research base for a socio-psycholinguistic approach to reading. Miscues, or unexpected responses to text, help show us how the reader is attempting to make sense. It is only when readers leave a word out, insert a word, or substitute one word for another that we can start to understand the cues they are using during reading. As Goodman (1967) puts it, "expected responses mask the process of their attainment, but his unexpected responses have been achieved through the same process, albeit less successfully applied. The ways that they deviate from the expected reveal this process" (p. 127).

In other words, when readers produce the words we expect as we look at the story, we really can't say how they did it. But when readers produce unexpected responses, we get important insights into what they are doing as they read. For example, one young reader substituted *wants* and *set* for *went* and *suit* in the following sentence:

wants   set
Jack Jones always went around in overalls or a sun suit.

What insights do these miscues give us? For one thing, the reader used visual or auditory cues. Both *wants* and *set* look and sound like *went* and *suit*. In addition, the reader used syntactic information: He substituted a verb for a verb and a noun for a noun. He even added an *s* to *want* to make it agree with the subject. In addition, he used semantic information. He knew that *sun* and *set* go together in many situations. Despite these strengths, this reader doesn't show a focus on meaning. He did not correct these miscues, and the result is a sentence that doesn't sound like English and doesn't make any sense. Of course, we can't evaluate this reading on just one sentence with two miscues. In miscue analysis, students read a complete text, and researchers look for general patterns in the miscue data.

Readers in every language make miscues. A number of researchers have carried out miscue investigations in Spanish (Barrera, 1981; Hudelson, 1981). In their research, they found Spanish readers making miscues such as the following:

tus

Gracias, Pedro, pero no quiero sus zapatos

ⓒ la

Mientras comía y fregaba los. . . .

Translation:

your (informal)

Thanks, Pedro, but I don't want your (formal) shoes

ⓒ the

While he was eating and washing the. . . .

In the first sentence, the reader again used visual and/or sound cues. *Tus* looks and sounds like *sus*. The reader also used syntactic information, substituting one possessive for another. In fact, the reader showed good knowledge of the semantic/pragmatic system by substituting the familiar form of *you*, *tus*, for the formal form, *sus*. This substitution is logical in the sentence, and the reader doesn't correct it. In fact, the familiar form makes more sense since this is a discussion about borrowing someone's shoes. In addition, the speaker calls the person by his first name, Pedro, something that would also indicate familiarity.

The substitution of *la* (*the*) for *y* (*and*) in the second sentence, shows that the reader was focusing on meaning more than on the visual or sound information. He used syntactic information to predict that a noun would follow *comía* (*was eating*) naming what was being eaten. When a verb instead of a noun occurred, the reader went back and corrected. This shows again that the reader was focusing on meaning.

Crowell (1995), a bilingual teacher/researcher, explains how miscue analysis allowed her to discover what her students "knew about reading and texts and which reading strategies they needed to learn to use more effectively" (p. 32). Two examples from one of her Spanish-speaking students reading *Los animales de Don Vicencio* (*The Animals of Don Vicencio*) (Cowley, 1987) are instructive:

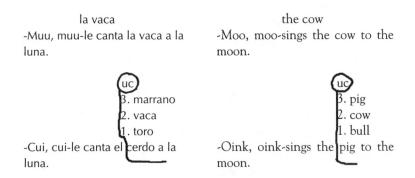

la vaca
-Muu, muu-le canta la vaca a la
luna.

the cow
-Moo, moo-sings the cow to the
moon.

3. marrano
2. vaca
1. toro
-Cui, cui-le canta el cerdo a la
luna.

3. pig
2. cow
1. bull
-Oink, oink-sings the pig to the
moon.

Crowell explains that in the first example the reader relied heavily on the picture cues in the book and the first words on the page, the sounds of the cow, to predict that the text that followed the *muu, muu* would be *la vaca*. Crowell points out that the reader, "did not self-correct on this page, but did read *canta* correctly on the next page, and thereafter" (p. 33). In the second example the reader does not self-correct but does finally substitute another word in Spanish for pig, *marrano*, for *cerdo*, relying on picture cues and her own background knowledge. Because this reader relied too heavily on picture cues, Crowell engaged her in strategy lessons which focused on integrating all the cueing systems. (We will discuss strategy lessons later in this chapter.)

As these examples show, our language is full of cues. We are seldom aware of just how redundant our language is. In a sentence such as "He walks to school," for instance, we have two clues that the subject is third person singular: the pronoun *he* and the *s* on the verb. We don't really need that *s*. Readers could easily understand "He walk to school," but our language has extra clues, like the *s* built in.

We keep making predictions as we read. We predict at both the micro and macro levels. That is, we are constantly guessing what letters we will see next in a word, what word will follow the one we are reading, where the sentence is headed, and what the whole text means. This is what the readers whose miscues we analyzed earlier were doing.

We rely on different kinds of information to make our predictions. For example, Smith (1971, p. 20) has pointed out that the last line on a page might read:

> The captain ordered the mate to drop the an-

We would have at least four ways of reducing uncertainty and getting at the meaning: We could use visual information. We could simply turn the page and see how the last word is finished. This is what is normally meant by *reading*. But even before we turn the page, we are making predictions about what we will see. On the micro level, we use orthographic (spelling) information for our prediction. We know that the next letter is unlikely to be *b, f, h, j, m, p, q, r, w,* or *z* because, combined with *an*, these letters do not produce common words in the English language. In addition, we could base our prediction on syntactic (grammatical) information. We know the word is likely to be an adjective or noun because other types of words such as articles, conjunctions, verbs and prepositions are unlikely to follow *the*. At a more macro level, we could use semantic information. If we stick to nouns and adjectives, we can continue to eliminate words with *an* plus one of the letters not eliminated by orthographic information. This would rule out words like *answer, anagram,* and *antibody* because our knowledge of the world tells us these are not the kinds of things that captains normally order mates to drop.

Let's look at an example from Spanish to demonstrate the same idea. Although it is highly unlikely that any editor or publishing house would hyphenate the last word on a page, we will imagine that the following sentence was at the bottom of a page:

> Todos los animales necesitan oxígeno para res-

Translation:

> All the animals need oxygen in order to br-

Again readers would have four ways to reduce uncertainty about the word. They could turn the page and use the visual information to see how the last word is finished. Remember that before we even turn the page, we are making a prediction about what we will see once we actually read the rest of the word. On the micro level, we use our knowledge of normal spelling patterns in Spanish to eliminate letters that are not likely to follow *res-*. Unless readers can think of some very unusual words, the letters *d, h, j,*

k, l, r, s, v, w, x, y, and *z* are not likely to follow *res-*. On the syntactic level we know that the word is likely to be a noun or a verb and less likely to be an adjective or adverb. It would not be possible for the word to be a conjunction, preposition, or article because none are spelled beginning with *res* (orthographic reasons) and they would not follow *para* (syntactic reasons). At the more macro level, we could use semantic information. Thinking of only nouns or verbs, we could eliminate *rescate* (ransom), *resecar* (to dry), *resfriado* (head cold), *residencia* (residence), and *restar* (to subtract), because none of those words makes sense when discussing why animals need oxygen. In fact, native Spanish speakers would realize that, although a verb or a noun could fit the sentence pattern, only a verb would make sense.

You might ask, "Why go through all this? Why not just look at the rest of the word? Wouldn't that be easier?" It might seem easier, but it's not very efficient. The more carefully we have to look at each word, the more slowly we read. And if we slow down too much, our short-term memory gets overloaded and we end up getting the words but missing the meaning. Good readers make use of all the available information to make their predictions and use just enough visual information to confirm their guesses. Making use of all the redundant cues language offers is particularly helpful to readers for whom the visual or sound information is not enough. Some of Alicia's students might not recognize <respirar> in the sentence above, and they might have trouble sounding it out. Going through the process of sounding the word out would certainly slow them down and might cause them to lose the meaning of the passage.

Using the Cueing Systems During Reading   As these examples show, readers use cues from different sources to make and confirm their predictions. As a result of his research in miscue analysis, Goodman (1996) identified three kinds of cues, which he calls graphophonic, lexico-syntactic, and semantic-pragmatic. Try reading the following "story" out loud.

> Arn tib a phev was larzing two sleks. Ambily, ek plobbed one. "Blars!" ek gliffed. "O hwez to glif sleks. Ern are avily quinzy. O will larz aloftil slek. O grun to larz sleks."

Could you read the story? At the least, you were probably able to say the words (even though you didn't recognize some of them). To pronounce the words, you used your knowledge of graphophonics. This includes your knowledge of orthography (the writing system), phonology (the sound system), and phonics (the relationships between patterns of letters and patterns of sounds). For example, you might have stumbled on *phev* because you knew something was wrong. English spelling conventions don't permit ending words in *v*. Another word that could have caused trouble was *hwez*. The *hw* spelling pattern looks unfamiliar even though we actually pronounce an *h* before the *w* in words like *when* or *where*.

Your knowledge of phonology allowed you to pronounce the *ed* of *plobbed* as a *d* sound and the *ed* of *gliffed* as a *t* sound. The *s* of *sleks* is pronounced as *s*, but the *s* of *Blars* has a *z* sound. Most of this knowledge is subconscious. It's something you have developed by reading and talking. It isn't a set of rules you needed to learn before speaking or reading. It's an effect, not a cause. If you ask other people to read this passage, you will find that there will be much agreement on the pronunciation of these invented words. That's because all of you are operating on the same social conventions of phonology, orthography, and phonics.

In order to read this story out loud, you didn't have to rely solely on graphophonic cues. This text also offers syntactic cues. For example, you probably predicted that a noun would follow *a* in the first line and that a verb would follow *was*. You might even have decided that *ek* was a pronoun referring to *phev*. Whether you really thought about nouns, verbs, and pronouns is not so important as the pattern of nouns and verbs you predicted based on your intuitive knowledge of English syntax. You probably looked for a pattern that starts with a noun as the subject, then has a verb as the predicate, and ends with another noun that serves as direct object. If the story were in Spanish, you'd expect the same basic pattern although you wouldn't be surprised if a sentence started with a verb since Spanish marks subjects on the verb forms. Your knowledge of syntactic patterns is what helps you predict as you read the story. While some of the words are nonsense words, others, like *a* and *was* are real words. These are the function words in the language that signal the syntactic patterns. So even though the story might not make sense, it does sound like English and follows a typical English syntactic pattern.

The third cue system is the semantic-pragmatic. Semantics refers to the meaning of words. But semantic knowledge also includes your knowledge of what words typically go together. In a sports story, if you see *baseball*, you can predict other words like *player*, *base*, or *run*. Pragmatics involves your knowledge of the world. In reading the sports story, you could rely on your general knowledge of baseball and how the game is played. Pragmatics also refers to the tone of a story. Is the writer being serious, humorous, sarcastic? This knowledge helps you make predictions and helps you construct meaning as you read.

Since the content words in the story above, the nouns, verbs, adjectives, and adverbs, are all nonsense words, you couldn't very well access your semantic or pragmatic knowledge as you read. You could only use two of the three cueing systems. Meaning is at the heart of reading, and without the semantic-pragmatic system, all you could really do here is what Goodman (1996) calls "recoding." When we decode we get at the meaning, but when we recode, we just change one code into another. In this case, you changed the written code into an oral code. But you did that without getting the meaning.

The students in many classes like Alicia's come to understand reading as recoding. They say the words, but they miss the meaning. This may seem hard to believe, but try the following exercise. Here are some *comprehension* questions based on the story above. See if you can answer them.

1. What was the phev larzing arn tib?

2. What did the phev do?

3. Are sleks avily quinzy?

4. What will the phev do?

5. What does the phev grun?

Many people can actually give complete sentence answers to these questions. For example, by looking back at the story, they can say that "The phev was larzing a slek arn tib." You can answer even when the words don't make any sense. For someone who knew the words (who spoke this strange language), your answers would sound good. You might get 100% on the comprehension test. However, as you are aware, you didn't really understand anything here. The danger is that kids can sometimes fool us (and themselves) by following this same procedure. They can appear to show *comprehension* when no real comprehending ever took place. If reading is a process of constructing meaning, then kids who simply recode texts aren't really reading.

Constructing Meaning During Reading   Reading and writing are interrelated processes, but there isn't a direct link between what is in the writer's head and what ends up in the reader's mind. The process, according to Goodman (1984), works something like this: The writer has certain experiences and ideas that lead to the formation of a mental text. These ideas and experiences (including previous reading and talk with others) constrain the creative potential of the writer. That is, a writer can only generate a certain

some of the pictures. As she began reading, Celia did not have to tell her students that the book was about animals who eat different food, live in different places, and look quite unalike. The pictures, the words, and the students' knowledge of the world all helped them infer that information. As the students listened and read with Celia, they were able to make use of the text pattern to predict that more and more oviparous animals and insects were going to be discussed.

Readers confirm or disconfirm their predictions as they read. For example, on one page there are illustrations of snakes and lizards, and the text reads, <Las gallinas no son las únicas. Casi todas las serpientes y los lagartos ponen huevos.> (Chickens aren't the only ones. Almost all snakes and lizards lay eggs.). If Celia had read *sirvientas* (servants) for *serpientes* (snakes), both the children and Celia would have noticed. Although *sirvientas* and *serpientes* look and sound alike, and even though they are both nouns, Celia would have relied on information from the semantic cueing system and self-corrected. This substitution looks and sounds like the text word, and it fits the sentence pattern, but it doesn't make sense.

Integration, the last step of the reading process, operates at both a micro and a macro level. On the micro level, Celia integrates the meaning of a word like *serpientes* (*snakes*) with the other words in the sentence, like *lagartos* (*lizards*); at another level, she integrates the information from this sentence with the ideas from other sentences in the text, and finally, after reading, as Celia and her students discuss the book, they integrate the new content knowledge with their past knowledge of animal reproduction. By reading to—and with—her students in this way, and then by talking about books with them, Celia helps her students construct meaning from texts. Alicia, on the other hand, takes an approach that focuses less on constructing meaning and more narrowly on getting the words right. As a result, her students sometimes miss cues available to them and fail to make sense of what they read.

Transactions During Reading and Writing   As readers go through the reading process, they construct a mental text. The form this text takes is mediated by both the meaning potential of the written text and the experiential background of the reader. Readers may discuss what they have read with others, and they may reread the text. In doing this, they may reshape their individual inventions to more closely fit with the socially accepted meanings—the conventions—created by others. Both the reader and the reader's mental text are changed through the process of reading and talking about what was read. In addition, readers may return to read a text at any time in the future and construct a new mental text. The meaning the reader constructs will be different because the reader is different as a result of added experiences, including talk and reading.

Because reading changes readers, the process has been called a transaction. This idea was first developed by Rosenblatt (1978). She pointed out that meaning is not simply in a text or in a reader's head. Instead, it is created during the process of reading. Both the text and the reader contribute to the meaning. Rosenblatt called the process a transaction, which she distinguished from an interaction. When readers interact with texts, they come away unchanged. During transactions, both the reader and the mental text the reader constructs are changed in the process of reading and then talking about what was read. That's why teachers like Celia give their students time to read and time to talk about what they have read.

In sum, from a socio-psycholinguistic view a writer has a certain potential for constructing meaning. Writers select from the ideas in their heads and create a text. The text (the words on the page) has a certain meaning potential. Readers have certain potential for constructing meaning from a particular text based on such factors as their background, purpose, and the text itself. Through transactions with the text, readers construct meaning. The chart in Figure 2–3 summarizes how both writers and readers are involved in constructing meaning.

A socio-psycholinguistic view of reading holds that meaning is not in the writer, the text, or in the reader. Instead, meaning is constructed and reconstructed in the process of reading and writing, and during these processes, readers and writers are changed. This view of reading is both personal and social. Readers reshape their individual inventions (their meanings) in response to social conventions (what others say). This perspective takes into account knowledge from linguistics and psychology. It is a universal view of reading that applies to all languages, not just English or Spanish.

A socio-psycholinguistic theory of reading is based on data from miscue analysis, which analyzes reading by looking at actual readers reading. Miscue analysis has been done in many different languages, including nonalphabetic languages like Chinese. The conclusion is that all readers construct meaning in the same general ways using information from the writing and sound systems, the wording and grammar systems, and the meaning systems of their languages. As Goodman (1984) states, "Though written language processes appear to vary greatly as they are used in the wide range of functions and contexts they serve, reading and writing are actually unitary, psycholinguistic processes" (p. 81). If the process of reading

Los lectores	Readers
tienen ciertas ideas/experiencias	have certain ideas/experiences
pasan por el proceso de iniciación, muestreo, inferencia, predicción, confirmación e integración a medida que realizan transacciones con el texto físico	go through a process of initiating, sampling, inferring, predicting, confirming, and integrating as they transact with a physical text
construyen un texto mental que se puede revisar mediante conversaciones con otros o al releer el texto	construct a mental text which may be revised through talk with others or through rereading

Los escritores	Writers
tienen ciertas ideas/experiencias las cuales forman un texto mental	have certain ideas/experiences which form a mental text
pasan por el proceso de crear un borrador, hablar o compartir con alguien sus ideas y luego revisarlo para crear un texto físico	go through a process of drafting, conferencing, revising to create a physical text
cambian el texto mental durante el proceso de la escritura	change the mental text in the process of writing

FIGURE 2–3: How Readers and Writers Construct Meaning

is the same for every language, the way reading is taught should also be the same.

Implications for Instruction

The two views of reading lead to two different approaches to instruction. Alicia sets up her reading program very differently than Celia does because Alicia has a different view of reading proficiency and reading instruction. Both Alicia and Celia want their students to comprehend what they read. However, because the two teachers operate on different theories of reading, they lead their students toward comprehension by two different routes.

Alicia's Class

Teachers like Alicia believe that students must first recognize words. Then they can comprehend a text. Reading proficiency from this view consists of two elements: accuracy and fluency. That is why Alicia sits with a small group of students and listens to them read. She wants them to be able to read fairly fast and smoothly with good expression and with few, if any, errors. In fact, she views all errors as bad and tries to help her students avoid making them. In Alicia's class, a good reader is a good oral reader because reading is an oral performance. Alicia assesses students' reading proficiency based on how well they can read aloud in the small group setting.

Instruction consists largely of lessons designed to help students identify words by using knowledge of phonics or by accessing a bank of sight words. Alicia does some whole class instruction in phonics. As her students read, Alicia encourages them to sound out words they don't know, and she corrects their errors. While some students read with Alicia, the others complete seatwork, including worksheets on phonics. These exercises closely parallel the questions on the reading test the school uses. Alicia's second graders do well on these tests. However, their test scores often drop at the intermediate grades where the test questions shift from a phonics focus to a comprehension focus.

Other teachers at the school do not use phonics as much as Alicia, but still take a word recognition view of reading. These teachers put more emphasis on helping students develop visual strategies. They expect students to know common words by sight. They may ask students to keep a list of the words they know. In some cases, teachers use flash cards in small group settings to help reinforce the sight words.

Alicia's program seems to combine phonics and sight-word instruction. Her program fits into the basal reading program at the school because activities from the teacher's guide include both worksheets on phonics and sight-word and vocabulary exercises. Teachers like Alicia, then, rely heavily on those program materials to encourage students to use both sound cues and visual cues to help recognize words.

Alicia and other teachers who take a word recognition view want their students to read without errors. For students who do make errors, these teachers attempt to intervene and provide the direct instruction in the skills the children appear to lack. They may also refer children to specialists who can provide additional support, usually in the form of early intervention programs.

Celia's Class

One of Celia's goals is the same as Alicia's. She wants her students to understand what they read. Since she defines reading as the construction of meaning, she can't really talk about reading without talking about comprehending. In addition, Celia has as a goal the development of a love of reading.

To serve as a guide for her reading/language arts program, Celia often refers to the Checklist for Effective Reading Instruction laid out in Chapter One. In addition, she refers to the second checklist, Characteristics of Texts that Support Reading, as she chooses the books she makes available to her students. Especially for Spanish materials, Celia considers whether the books were originally written in Spanish or translated from English. If the books are translated, she checks on how good the translation is. In some cases, she chooses books originally written in English by Latino authors like Gary Soto or Alma Flor Ada because these authors write on topics familiar to Latino children who have grown up in the United States. Because some of Celia's students were born in various parts of Latin America and others were born into Latino families in the United States, Celia chooses texts that represent the experiences of all of her students. In addition, Celia works to ensure that her students have easy access to a variety of books appropriate for readers at different proficiency levels.

Celia's students spend most of their time reading silently. Celia knows that when students sit in a group and listen to one another read aloud, some students get bored because the pace is too slow while others get frustrated because they can't keep up. Celia also knows that it is important to help students learn to make good choices of what they read. She has a great number of books in her room in both English and Spanish, and she also takes her students to the library on a regular basis. She has a listening center in her room where students can listen to a story on headsets as they look at the book. Much of the reading is individual and silent, but some students read in pairs. Celia's students usually have at least three books at their desks to pick from during reading time. One of these is a bit challenging, one is somewhat easy, and the third is about at the students' comfort level. Celia knows that students can only develop a love of reading if they have experience with a variety of books that represent a range of difficulty.

Reading Proficiency

Celia has come to understand that readers construct meaning during transactions with texts by using cues from the three cueing systems. Alicia views proficiency as a combination of accuracy and fluency, but Celia takes a different approach. She defines a proficient reader as one who is both effective and efficient. An effective reader makes balanced use of cues from all three systems. Celia has seen readers who rely too much on one system, often the graphophonic system. They miss many of the other available cues. They often slow down and start concentrating on the words. When that happens, they lose their focus on constructing meaning.

Proficient readers are also efficient. They know that the goal of reading is to make meaning from a text, not to get all the words right. Efficient readers use the fewest cues possible to get to the meaning. Both oral and written language offer many redundant cues. Proficient readers use just as many of these cues as they need to make sense of what they are reading. If their predictions go wrong, and the text no longer makes sense, they go back and look for additional cues. But as long as they are comprehending a text, they read fairly rapidly.

Like Alicia, Celia meets regularly with small groups of children. At this time, they talk about what they have read. This allows Celia to monitor progress. How much have students read? How much did they understand? Are they learning to talk about literature in more sophisticated ways? Can they tie the information from stories and from content texts to the themes they are studying? Can students rethink what they have read in light of their classmates' comments? Do they go back and reread after some of the discussions? Does their writing reflect their reading in style or content? As her students read, talk, and write, Celia keeps anecdotal records for use during conferences with individual students or small groups.

Celia also conducts whole class lessons to demonstrate how to choose books and how to respond to books. For example, she might engage the whole class in a brainstorming session on how to act during the discussion group (for example, look at the child who is speaking, come with something to say), and what kinds of comments lead to good discussion. She also reads to the whole class on a regular basis. Each day, she plans a number of activities to help her students become more proficient readers and to help them develop a love of reading.

Strategies to Support Efficient and Effective Reading   Despite the rich context Celia creates for literacy development, some of her students still struggle with reading. They don't stick with it for long, even with highly predictable picture books. During small group discussions, it is evident that they haven't understood much of what they have read. In order to get insights into the strategies these students are using, Celia may use informal

- Los venezolanos comen hallacas durante todo el mes de diciembre pero durante la Nochebuena de Navidad y de Año Nuevo es el plato que nunca falta en la mesa.

Translation:

HALLACAS

- Everyone likes hallacas.

- The word *hallaca* is a combination of two words, *there* (Spain) and *here* (The New World). Hallacas represent the influence of the Spanish and the indigenous people.

- One can buy them, or make them at home.

- Many families make them together.

- They are more delicious made at home.

- They are a typical Christmas dish.

- It is necessary to gather a lot of ingredients to prepare them.

- A special dough made of corn flour is used.

- This dough is made very thin and formed in a circle and then is filled with a mixture of chicken, pork, tomatoes, red peppers, onions, garlic, and other spices that give the dish flavor.

- The dough is doubled over with this filling inside and wrapped in banana or plantain leaves. It is tied with a string and then put in hot water to cook for approximately an hour.

- Venezuelans eat hallacas during the entire month of December but on Christmas and New Year's Eve it is a dish that is never missing from the table.

Students enjoy these lessons. What is important is for students to discuss with classmates why they made certain predictions and what clues helped them confirm their predictions or helped them decide they had not made a good guess. Less proficient readers are helped to see that even the good readers don't know all the words. They also come to understand the process good readers use to make guesses about words they don't know. Finally, they start to see the importance of reading on for more information instead of stopping to wait for help. Of course, they also understand that sounding out words like *hallacas* won't help them make sense of text.

Strategy lessons, like this one, focus on one particular cueing system. Others are more general and might be appropriate for readers with a variety of difficulties. Watson (1987) has compiled a number of useful strategy lessons in her book *Ideas and Insights: Language Arts in the Elementary School.*

Three general kinds of strategy lessons that teachers like Celia have found useful are cooperative Cloze, read and retell, and retrospective miscue analysis. The cooperative Cloze technique has been developed by Y. Goodman and Cambourne. Teachers prepare materials for these lessons by finding a short reading passage and retyping it, leaving out some words. Students then work in small groups to decide what words might logically fit in the blanks. What is important is that students talk together about why they chose a certain word. When they finish working through the passage, they go back to see if they want to change any of their answers. Often, students find that information from later in a text gives them insights into earlier sections.

For example, the story "The Peddler and the Tiger" starts this way:

> One night an old tiger was out in the rain. It was very dark and the rain was falling very fast. The ___ was wet and cold. He tried to find a ____ place so that he could get out of the rain.

Many students would suggest putting *tiger* in the first blank. However, some students might think *night* fits better. Students could discuss their choice and talk about why they made it. For the second blank most students choose *dry*, but some give other words like *sheltered* or *warm*.

A parallel example in Spanish comes from *El tigre Carlitos* (*The Tiger Carlitos*) (Dobbs, 1993):

> Una mañana, el tigre Carlitos se despertó sin su rugido. Se sentía tan triste que _____ a buscarlo. Subió a la cima de una loma muy _____ y encontró _____ oso pero no su rugido. Buscó en la hierba espesa y encontró una serpiente, pero no su _____.

Translation:

> One morning the tiger Carlitos woke up without his roar. He felt so sad that _____ _____ to look for it. He went up to the top of a very _____ hill and found _____ bear but no roar. He looked in the thick plants and found a snake but not his _____.

In this passage students might use different verbs for the first blank including *fue* (went) or *salió* (went out). The adjective for the next blank could be *alta* (high) or some other word such as *lejos* (far). The next two blanks would really give the reader less choice. Probably, the indefinite article *un* (a) fits better than *el* (the) before *oso* (bear) because this is the first reference to the bear. The last blank must be filled with *rugido* (roar) to continue the story pattern.

Again, what is important is for students to talk about the cues they used to make their decisions. It is particularly important for less proficient readers to become aware of the process their more proficient classmates use to make sense of text. They often see that as they continue to read, they get additional cues. Once they finish the passage, they go back through and make any changes they agree on. Teachers may choose to pass out the original passage and have students compare their answers with what the author wrote. Often students like their words better than the original. This activity helps students see reading as a process of constructing meaning for themselves, not just getting someone else's meaning.

A second general strategy lesson developed by Brown and Cambourne (1987) is called read and retell. First, students read a number of texts from a certain genre, such as fables, fairy tales, science fiction, social studies texts, or science texts, to become familiar with the general organization and vocabulary of this kind of literature. The strategy lessons emerge out of this background of intensive reading.

The teacher begins by writing the title of a short, complete story or nonfiction text on the board. Students then write down one or two sentences telling what they think the reading might be about. Then they write down any words or phrases they might expect to see in the story. Students sit in groups of four or five, and each student reads his or her predictions to the group. The other students in the group comment on the predictions. This oral activity moves fairly fast, usually taking about five minutes.

Then everyone reads the story silently. After the reading, and without looking back at the story, students do a written retelling. Teachers allow about fifteen minutes for students to rewrite as much as they can remember from the passage. When they finish with their writing, students work in pairs to compare retellings. Brown and Cambourne suggest that students ask each other some or all of these questions during the pair activity:

1. What did I include or leave out that is different from what you included or left out?

2. Why did you leave out a certain part?

3. Are there any parts that I got mixed up? Does it change the meaning of the story in a significant way?

4. Did you paraphrase effectively (use words or phrases that are different but mean the same thing)?

5. If you could take part of my retelling and put it in yours, what would you borrow?

Translation:

1. ¿Qué puse/dejé por fuera que sea diferente a lo que tú pusiste o dejaste por fuera?

2. ¿Por qué dejaste por fuera o por qué no mencionaste esta/aquella parte?

3. ¿Crees que hay partes en las que yo me equivoqué? ¿Crees que esto cambia mucho el significado del cuento?

4. ¿Usaste alguna/s palabra/s o frase/s que es/son diferente/s pero que significa/significan lo mismo?

5. Si tú pudieras intervenir o participar en mi recuento y ponerlo en el tuyo, ¿Qué te gustaría tomar prestado en mi recuento?

Read and retell strategy lessons involve students in authentic reading and writing. In addition, students interact with classmates and start to develop a sense of how others make sense of their reading. These lessons help focus students on making sense of text. At the same time, the lessons increase students' awareness of the importance of good word choices. They realize that they can make predictions about both general concepts and about specific words and phrases. Brown and Cambourne offer a number of short texts of different types that teachers can use, and they also show samples of students' written retellings that show normal developmental patterns. Teachers of Spanish reading can choose similar short passages from different Spanish language textbooks.

Probably the most effective strategy that teachers like Celia use is retrospective miscue analysis (Goodman and Marek, 1996; Marek, 1989). Teachers who have studied miscue analysis use that procedure to gain insights into readers' uses of the cueing systems. But it is not only teachers who need this increased awareness. In retrospective miscue analysis, teachers ask students to listen to their own taped readings. Celia, for example, might have one of her students listen to certain parts of a tape. To build students' confidence, she might choose good miscues, substitutions that make sense like *tus* for *sus* in the sentence discussed above <Gracias, Pedro, pero no quiero sus zapatos.> (Thank you, Pedro, but I don't want your shoes.). Listening to this type of miscue could help a student realize that this *error* is a good one because getting the meaning is more important than getting all the words right. She might also choose some miscues that cause students to lose meaning. For instance, one reader substituted *parece* (seem) for the *pasa* (going) in the question, <¿Qué te pasa?> (How is it going (for you)?). The two words look and sound alike, but *parece* doesn't make any sense in that sentence. Having students focus on this kind of miscue reminds them of the importance of reading for meaning.

As students listen to themselves read, they attempt to answer a series of questions. At first teachers may help students by asking them some or all of the questions. Over time, students learn to use the questions to check their own miscues. Marek (1989) suggests using the following questions to help students focus on making sense as they read:

1. Does the miscue make sense?

2. Was it corrected? Should it have been?

3. Does the miscue look like what was on the page?

4. Why do you think you made this miscue?

5. Did the miscue affect your understanding of the story? (p. 160)

Translation:

1. ¿Tiene sentido esta palabra?

2. ¿La corregiste? ¿Tú crees que debías haberla corregido?

3. ¿Se parece la palabra que leíste a la que estaba en la página del libro?

4. ¿Por qué crees que leíste esta palabra y no la otra?

5. ¿Afectó de algún modo la palabra que leíste la comprensión del cuento?

Teachers have reported that even second graders can benefit from listening to themselves read and asking these questions. They also report that students start to read for meaning once they realize that what they are saying as they read aloud doesn't make sense.

Strategy lessons and procedures like read and retell or retrospective miscue analysis are important components in Celia's class. She knows that it is crucial that children learn to choose appropriate books to read, that they have time to read, and that they have opportunities to talk with their classmates about what they have read. However, she also knows that not all students will become proficient readers simply by engaging with literature. She uses procedures like miscue analysis in Spanish or English to determine how her troubled readers are using the different cueing systems. If students are not making a balanced use of all three systems, she then chooses strategy lessons that will build on what these readers do well and will also strengthen them in the cueing systems they are using ineffectively.

Conclusion

Both Alicia and Celia provide reading instruction. In Alicia's class the instruction centers on techniques to help children recognize words. In Celia's class the instruction centers on techniques to help children construct meaning. The difference is important. In classes like Alicia's the instruction can include words out of context. Developing reading skills can be separated from actual reading. In fact, troubled readers may be required to spend so much time developing skills that they never get to reading. Many students who can successfully complete skills exercises can't transfer those skills into their reading. On the other hand, in Celia's class instruction is always carried out in the context of reading. Her goal is to help her students become skilled readers, not to become good at performing decontextualized reading skills.

Unfortunately, many teachers take Alicia's approach rather than Celia's. This is particularly true of teachers who follow traditional methods of teaching reading in Spanish. Since phonics patterns are more consistent and less complex in Spanish than in English, most methods for teaching reading in Spanish emphasize using sound clues to identify words. In the next two chapters we review these traditional Spanish reading methods as well as popular programs that have been developed to teach Spanish reading. After describing each method, we present an alternative that shifts the focus from word recognition back to meaning construction.

3
Synthetic Spanish Reading Methods

La enseñaza de la lectura y de la escritura sigue siendo el rompecabezas para muchos maestros, y muy especialmente para los que habiendo terminado la carrera normalista, se inician en la docencia como profesores de primer grado de primaria. La falta de experiencia profesional y el desconocimiento de las técnicas más adecuadas para enseñar a leer y escribir a sus alumnos, los llena de desasosiego y de incertidumbre y los conduce, no pocas veces, a resultados menos que mediocres al término del año escolar (Heldt, 1971, p. 15).

Translation:

The teaching of reading and writing continues being the puzzle for many teachers, especially for those who, having finished their teacher education training, begin their teaching as first-grade teachers. The lack of professional experience and the lack of knowledge of adequate techniques for teaching reading and writing to their students, fills them with worry and uncertainty and leads them, quite often, to less than mediocre results at the end of the school year.

This quote was written in 1971. The work in psycholinguistics and reading was just beginning. As Heldt points out, many teachers did not know the best way to teach reading. We have found as we have worked with teachers in schools that the above quote may be as true today as it was twenty-five years ago. This last year we were invited to work with teachers in a rural school district with a 90 percent Hispanic population. After spending time observing classrooms, our major conclusion was that students, though busy during language arts time, were not doing much reading or writing.

First- and second-grade teachers in both Spanish and English language arts were using a variety of methods to teach sound-letter correspondence and word identification. Because the district had provided a *Zoo-phonics* workshop in the summer, several bilingual teachers worked with students doing hand signals related to sounds as students spelled out words. Other teachers had students in groups working on sounds and building words through different phonics exercises. Still others were using the traditional syllabic method, working on basic syllables in Spanish and combining them to make words. However, the children were reading few, if any, books and doing no writing beyond tracing, filling in single word blanks, or illustrating pattern books where words were already provided.

A major concern we had as we watched the children was that so little was expected of them. The teachers were convinced that students needed more structure, and they combined methods and materials to give students reading skills, but they could not really tell us why they had chosen the methods they were using. When we talked to teachers about reading as the construction of meaning, they agreed that meaning was essential, but they added that most of their first- and second-grade children just weren't ready to read yet.

Experiences like this convince us that when teachers understand the approaches to reading that different methods and materials represent, they can make better choices about literacy instruction in their classrooms. Even when teachers study and understand a socio-psycholinguistic view of reading, they often have trouble knowing how to implement that approach. Both young bilingual teachers just finishing their student teaching and experienced bilingual teachers feel insecure about what method will best help children learn to read in Spanish. They are influenced by methods other teachers are using or by the materials the school has adopted. Teachers who were originally taught to read in Spanish often teach as they were taught. Seldom do teachers really evaluate which methods reflect their beliefs about how reading happens.

In this chapter and the next we provide an overview of Spanish reading methods. This review is designed to help teachers evaluate traditional methods and to consider alternatives to these approaches to teaching reading. Generally, traditional methods can be divided into two types: synthetic and analytic.

Synthetic approaches go from the parts, usually sounds, letters, or syllables, to wholes. In most cases, the *whole* is a word. A second group of methods, those that are analytic, go in the opposite direction, from whole to part. However, the wholes that these analytic methods begin with are usually no bigger than words or, at most, sentences. Even though these two types of methods seem to be opposites, they really are more alike than they are different because both the analytic and synthetic methods are based on a word recognition view of reading. Synthetic methods often build up to words, and analytic methods begin with words and break them into parts.

In this chapter, we look at several synthetic methods for teaching reading in Spanish and in Chapter Four we consider analytic methods. For each method, we present a scenario of what a reading lesson might look like. We then analyze each of the lessons we present using the Checklist for Effective Reading Instruction, which we introduced in Chapter One. If teachers can answer yes to most items on the checklist when evaluating a particular method or set of materials, they can be assured that the method or materials are consistent with a socio-psycholinguistic view of reading. A series of no answers indicates that the method and materials emphasize a word recognition view.

Before beginning our discussion of specific methods, we give a brief historical overview of Spanish reading instruction. This overview provides the context for our discussion of current methods.

A Brief Historical Overview of Spanish Reading Methods

In his book, *Los métodos de lectura* (*Reading Methods*), Bellenger (1979) provides a history of reading instruction. According to Bellenger, reading was taught using a synthetic, part-to-whole, approach for over two thousand years beginning with the ancient Greeks. In this synthetic approach children were taught to read by first identifying letters, then syllables, then isolated words, then phrases, and finally whole texts. Recitation, memorization, and careful pronunciation were important parts of the pedagogy. The Romans followed the same practices, and, in fact, these practices continued through the Middle Ages.

In earlier times, literacy was restricted to the upper classes and members of the church. Bellenger explains that the French had an important influence on the teaching of reading, especially in the Spanish-speaking world, when in the 1660s religious schools devised reading methods to educate the common people. Reading was approached synthetically, as it had been in the past, beginning with the parts and moving toward the whole because it was believed that the lower classes needed a very regimented, step-by-step progression in order to learn.

During this period in Mexico, the famous *Silabario de San Miguel* (*San Miguel's Reader*) was developed to teach religion to the masses. It was a religious pamphlet used in parochial schools, and the last page was a catechism including questions and answers about the faith. The front of the *Silabario* is known for its depiction of the archangel Saint Michael beating Satan (Heldt, 1971). The *Silabario de San Miguel* is a classic text used to teach reading. Heldt describes it as <un verdadero documento de la pedagogía tradicionalista y anticientífica, cuyo origen se remonta a siglos pasados> (p. 29) (a true document of the traditional and antiscientific pedagogy whose origin comes from past centuries). Reading is presented through a part-to-whole approach. Students memorize the names of vowels listed in different orders, and then combinations of vowels with letters. Despite the rejection of this approach by Heldt and other educators, the text is still available today in some parts of the Spanish-speaking world as are other *silabarios* such as the *Silabario de San Vicente*. It is obvious that there is still a market for these traditional materials. In fact, in 1994 two silabarios were published in Venezuela.

In 1828 a Frenchman named Laffore devised what might have been the first phonics method, which, he claimed, produced instantaneous reading. In essence, Bellenger explains that this phonics method was <el último aspecto del viejo y antiguo sistema sintético> (p. 68) (the latest representation of the old and ancient synthetic system), the same synthetic approach that had been used since the time of the Greeks.

However, some French educators were not satisfied with this synthetic method of teaching reading. In the sixteenth and seventeenth centuries, during *La Edad de Oro* (The Golden Age), when writers produced an abundance of literature—poetry, plays, and novels—criticism of synthetic methods arose because these methods were artificial and mechanical. In the early seventeenth century, at about the time Laffore was proposing his phonics method, Comenio presented a new method in his *Orbis Pictus*. He proposed starting with the whole rather than the parts. Others followed with critiques of the synthetic approach. In *De la maniere d'apprendre les langues* (*The Way to Learn Languages*), Radonvilliers rejected the idea that children should be spelling and sounding out syllables and words and proposed they could directly recognize whole words. Adams agreed with this view insisting that the synthetic method should be abandoned because:

> Se atormenta insistentemente a los niños para hacerles conocer y retener un elevado número de letras, de sílabas y de sonidos, de lo cual nada pueden comprender porque estos elementos no contienen en sí mismos ninguna idea que les atraiga ni les divierta (Adams in Bellenger, 1979),

Translation:

It constantly torments children to make them learn and remember a high number of letters, syllables, and sounds, which they do not understand at all because those elements do not have in them anything that is interesting or enjoyable (for children).

In 1880, Block, borrowing from these scholars and the German Schuler Method, introduced a daring new reading method that used whole words to illustrate the sounds and letters students were to learn. Because the method began with whole words and then broke the words into parts to be analyzed, it was considered an analytic approach to reading. In Mexico this method was introduced by Rébsamen in 1899, when he published his *Guía metodológica de la enseñaza de la escritura y lectura* (*Methodology Guide to Teaching Reading and Writing*). Heldt (1971) explains how this method works:

A Rébsamen, pues, se debe la introducción a México del Método llamado de Palabras Normales . . . Es analítico-sintético, porque sigue un orden en que se presenta primero la palabra, pasando luego a su división en sílabas y por último a las letras, representadas por sus sonidos, para regresar a las sílabas y retornar a la palabra (p. 38).

Translation:

Rébsamen introduced the Method, *Palabras Normales*, to Mexico . . . It is an analytic-synthetic method because it follows the order of first (teaching) the word, going next to dividing it into syllables, and lastly into letter-sounds, and (then) building back to syllables and returning to the word.

Although this analytic method was popular in France for over seventy-five years, and was still referenced in the government-approved beginning reading text in Mexico in the 1980s (Alvarez, 1979), it was also criticized because of the nonsense children read and analyzed in order to learn sounds and letters. Block's method was rejected, then, because of <su negación de la lectura como medio de comunicación utilizable por el niño> (p. 70) (its negating of reading as a means of useful communication for the child) (Bellenger, 1979).

While most reading pedagogy was dominated by these analytic-synthetic methods, the work of scholars like Radonvilliers and Adams brought forth new ideas about teaching reading based on the idea of perceiving words and phrases globally, by drawing on the child's background knowledge. This led to Decroly's método ideovisual in 1936 that <Se trataba de hacer

que los niños comprendiesen lo que leían y de orientarles hacia la iden-tificación del texto> (p. 76) (It tried to help children comprehend what they read and relate to the texts.) (Bellenger, 1979). In 1947 the French educator, Hendrix, wrote a book to help French speakers teach using the Global Method. This was translated into Spanish in 1952 as *Cómo en-señar a leer por el método global* (*How to Teach Using the Global Method*) (Hendrix, 1952), and was widely read throughout Latin America. The book shows educators how to teach reading beginning with the sen-tence or phrase and moving to the word, then the syllable, and finally, the letter.

If one considers the historical influences on reading methodology, it is not surprising that methods of teaching reading in the Spanish-speaking world are a reflection of a mixture of influences. It is also important to point out that the synthetic and analytic methods and, in fact, even the global methods that were considered so revolutionary, all view reading as recognizing words. The synthetic approaches start from the parts to build up to identifying the whole, but the whole is the word. In the same way, most of the analytic approaches begin with words and then break those down for analysis. Even when sentences and phrases are presented, indi-vidual words are analyzed. Little evidence exists that the construction of meaning was ever a consideration in most of the methods, although educa-tors may have assumed that readers would comprehend once they got the words.

Most methods, then, are based on a word recognition view of reading. The alternative view of reading as a socio-psycholinguistic process that centers on comprehension has been largely misunderstood until very re-cently. In both the United States and Latin America, reading research de-bates have centered around the best way to recognize words. For English reading, Chall's famous *Learning to Read: The Great Debate* (1967), which is still often quoted by opponents of whole language, was, in fact, a study on the difference between two word identification approaches to reading, phonics and sight words. It was never a comparison between a word identi-fication approach and a socio-psycholinguistic approach. For the Spanish-speaking world, Braslavsky (1962) published *La querella de los métodos en la enseñanza de la lectura* (*The Debate of the Methods for Teaching Reading*). This book is basically about the identification of words as well. Braslavsky com-pares the synthetic methods with the Global Method, which she calls ana-lytic. She uses Simon's definition to distinguish the two methods to be debated:

A pesar de las apariencias, no existen verdaderamente más de dos métodos de lectura. Ambos tratan de hacer comprender al niño que existe cierta correspondencia entre los signos de la lengua escrita y los sonidos de la lengua hablada; pero, para ello, uno de estos métodos comienza por el estudio de los signos o por el de los sonidos elementales, y el otro busca por el contrario obtener el mismo resultado colocando de repente al niño pequeño frente a nuestro lenguaje escrito (Simon, 1924, p. 101).

Translation:

In spite of appearances, there do not exist more than two methods of reading. Both deal with helping children understand that there exists a certain correspondence between the signs of the written language and the sounds of the spoken language, but in order to arrive at this understanding, one of those methods begins with the study of the signs or the basic sounds and the other sets out by contrast to get the same results by suddenly giving the small child our written language.

Braslavsky's choice of words shows her bias from the start. She feels that giving students whole words, phrases, and stories from the beginning is unfair and that the phonetic approach, moving from part to whole is much more effective. Even in the analytic approach she opposes, however, it is really the word that is the basic unit to be picked out, broken down, and analyzed.

In the last fifteen years, publications about literacy in Spanish reflect a growing understanding of the socio-psycholinguistic view. As early as 1984 Dubois (1984) was questioning more traditional approaches of teaching reading in favor of taking a psycholinguistic view. In 1989, Goodman's classic, *What's Whole in Whole Language* was translated into Spanish in Venezuela and widely distributed throughout Latin America. The demand for the book has continued and has generated a newer translation into Spanish (Goodman, 1995).

In Latin America the whole language movement and the socio-psycholinguistic view of literacy are closely connected to a movement called *constructivismo* (constructivism). In fact, the same Braslavsky who wrote *La querella de los métodos en la enseñanza de la lectura* has more recently published a book which supports this view. In her 1992 publication, Braslavsky describes *constructivismo* as a model for literacy which is "didáctico, holístico, encuadrado en el contexto sociocultural y político" (p. 13) (didactic, holistic, and framed by the sociocultural and political context). Braslavsky describes the basic philosophy of constructivism which involves both drawing on the strengths of the student and the understanding of the teacher:

> El alumno es el agente de la construcción del conocimiento, ya que sin su actividad mental no habría elaboración de significados. Pero es el profesor quien conoce en principio los significados que espera compartir y ese conocimiento le permite planificar la enseñanza (p. 26).

Translation:

> The student is the agent of the construction of knowledge since without his/her mental activity there would not be a construction of meaning. But it is the teacher who first knows the meanings he/she hopes to share and that knowledge permits him/her to plan his/her teaching.

Recent issues of the International Reading Association's Spanish-language journal on literacy, *Lectura y Vida* (*Reading and Life*), contain articles that show wide acceptance of a socio-psycholinguistic approach to reading and writing (Castedo, 1995; Dubois, 1995; Freeman et al., 1995; Rodríguez, 1995; Sequeida and Seymour, 1995; Solé i Gallart, 1995). Ferreiro (1994), for example, states clearly how literacy has changed:

> La alfabetización ha dejado de ser vista como la simple transmisión de una técnica instrumental, realizada en una institución específica (la escuela). La alfabetización ha pasado a ser estudiada por una multitud de disciplinas: la historia, la antropología, la psicolingüística, la lingüística . . . (p. 5).

Translation:

> Literacy is no longer seen as the simple transmission of an instrumental technique realized in a specific institution, the school. Literacy is now being studied by a wide variety of disciplines including history, anthropology, psycholinguistics, linguistics. . . .

Heldt (1971) reminded readers that many of the reading educators of his time, including himself, fought to change the traditional reading instruction of the past because they themselves were submitted to painful and mechanical instruction:

> Muchos de quienes aprendimos a leer y a escribir con métodos mecánicos y rigidos, recordamos ahora el deletreo difícil, "la tonada" que aprendimos paralelamente al conocimiento del signo gráfico y rememoramos los castigos que se nos imponían para dar validez al refrán de que la letra con sangre entra (p. 12).

Translation:

Many (of whom) of us learned to read and write with mechanical and rigid methods, we remember the difficult spelling, the melody that we learned at the same time as (we gained) an understanding of the graphic symbols and we remember the punishment that teachers imposed upon us to give validity to the saying that literacy enters only with blood (shed).

Certainly, we do not want our students to suffer through reading instruction based on the philosophy of <la letra con sangre entra.> Theories of teaching of reading in Spanish have moved away from methods or approaches that are <tradicionales y anticientíficos> (traditional and antiscientific). Nevertheless, in many schools, traditional practices still flourish. To help teachers evaluate their own teaching, we discuss the traditional methods. First we describe each one. Then we present a scenario of an actual lesson using the method and analyze it with the Checklist. Finally, we present a positive alternative for the method that reflects a socio-psycholinguistic view of reading and includes a list of suitable literature.

In this chapter we examine synthetic methods for teaching reading in Spanish. These methods begin with different elements—letters, syllables, or words—and then combine the elements to form short texts, usually single sentences. Although the synthetic methods use different starting points, they all have in common the belief that reading is learned by starting with the parts and then moving toward the sentence, which is considered the whole.

El método alfabético (The Alphabetic Method)

This method begins with the teaching of the names of the letters. In its purest form, students begin by learning the names of the vowels and consonants. Next, the vowels and consonants are joined to create syllables and then words. Students are asked to repeat the spelling of the syllables or words and then pronounce them. This procedure is repeated for the many different words students are given to learn to read. The *Silabario de San Miguel* is the classic version of this method. Below we give a scenario of what this method looks like in classrooms today.

Scenario for el método alfabético

The teacher writes three words on the blackboard, *mamá* (mother), *mano* (hand), and *ama* (he/she loves). Then she begins:

MAESTRA: Buenos días, niños.	TEACHER: Good morning, children.
NIÑOS: Buenos días, maestra.	CHILDREN: Good morning, teacher.
MAESTRA: Hoy vamos a aprender a leer las palabras escritas en el pizarrón. Las voy a leer. <mamá> <mano> <ama.> Repitan mientras yo señalo las letras con mi dedo: <eme> <a> <eme> <a> – <mamá>.	TEACHER: Today we are going to learn to read the words written on the chalkboard. I am going to read them. "mamá" "mano" "ama". Repeat while I point to the letters with my finger. "eme" (m) "a" (a) "eme" (m) "a" (a) – "mamá".
NIÑOS: <eme> <a> <eme> <a> – <mamá>.	CHILDREN: "eme" (m) "a" (a) "eme" (m) "a" (a) – "mamá".
MAESTRA: Muy bien. Ahora seguimos con la segunda palabra: <eme> <a> <ene> <o> – <mano>. Repitan.	TEACHER: Very good. Now, let's continue to the second word. "eme" (m) "a" (a) "ene" (n) "o" (o) – "mano". Repeat.
NIÑOS: <eme> <a> <ene> <o> – <mano>.	CHILDREN: "eme" (m) "a" (a) ma "ene" (n) "o" (o) no – "mano".
MAESTRA: Muy bien. Ahora seguimos con la tercera palabra: <a> <eme> <a> – <ama>. Repitan, por favor.	TEACHER: Very good. Now, let's go on to the third word: "a" (a) "eme" (m) "a" (a) – "ama". Repeat, please.
NIÑOS: <a> <eme> <a> – <ama>.	CHILDREN: (a) "eme" (m) "a" (a) – "ama".

The students continue repeating the letters and pronouncing the words after the teacher.

Analysis of el método alfabético
Using the Checklist for Effective Reading Instruction, it appears that the answer to all twelve questions on the checklist is *no*. The only reading materials are the words the teacher has written on the blackboard and students are given no choice. The students are not making meaning as they repeat letters and words after the teacher. Even other traditional reading educators saw how this method was senseless. Heldt (1971) pointed out that spelling a word like *hijo*, for example, caused serious problems:

El niño lee y pronuncia por ejemplo: hache, i, jota, o, y se le pide el milagro, que al reunir todo eso pronuncie HIJO, y pobre de él si sale o resulta con un HACHEIJOTAO (p. 22).

Translation:

The child reads and pronounces, for example, *h, i, j, o* and one asks of him the miracle of uniting all that to pronounce *hijo*, and poor him if out comes, *h, i, j, o*.

This method only uses the graphophonic system. Students can't access the syntactic or semantic systems since they only read isolated words. While it might be argued that the children have a *mamá* (mother) and a *mano* (hand) and that love each one, *amas*, the teacher chose the words based on their letters and made no real attempt to relate the words to the students' lives. All students do is repeat the words, and this is not likely to spark their imagination nor make connections to other topics or areas of study. After this kind of reading lesson, children have no reason to talk about what they have read.

A Positive Alternative to *el método alfabético*

Rather than learning letter names and sounds by spelling out individual words, students can learn the alphabet as they engage in meaningful reading and writing. Teachers of younger children usually have the alphabet up around the room. They also provide students with alphabet books such as *Libro del ABC* (ABC Book) (Detwiler and Rizo-Patrón, 1993) which students can refer to as they do their own writing. Although the direct teaching of the alphabet is not an effective way to teach reading, there are appropriate activities and materials to use with students that are related to the alphabet and that promote learning and literacy. Several engaging alphabet books in Spanish encourage children to use letters and language creatively.

De la A a la Z por un poeta (From A to Z by a Poet) (Del Paso, 1990) is one such book that is especially good for older learners. This book devotes two pages to each letter. The first page has an artistically decorated letter that forms the basis for the poem, which appears on the second page. For example, for the letter *D*, there are colorful flowers and grasses within and surrounding a large *D* with *delfines* (dolphins) swimming out of the center of the letter. The poem reads:

El Delfín:	The Dolphin:
con pasto y flores,	with grass and flowers
se hace jardín.	a garden makes.
La *D*	The *D*
Es la «D», ya lo verás,	It is the *D*, now you will see it
un tanto desordenada:	a bit disordered:
está en todo y está en nada,	It is in *todo* (all) and it is in
está delante en detrás	*nada* (nothing)
y, siempre en actividad,	It is in front in *detrás*
se aparece, por igual,	and, always in *actividad*
dos veces en un dedal,	(activity),
y entera en una mitad (p. 10).	It appears, equally
	two times in *dedal* (thimble)
	and whole in a *mitad* (half).

Another alphabet book appropriate for middle-grade students working on environmental themes, especially the rain forest, is a bilingual alphabet book, *Un paseo por el bosque lluvioso* (*A Walk in the Rain Forest*) (Pratt, 1993). This book, originally in English, was written and illustrated by a high school student. It is beautifully illustrated and includes a wealth of information about the flora and fauna of the rain forest. Though not every letter of the alphabet works in translation into Spanish, discussion about the few words that do not start with the same letter such as *perezoso* (sloth), *ranas venenosas* (poison-arrow frogs), or *helecho* (fern) would create interesting linguistic and vocabulary discussion.

Less complicated alphabet books such as *ABC animales* (*ABC Animals*) (Broeck, 1983) and *ABC* (Sempere, 1987) also have delightful rhymes and pictures. In the former, for example, the M is illustrated with a colorful *mariposa* (butterfly) and the poem is <M de *mariposa*, que sobre las flores se posa y es, por sus colores, hermosa.> (The M of *mariposa* that settles on the flowers and is, because of its colors, beautiful.). In the latter, the poem for the letter V is illustrated with black and white drawings:

A volar me llevó el viento	The wind took me flying
y todo chiquito lo vi:	and I saw everything tiny:
veinte ovejas, diez venados	twenty sheep, ten deer
y una vaca con violín (p. 53).	and a cow with a violin.

When students are exposed to alphabet books such as these, they often choose to make their own alphabet books. Children make up their own alphabet text for each letter and then illustrate the pages. Sometimes a whole class works on a big book and all the children illustrate pages or help cut out pictures from magazines to paste on the letter pages. These

Broeck, Fabricio Vanden. *ABC animales, Colección Piñata*. México, D.F.: Editorial Patria (1983).

Del Paso, Fernando. *De la A a la Z por un poeta*. México, D.F.: Grupo Editorial Diana (1990).

Detwiler, Darius, and Rizo-Patrón, Marina. *Libro del ABC*. Boston: Houghton Mifflin (1993).

Pratt, Kristin Joy. *Un paseo por el bosque lluvioso*. Nevada City: Dawn Publications (1993).

Sempere, Vicky. *ABC*. Caracas, Venezuela: Ediciones Ekaré-Banco del Libro (1987).

TABLE 3–1: Alternatives to Método Alfabético

pages are then laminated, and the book remains in the classroom. Children enjoy looking at the pages and repeating the names of the pictures.

Several teachers we have worked with have students and parents work together at home to make individual alphabet books. Together parents and children cut out pictures from magazines and newspapers or draw pictures that begin with the letters of the alphabet. These activities familiarize children with the alphabet in a purposeful and enjoyable way. If teachers are concerned that parents may not have access to newspapers or magazines, they make these available in the class for students to take home. Teachers can usually get old magazines from church groups or other organizations. Newspaper ads are another good source of print materials.

Young readers do need to learn the letters of the alphabet. The alphabetic method is based on the idea that reading should start with small parts, letters, and build up to words. We prefer an approach that keeps letters and words in meaningful contexts. Reading and making alphabet books are authentic alternatives to the decontextualized exercises that characterize the alphabetic method. Table 3-1 lists literature alternatives for *el método alfabético*.

El método onomatopéyico (The Onomatopoeic Method)

Onomatopoeia refers to words that represent sounds. In English, examples would include *hiss* or *buzz* and in Spanish, words like *zas* or *cataplán*. In the onomatopoeic method of teaching reading, sounds in the environment are associated with letters and sounds in the language. For example, the Spanish vowel sound for *i* might be taught in connection with the squeal of an animal like a pig, monkey, or mouse, and the sound for *a* in connection with people laughing. The idea is similar to Zoo-phonics in English, where students are asked to associate English sounds with sounds that animals make. In *el método onomatopéyico*, consonants are often taught by having students repeat them in alliterative sentences. For example, *m* could be presented in the sentence <Mamá amasa la masa> (Mother kneads the dough) or *p* with <Pepe es mi papá>. (Pepe is my dad). Once the students are able to identify individual sounds, it is assumed they can combine them to identify words.

Scenario for el método onomatopéyico
The teacher brings into the classroom a picture of monkeys in a cage surrounded by a group of laughing people. The cartoon bubbles above the monkeys performing their antics, saying, <hi, hi, hi>. The people watching and laughing are saying <ja, ja, ja>.

MAESTRA: ¿Qué ven en este dibujo?	TEACHER: What do you see in this picture?
NIÑO: Una jaula con monos.	BOY: A cage with monkeys.
MAESTRA: ¿Qué más?	TEACHER: What else?
NIÑA: Hay gente mirando a los monos jugar.	GIRL: There are people watching the monkeys playing.
MAESTRA: ¿Qué está haciendo la gente?	TEACHER: What are the people doing?
NIÑO: Todos están riéndose.	BOY: Everyone's laughing.
MAESTRA: ¿Qué sonido hacen las personas allí?	TEACHER: What sound are the people there making?
NIÑO: ¡Ja! ¡Ja! ¡Ja!	BOY: Ha! Ha! Ha!
MAESTRA: ¿Y qué sonido hacen los monos?	TEACHER: And what sound are the monkeys making?
NIÑA: Hi, hi, hi.	GIRL: Hē, hē, hē.
MAESTRA: Muy bien. El sonido que hacen los monos es el sonido de la letra *i*. hi, hi, hi. ¿Qué sonido hace la gente?	TEACHER: Very good. The sound the monkeys are making is the sound of the letter *i*. hi, hi, hi. What sound do the people make?
NIÑOS: ¡Ja! ¡Ja! ¡Ja!	CHILDREN: Ha! Ha! Ha!
MAESTRA: Sí. Este es el sonido de la letra *a*. ¡Ja! ¡Ja! ¡Ja!	TEACHER: Yes. This is the sound of the letter *a*. Ha! Ha! Ha!

Analysis of el método onomatopéyico

This is an interesting lesson to analyze with the checklist because the only text the students see appears in cartoon bubbles and represents the sounds made by monkeys and people. The students are only using the graphophonic cueing system because there is no linguistic context to provide syntactic or semantic cues. Students are asked to make connections and predictions using the background knowledge of the sounds people and monkeys make as they identify the words in the picture. Students might be interested in the pictures. However, since the students really have no text to read and are only identifying sounds that might later be found in other words, one could not say they are really reading.

A *Positive Alternative* to el método onomatopéyico

Many creative and imaginative books written for young children use onomatopoeia. These could be incorporated into an effective Spanish reading program. One excellent example is *¿Qué dice el desierto?* (*What Does the Desert Say?*) (Mora, 1993), a book available in big book form. In this predictable book the author writes about the sounds of the desert. The illustrations help support the meanings of the onomatopoeic words and phrases. For example, on one page an owl sits atop a saguaro cactus in the desert, and the text reads:

> Oye la lechuza, uuu, uuu, uuu.
> Oye la lechuza, uuu, uuu, uuu (p. 5).

Translation:

> Listen to the owl, uuu, uuu, uuu.
> Listen to the owl, uuu, uuu, uuu.

Reading a text such as this one chorally, encouraging discussion of the pictures, and drawing on the children's knowledge of deserts and desert animals would be an excellent way for a teacher to support reading and learning at the same time. Children could read the book in parts and read more about the desert and desert animals in other books such as *El desierto* (The Desert) (Torres, 1994). Using wordless books like *En el bosque* (In the Woods) (Cristini and Puricelli, 1983), children could talk about the animals and sounds in other environments and then make their own book about some place they know and would like to write about. In their books, students could feature the sounds of nature and animals from the place they choose.

Books such as *El chivo en la huerta* (*The Goat in the Garden*) (Kratky, 1989) and *Doña Carmen* (Bragado, 1993) encourage children to read and make the sounds of the farm animals. Both of these books are highly predictable, and teachers can involve students in readers' theatre and the writing of their own stories following similar patterns. In addition, poetry often includes playful sounds. In *El cuento del gato y otras poesías favoritas* (*The Story of the Cat and Other Favorite Poems*) (Ada, 1992), the poem *Los sapitos* (*The Little Frogs*) incorporates the sounds of the frogs themselves as in the verse, <La ranita soy yo, glo, glo, glo> (Little frog am I, glo, glo, glo) (p. 9).

Songs provide opportunity for the natural and enjoyable use of onomatopoeia. Many songs draw on natural sounds. An especially charming one is *Los instrumentos* (*The Instruments*) (Aron, 1988). This song not only involves students in the sounds of the language but also teaches them about musical instruments. As they sing the song, children identify the trumpet, the maracas, the guitar, and the drum with the sound each one makes. The lyrics are as follows:

La trompeta, (The trumpet)
tu, tururu, tu
tu, tururu, tu

Las maracas, (The maracas)
chucu, chucu
chucu, chucu

La guitarra, (The guitar)
chunta, chunta
chunta, chunta

El tambor, (The drum)
pomporo, rom, pom, pom
Pomporo, rom, pom, pom, pom
pomporo, rom, pom, pom, pom
pomporo, rom, pom, pom, pom
pomporo, rom, pom, pom (p. 26).

A song like this one would be excellent for young children to mime the use of the instruments at the same time they sing the song from a chart. Ideally, students would have access to the instruments too and actually be able to play them at some point in the lesson. Students in this case would be learning about musical instruments and their sounds at they same time they are learning about the sounds of Spanish.

Children love to play with the sounds of language. As they learn to read, they make connections between patterns of sounds and patterns of

ALTERNATIVES TO METODO ONOMATOPEYICO

Ada, Alma Flor. *El cuento del gato y otras poesías favoritas, Días y días de poesía.* Carmel: Hampton-Brown Books (1992).

Aron, Evelyn. *Cántame en español: Sing to me in Spanish.* México, D.F.: Multidiseño Gráfico (1988).

Bragado, Manuel. *Doña Carmen.* Boston: Houghton Mifflin (1993).

Cristini, Ermanno, and Puricelli, Luigi. *En el bosque.* New York: Scholastic (1983).

Kratky, Lada Josefa. *El chivo en la huerta.* Carmel: Hampton-Brown (1989).

Mora, Pat. *¿Qué dice el desierto?* Boston: Houghton Mifflin (1993).

Torres, Edna. *El desierto.* (Fonseca, R., ed., *Educación ambiental.*) México, D.F.: CONAFE (1994).

TABLE 3–2: Alternatives to Método Onomatopéyico

spelling. The onomatopoeic method capitalizes on children's interest in language play. However, the method takes natural sounds out of context and uses them as building blocks to help students identify words. Teachers can draw on children's interest in sounds by finding rhymes and songs that are onomatopoeic. This element is part of a love of reading but not the key for learning to read. Table 3-2 lists literature alternatives for *el método onomatopéyico.*

El método fónico o fonético (The Phonics or Phonetic Method)

Like *el método onomatopéyico*, this method focuses on the sounds that letters make. In this part-to-whole synthetic method, the students first learn the names of the letters of the alphabet. Then they identify the sounds of letters and put those sounds together to make syllables and then words. Generally, in Spanish this method has been used to teach the vowels only. Then, once the vowels are learned, the syllabic method is used to teach syllables and words.

Scenario for el método fónico o fonético
Most of the teacher's words in the dialogue for this lesson are taken from the teacher's guide for the readiness for reading level of the *Vamos: Programa de lectura en español de Houghton Mifflin* (*The Spanish Reading Program from Houghton Mifflin*) (Barrera and Crawford, 1987, pp. 188–190).

The teacher has a series of cards that she can put in a pocket chart or put up where the students can easily see them. One card has only the letter *a* on it. Some cards have pictures of objects beginning with the letter *a*. Other cards have a word beginning with an underlined *a*. For example, there are cards for the words *abeja* (bee), *astronauta* (astronaut), and *avión* (airplane). Finally, there is a series of cards with the picture of an *a* word with the letter *a* superimposed upon the picture. These cards are called *dibujos mágicos* (magic pictures).

The teacher begins by putting up the picture of the bee (*abeja*), the word card *abeja* with the *a* underlined, the magic picture card of the bee with the *a* superimposed, and a letter card with the letter *a*.

MAESTRA: Ustedes conocen la letra *a* y también conocen el sonido que oyen al principio de la palabra *abeja*. Ese sonido es el sonido de la *a*. En esta tarjeta está escrita la palabra *abeja*. La letra que ustedes ven al principio de *abeja* es la *a*. El sonido que ustedes oyen al principio de *abeja* es el sonido de la *a*. Cuando vean la letra *a*, piensen en el sonido que oyen al principio de *abeja*. Así ustedes siempre recordarán el sonido de la *a*. ¿Cuál es el dibujo que nos ayuda a recordar el sonido de la letra *a*?

TEACHER: You know the letter *a* and you also know the sound you hear at the beginning of *abeja*. This sound is called the sound of the *a*. On this card is written the word *abeja*. The letter that you see at the beginning of *abeja* is the *a*. The sound that you hear at the beginning of *abeja* is the sound of the *a*. When you see the letter *a*, think of the sound that you hear at the beginning of *abeja*. In that way, you will remember the sound of the *a*. What is the picture that helps us remember the sound of the letter *a*?

NIÑOS: abeja

CHILDREN: Bee

MAESTRA: Muy bien.

TEACHER: Very good.

The teachers points to the magic picture (the picture of the bee with the letter *a* superimposed).

MAESTRA: Este es el dibujo mágico de la *a*. La *a* está en <abeja> porque <abeja> comienza con el sonido de la *a*. Cuando vean la letra *a*, piensen en el sonido que oyen al principio de <abeja>. De esa manera, ustedes recordarán el sonido de la *a*.

TEACHER: This is the magic picture for *a*. The *a* is on *abeja* because *abeja* begins with the sound for the *a*. When you see the letter *a*, think of the sound you hear at the beginning of *abeja*. In this way, you will remember the sound for *a*.

The teacher then puts up pictures of an astronaut (*astronauta*); airplane (*avión*), a blotch of blue paint (*azul*), and a bird (*pájaro*).

MAESTRA: Algunos de los nombres de estos dibujos comienzan con el sonido de la *a*. Piensen en el sonido de la *a*, el sonido que oyen al principio de *abeja*, mientras decimos los nombres de los dibujos.	TEACHER: Some of the names of these pictures begin with the sound of *a*. Think about the sound of the *a*, the sound that you hear at the beginning of *abeja* while we say the names of the pictures.

After this, the teacher puts up the letter *a* by itself on a row of the pocket chart.

MAESTRA: ¿Qué letra es ésta?	TEACHER: What letter is it?
NIÑOS: Es la *a*.	CHILDREN: The letter is *a*.
MAESTRA: Voy a pedirle a uno de ustedes que diga el nombre de estos dibujos. Si el nombre del dibujo comienza con el sonido de la *a*, debe colocarse el dibujo en la misma línea que la *a*.	TEACHER: I am going to ask someone to say the name of the pictures. If the name of the picture begins with the sound of the *a*, put the picture on the same line as the *a*.

Analysis of el método fónico o fonético

Again, in this lesson, the text only consists of isolated words that begin with *a*. Since students are looking at pictures, they may, in fact, see some meaning in the lesson. However, they are not really constructing meaning through the use of the three cueing systems. The only context is single words, so there is no sentence support for syntax or semantics. Students are focused on the graphophonic system because they are asked to identify pictures and match the beginning sounds of the pictures with a letter. At this stage they have not even reached the level of word recognition. No attempt is made to connect the lesson with the students' background experiences. While the pictures used may be attractive and colorful, the method does not involve students in reading extended text. In fact, the uses of the different pictures, combined with the type of questioning that is done, probably confuses children. They expend more energy deciding what answer the teacher is looking for than in working on any sound concepts.

A Positive Alternative to el método fónico o fonético

The goal of *el método fónico* is to help beginning readers use initial sounds to identify words. Sounds provide important cues for readers, and publishers have created materials that can help emergent readers develop an awareness of sounds. Several companies have responded to the need expressed by Spanish bilingual teachers in the United States for predictable reading materials that have limited text for emergent Spanish readers. Two of these series, *Pan y Canela* (*Bread and Cinnamon*) (Kratky, 1995), and *Literatura 2000* (*Literature 2000*) (Cappellini and Almada, 1994) consist of a series of little books with colorful pictures closely tied to the texts, repetitive patterns of language, and interesting themes relevant to young learners. Students naturally begin to associate letters and sounds as they work with these books. Examples of two books from the *Pan y Canela* series show how beginning readers are supported through these books.

In *Uno, dos, tres y cuatro* (*One, Two, Three and Four*) (Kratky, 1995) there is a repetitive pattern with contrasting sounds highlighted through rhyme as on the page with the cat carrying a dish:

Uno, dos, tres y cuatro.	One, two, three and four
Sale un gato	Out comes a cat
con un plato (p. 2).	with a plate.

Another page depicts a mouse dragging a big ham. The text reads:

Uno, dos, tres y cuatro	One, two, three and four
Sale un ratón	Out comes a rat
con un jamón (p. 5).	with a ham.

In *Papi y yo* (*Dad and I*) (Garza-Williams, 1995) photographs show an Hispanic boy and his father dressing for a mariachi concert they both will play in. The repetitive text is closely related to the photographs and varies only slightly for each page:

Papi se pone los pantalones.	Daddy puts on his pants.
Yo me pongo los pantalones.	I put on my pants.
Papi se pone la camisa.	Daddy puts on his shirt.
Yo me pongo la camisa (pp. 2–3).	I put on my shirt.

A book from *Literatura 2000* that supports theme study is *Patas* (*Animal Feet*) (Almada, 1994). In this book colorful photographs feature animals and the characteristics of their feet beginning with the large feet of the mother buffalo and the small ones of her calf. The short feet of a lizard are

ALTERNATIVES TO METODO FONICO O FONETICO

Almada, Patricia. *Patas, Literatura 2000.* Crystal Lake: Rigby (1994).

Cappellini, Mary, and Almada, Patricia. *Literatura 2000.* Crystal Lake: Rigby (1994).

Garza-Williams, Liz. *Papi y yo, Pan y Canela, Colección A.* Carmel: Hampton-Brown (1995).

Kratky, Lada Josefa. *Pan y Canela.* Carmel: Hampton-Brown Books (1995).

Kratky, Lada Josefa. *Uno, dos, tres y cuatro, Pan y Canela, Colección A.* Carmel: Hampton-Brown (1995).

TABLE 3–3: Alternatives to Método Fónico o Fonético

contrasted next with the long ones of a giraffe followed by the fast feet of a cheetah and the slow ones of a turtle. The last two pages have the many feet of a centipede and the lack of feet of a snake. The limited text is supported by the photographs:

Patas grandes y patas chicas.	Big feet and little feet.
Patas cortas y patas largas.	Short feet and long feet.
Patas rápidas y patas lentas.	Fast feet and slow feet.
Muchas patas y ni una pata.	Many feet and not one foot.

Texts such as these allow emergent readers to experience success while reading books on topics of interest to them. These small books are imaginative, relevant, and informative. As students engage with these texts, they begin to develop phonemic awareness. We prefer this approach to one that isolates phonemes and teaches them out of context. Table 3-3 lists literature alternatives for *el método fonico o fonético.*

El método silábico (The Syllabic Method)

The syllabic method moves beyond the individual letter sounds and uses the syllable as the basic unit. As syllables are introduced and learned, they are combined to form words and sentences. Many teachers prefer this method to *el método fonético* because consonants can be pronounced only in combination with vowels. Also, Spanish speakers point out that Spanish is a naturally syllabic language. The words can easily be broken up into syllables of a consonant and a vowel.

In the syllabic method, the sounds of the five vowels are usually taught first. Then words are learned by teaching syllables and putting the syllables together into words. In this method, many texts for beginning readers begin with the letter *m*. This letter is joined with the vowels, and students repeat, *ma, me, mi, mo, mu*. These syllables are then put into words, such as, *mamá, mimo, memo,* or *mami*. Next, these words are put into sentences: *Mi mamá me mima. Mi mamá me ama. Amo a mi mamá.* (My mother pampers me. My mother loves me. I love my mother.) During the course of the lesson the students repeat syllables, words, and the basic sentences.

The syllabic method is taught sequentially. Each lesson builds on the one before by adding a new consonant. For example, in the second lesson there would be words with both *m* and *p*, so students would read sentences like *Mamá ama a papá* (Mother loves father).

Scenario for el método silábico

In earlier lessons, the students have already been taught the syllables *ma, me, mi, mo, mu* and *sa, se, si, so, su*. For this lesson the students are learning the syllables with the letter *p*. The children have their books open to the page which is introducing *p*. There is a picture of a father with his son. The word, *papá* is written next to the drawing. Under it, on the page follow the syllables *pa, po, pu, pe, pi* and words and sentences. On the opposite page is a picture of a map, a father, a cat, a dish of soap suds (foam), and a box of raisins. Under each picture are lines where students can write the words.

The teacher begins the lesson:

MAESTRA: Lean conmigo. <papá>	TEACHER: Read with me. "father"
NIÑOS: papá	CHILDREN: father
MAESTRA: Repitan: pa, po, pu, pe, pi.	TEACHER: Repeat: *pa, po, pu, pe, pi.*
NIÑOS: pa, po, pu ,pe, pi	CHILDREN: *pa, po, pu, pe, pi.*
MAESTRA: papá	TEACHER: father
NIÑOS: papá	CHILDREN: father
MAESTRA: pesa	TEACHER: weighs
NIÑOS: pesa	CHILDREN: weighs

MAESTRA: mapa	TEACHER: map
NIÑOS: mapa	CHILDREN: map
MAESTRA: pipa	TEACHER: pipe
NIÑOS: pipa	CHILDREN: pipe
MAESTRA: pasas	TEACHER: raisins
NIÑOS: pasas	CHILDREN: raisins
MAESTRA: espuma	TEACHER: foam
NIÑOS: espuma	CHILDREN: foam
MAESTRA: Pepe	TEACHER: Pepe
NIÑOS: Pepe	CHILDREN: Pepe
MAESTRA: pisa	TEACHER: steps (on)
NIÑOS: pisa	CHILDREN: steps (on)
MAESTRA: Pepe es mi papá.	TEACHER: Pepe is my father.
NIÑOS: Pepe es mi papá.	CHILDREN: Pepe is my father.
MAESTRA: Papá ama a mi mamá.	TEACHER: Father loves my mother.
NIÑOS: Papá ama a mi mamá.	CHILDREN: Father loves my mother.
MAESTRA: Memo usa ese mapa.	TEACHER: Memo uses that map.
NIÑOS: Memo usa ese mapa.	CHILDREN: Memo uses that map.
MAESTRA: Ema pesa esas pasas.	TEACHER: Ema weighs those raisins.
NIÑOS: Ema pesa esas pasas.	CHILDREN: Ema weighs those raisins.
MAESTRA: Susú pisa esa espuma.	TEACHER: Susú steps on that foam.
NIÑOS: Susú pisa esa espuma.	CHILDREN: Susú steps on that foam.
MAESTRA: Ahora, en la otra página van a escribir debajo de cada dibujo el nombre que le corresponde. (Señalando los dibujos) ¿Qué van a escribir debajo de los dibujos?	TEACHER: Now, on the next page, under each picture, you are going to write the name of the picture. (Pointing to the pictures) What are you going to write under the pictures?

NIÑOS: mapa, papá, gato, espuma, pasas

CHILDREN: map, father, cat, foam, raisins

MAESTRA: Está bien, pero uds. todavía no han visto las sílabas para la palabra <gato>. ¿Recuerdan el nombre del gato en la última lección?

TEACHER: OK, but you haven't studied the syllables for the word "cat" yet. Do you remember the name of the cat in the last lesson?

NIÑO: ¿Susú?

CHILD: Susú?

MAESTRA: Sí, Juan, <Susú>. Entonces, deben escribir la palabra <Susú> debajo del gato y no la palabra <gato>.

TEACHER: Yes, Juan, "Susú." Then, you should write the word "Susú" under the cat and not the word "cat."

Analysis of el método silábico

When analyzing the syllabic method with the Checklist for Effective Reading Instruction, it is clear that the students have little choice or variety in what they read. Although the students can access picture cues and although they do read whole sentences, the sentences are not connected. It would be hard to describe the lesson as one in which students are making meaning as they read. The lessons are designed to help develop the graphophonic cueing system. For the most part, the sentences consist of words that reflect everyday experiences a child might have. However, the words and sentences are presented in isolation with no real connection to one another, making prediction difficult. The exercise following the presentation of the vocabulary and basic sentences is merely a labeling exercise and could hardly be called either authentic writing or a true strategy lesson that supports reading.

The lesson presented above was not really interesting or imaginative. Sometimes basal reading programs have attempted to make lessons more imaginative and visually attractive to students despite the extreme limitations of the controlled vocabulary. For example, one beginning story in a syllabic series presents a short story about Manolo watching a *mono* (monkey) do funny tricks on television. Still, these stories are hardly predictable and the language is far from natural.

Pellicer (1969) discusses the pros and cons of the syllabic method, pointing out that it is good because it presents the material in a logical order; it requires very little in the way of materials; and teachers report they are satisfied with the method for both children and adults. However, he explains that the method depends too much on the student's memory in the first stages; the student can lose interest if meaningful words are not introduced early; there is the danger of a sort of mechanical learning, especially if the material is difficult or taught too quickly; and the method is not consistent with child psychology. It is interesting to note that all of the pros are aspects that appeal to teachers. On the other hand, the cons center on potential problems for students.

A Positive Alternative to el método silábico

The emergent literacy series books suggested above in the positive alternative section for *el método fonético* would also be appropriate for this method. The texts of songs such as *Los instrumentos* or the ever popular favorite *Los pollitos* emphasize syllables in a natural way. (The trumpet sound is *tururu tu*. The little chicks say *pio, pio, pio*.) In fact, there are many lovely versions of *Los pollitos* including one in big book format (Fernández, 1993).

Another type of support reading is predictable books with a pattern that also plays on sounds. A favorite in many bilingual classrooms is *Pinta, pinta, Gregorita* (*Paint, Paint, Gregorita*) (Kratky, 1990), the imaginative and colorfully illustrated story of a young girl's painting coming to life. This big book story is especially delightful because its artwork captures the imagination, and there is a surprise pop-out page toward the end. The repetitive patterns and the rhyme, along with the illustrations, help emergent readers make sense of the story.

> Pinta, pinta, Gregorita,
> ¿A dónde vas tan solita?
> Con mi boina y mi papel,
> con mi pintura y pincel,
> voy a mi cuarto a pintar.
> Pinto, pinto, pinto, pan (pp. 3–4).

Translation:

> Paint, paint, Gregorita,
> Where are you going all by yourself?
> With my beret and my paper
> with my paints and my paint brush
> I'm going to my room to paint.
> Pinto, pinto, pinto, pan.

Later in the story, all the things Gregorita has painted and balanced on top of each other tumble down and fall upon one another. This is the pop-out page of the book. The objects are paired according to their rhyming sounds. The text for this section reads:

Cae el tornillo
en el anillo,
el caracol,
en el girasol,
la chuleta,
en la maleta,
el calcetín,
en el patín (p. 14).

Translation:

The screw falls on top of the ring,
the snail on top of the sunflower,
the pork chop into the suitcase,
the sock on top of the skate.

Though books such as this one are not about the real world, their bright pictures, patterns, imagination, and rhyme support both the creativity and the reading development of children.

Another book that plays with the sounds of language but is about the real world too is a big book, *Voy a la escuela* (*I Go to School*) (Cervantes, 1996). The book is full of color photographs of children in and around their school and in a Spanish/English bilingual classroom. The limited text has a predictable story line like <Esta es mi escuela, donde yo aprendí, a decir 'buenos días' así, así, así.> (pp. 3–4) (This is my school, where I learned to say 'good morning' like this, like this, like this.). Because the pictures and text are so closely aligned, emergent readers could read the book in chorus as a group, in pairs, or even on their own.

Texts like this allow for the playful use of the language, encourage children to use their imagination, and allow them to connect their experiences to the reading. These books support readers as they construct meaning more fully than the controlled texts of syllabic method readers. Table 3-4 lists literature alternatives to *el método silábico*.

Commercial Programs Developed by Private Companies

The four synthetic methods we have described have been widely used throughout the Spanish-speaking world. In fact, they are still being used in many bilingual classrooms in the United States. In some schools, these traditional methods are being replaced by newer programs that compensate for a short history and a limited theoretical base with a large advertising bud-

ALTERNATIVES TO METODO SILABICO

Cervantes, Jesús. *Voy a la escuela.* Carmel: Hampton-Brown (1996).

Fernández, Laura. Pío, pío. In *Yo soy yo* (Barrera, R., Crawford, A., Mims, J.S., and de Silva, A.D., eds.) Boston: Houghton Mifflin (1993).

Kratky, Lada Josefa. *Pinta, pinta, Gregorita.* Carmel: Hampton-Brown (1990).

TABLE 3–4: Alternatives to Método Silábico

get. Many such programs have been developed over the years by one or two people who have their own unique ideas about how best to teach reading. These programs are broadly advertised to the general public as solutions to any reading problems that any child or adult might have. Often, the program developers have little to no background in reading, and the programs themselves are based on different gimmicks that the developers are convinced help to teach reading.

One such program is *Hooked on Phonics* (1984). The developers of this program spent a great deal more money on publicity than on research. In fact, some of the claims in the ads were so questionable that they were banned by the Federal Communications Commission. Still, the ads did work, and the program is in use in many school districts.

Although *Hooked on Phonics* is an expensive program, the actual materials that buyers receive are relatively inexpensive. They consist of some instructions, a set of flash cards, and a set of short audio tapes. The two sides of the fifteen minute tapes are identical; that is, what is on one side is repeated. The plan for instruction is as simple as the program components. Students listen to the tapes as they flip through the flash cards. Once they master a level they move on to the next level. At the earlier levels, the cards have words. At higher levels, students work on sentences. This program does not move to the level of complete stories, even in simplified form.

The hook in *Hooked on Phonics* is the catchy music on the tape. What would otherwise be dull, repetitive exercises are jazzed up by the rhythms and the lively voice on the tape. In many ways, this program is similar to many older programs that combine phonics methods with the look/say feature of the flash cards. The difference is the advertising hype and the music.

Hooked on Phonics is often used in special education programs or in programs for low level readers. This includes many Spanish readers transitioning into English. Often, parents wishing to help their students become better readers have purchased the program. The program is clearly based on a word recognition view of reading. The assumption is that students need to get the words first, and the meaning will come later. Students are told they must master each level before they move on to the next one. This puts all the responsibility on the student. The program can't fail, but the student can if he or she skips a level or moves ahead before achieving complete mastery. This approach almost ensures that some students will not only fail but also blame themselves for their failure.

Another program that has been widely used in California to teach reading both in English and Spanish is *Zoo-phonics* (Clark, 1994). This program draws on children's natural love of animals and uses gesture and music as mnemonic devices. In the Spanish version of this method children associate letter names with animals. For example, they learn the letter *a* by associating it with *Ana Ardilla* (Ana Squirrel) as they make the gesture of cracking nuts by pounding one fist into a palm. The sound of *b* is associated with *Beto Burro*; so the children flip one ear as they say the *b* sound. A tape that accompanies the program has children sing and gesture through the alphabet. After the children have mastered the gestures, they sound out words systematically making the gesture for each letter in the word. Additional gestures are used for accent marks.

Several serious concerns about this type of program arise. In the first place, the gesture and the sound are really not related at all, so the purpose of the gesture is lost from a pedagogical perspective. Students spend time practicing the gestures and the letters, but very little time is spent even reading isolated words. In many ways, this method takes educators back to the alphabetic method but makes it more complicated because students are signaling letters and trying at the same time to sound out words. Students in this program sing catchy songs. They even do "animal aerobics," but spend little to no time reading real texts.

Still another popular program, *Estrellita* (Myer, 1995), has been written and advertised by a bilingual teacher who has developed her own system of teaching reading using an eclectic method consisting of the teaching of all the initial sounds, establishing the association of the sounds with pictures, learning syllables, and moving to short, controlled stories. Though the method claims to include whole language strategies, in reality the method is an adaptation of the syllabic method using sound charts, picture and letter cards, and vocabulary flash cards to prepare students to read controlled story books. Although reading real literature is the goal, the program is based on the belief that first students must master the sounds and syllables to be able to read.

Commercial programs such as the three described above come and go. They are usually quite expensive. It is important that educators closely examine the claims of such programs, the rationale for the programs, and the materials themselves. Evaluation of the three programs above with the Checklist for Effective Reading Instruction would quickly show that they do not meet the criteria to support emergent readers. The alternative to such programs is the use of authentic literature to teach reading.

Conclusion

The methods described so far are all considered synthetic because readers are presented with letters, syllables, or words and asked to combine them to create larger units. These traditional methods of teaching reading in Spanish have as their goal the recognition of words. In most cases, students are working with parts of words, words, or individual sentences rather than with connected text. The textbooks present reading exercises rather than engaging students in authentic reading experiences. None of the synthetic methods we have described in this chapter meet the criteria for effective reading practices as outlined in the checklist. Synthetic methods generally present reading as a process of recognizing words instead of constructing meaning.

4

From Analytic Methods
to El lenguaje integral

In this chapter we continue to examine methods that have been used to teach reading in Spanish. The first methods we consider here are analytic. That is, they begin with some whole, and students are asked to find the parts within the whole. Analytic methods may at first appear to be more consistent with a socio-psycholinguistic approach to reading than synthetic methods. As we explain, however, analytic methods, like synthetic methods, do not represent effective practice because the goal is still word recognition. In analytic methods students seldom get to engage with connected text longer than a sentence, and our claim is that students need to engage with complete texts to develop the strategies they need to become proficient readers.

We follow the same format here for reviewing the various methods. We start with a short description, present a sample lesson scenario, analyze the lesson using the checklist, and then offer a positive alternative, including a list of appropriate literature. We end this chapter with *el lenguaje integral* (Whole Language), which is actually an approach based on a philosophy of learning, not a method. As we explain, we advocate *el lenguaje integral* because it is consistent with a socio-psycholinguistic approach to literacy.

El método de palabras generadoras (Generative Word Method)

This method involves both analysis and synthesis. Students begin with whole words, often presented in sentences that they repeat and memorize. Then the students are asked to analyze the sentences and words. They break down the basic parts of words, going from syllables to individual sounds. After taking apart the words, the students manipulate the parts to form new words and new sentences.

Scenario for el método de palabras generadoras

The teacher begins by reading a sentence he has written on the board, <Tomás mete la pelota.> (Tomás places the ball.). The sentence is then broken down into the four words, which are read in isolation. From that point the syllables from each word are taken and paired with another syllable beginning with the same letter. Finally, the syllables are broken down into vowels and consonants. Then there is a reverse build up from those letters to syllables to words to a new sentence.

MAESTRO: Repitan, por favor, <Tomás mete la pelota.>	TEACHER: Repeat, please. "Tomás mete la pelota."
NIÑOS: <Tomás mete la pelota>.	CHILDREN: "Thomas puts the ball." (in something or in some place)
MAESTRO: Ahora presten atención. Voy a dividir la oración en palabras, en sílabas, y después en letras. Con las letras voy a formar nuevas sílabas y palabras para formar una oración nueva. Entonces, vamos a comenzar con una oración y luego, vamos a terminar con otra oración.	TEACHER: Now, pay attention. I am going to divide the sentence into words, syllables and letters. With the letters I am going to form new syllables and words in order to make a new sentence. So, we're going to begin with one sentence and end with another sentence.
(El maestro escribe lo siguiente en el pizarrón.)	(The teacher writes the following on the board.)

Tomás mete la pelota.

Tomás
mete
la pelota
to ta
ta te
ma me
la lo
lo le
pe pa
a e i o u t m s p l
pe pa
lo le
la lo
ma me
ta te

Tomás mete la pelota.
(Thomas places the ball.)

Tomás
mete
la pelota
to ta
ta te
ma me
la lo
lo le
pe pa
a e i o u t m s p l
pe pa
lo le
la lo
ma me
ta te

to ta	to ta
Papá	Papá
toma	toma
atole	atole
Papá toma atole.	Papá toma atole.
	(Papa drinks atole.)

MAESTRO: Ahora voy a señalarles con la mano lo que ustedes van a leer después de mí. (El maestro lee cada línea y los estudiantes repiten después de él.)	TEACHER: Now, I am going to point with my hand to what you are going to read after me. (The teacher reads each line and the students repeat after him.)

Analysis of el método de palabras generadoras

Certainly, there appears to be little meaning making in this process of repetition of sentences, words, and sounds. Students are given no choice or variety in what they read. While one might say students are using the syntactic system because they are separating sentences into words and then forming new sentences from the parts, they are not really using clauses or phrasal units to do this, but instead, are mechanically taking the sentences and words apart. In fact, they don't even do this for themselves. Rather, they follow along after the teacher has divided the sentence into words, the words into syllables, and the syllables into letters.

The sentences themselves have no relation to the students' lives or interests. The mechanical process depends entirely on the letters, syllables, and words in the sentence the teacher chooses. Even though the procedure might appear to follow a predictable pattern, the reading material is not predictable because it consists of only one sentence. As a result, students don't build competence in the use of the cueing systems. This method seems to have been created as a type of linguistic exercise. However, it consists of manipulating linguistic units rather than reading for meaning. If reading involves construction of meaning, this method doesn't prepare students to read real texts.

A Positive Alternative to el método de palabras generadoras

Many stories do have a cumulative pattern that helps students predict and make sense of the text they are reading. Unlike the patterns in *el método de palabras generadoras*, these patterns are based on the overall story line and are dependent upon the whole text (see Table 4-1).

For example, in *Pan, pan, gran pan* (*Bread, Bread, Huge Bread*) (Cumpiano, 1990), two children are bored, so their grandmother suggests they make some bread. Without them noticing, a great deal of yeast falls into the dough. When the bread bakes it expands to unbelievable proportions that the children, Julieta and Julián, and their grandmother cannot control. The bread grows out of the house and into the street where not even the policeman, Sargento Todo de Talle, the teacher, doña Cara Mela, or the zoo keeper, don Dominales, can control it. Finally, a large bird pecks the bread, and the air explodes out of it, leaving lots of pieces of bread for everyone. The text that closes the story has a natural rhyming, repetitive pattern that draws upon all these characters. Children love reading these lines together or choosing parts:

Y don Dominales	and Don Dominales
que cuida los animales,	who takes care of the animals,
y doña Cara Mela	and Doña Cara Mela
que enseña en la escuela,	who teaches in the school,
y el sargento Todo de Talle	and Sergeant Todo de Talle
el policía de la calle,	the policeman on the street,
y sobre todo Abuelita,	and above all grandmother,
y Julieta	and Julieta
y también Julián,	and also Julián,
todos comieron	everyone had something to eat
de aquel gran pan (p. 16).	from that huge bread.

Another cumulative story is a folk tale about a chicken, a rooster, and a bean, *La gallinita, el gallo y el frijol* (*The Hen, the Rooster and the Bean*) (Kratky, 1989). In this story the rooster gets a bean stuck in his throat and tells the hen to ask the river for some water. The river will not give water until the hen brings it a flower from a jasmine plant. The plant will not give a flower until the hen brings some string to help hold up its vines from the girl weaving. The girl will not give the hen string until the hen brings her a comb from the comb maker. The comb maker wants a roll from the baker, and the baker wants wood from the woodcutter. Finally, the woodcutter gives the hen wood, and the hen then goes back through the sequence of characters to finally get the water from the river for the rooster who is still choking on the bean.

This kind of backward buildup story is predictable and enjoyable. The pattern helps readers construct meaning. Teachers can point out how the pattern works, and students can see the parts within a complete text rather than trying to make sense out of the parts of a single sentence that has been manipulated to form words or sentences.

El método global o ideovisual (The Global or Visual Concept Method)

In the early 1900s Decroly and Degand suggested the globalization method of teaching, explaining that reading <. . . no tiene relación alguna con el

ALTERNATIVES TO METODO DE PALABRAS GENERADORAS

Cumpiano, Ina. *Pan, pan, gran pan.* Carmel: Hampton-Brown Books (1990).

Kratky, Lada Josefa. *La gallinita, el gallo y el frijol.* Carmel: Hampton-Brown (1989).

TABLE 4–1: Alternatives to Método de Palabras Generadoras

sentido del oído que, por el contrario, es una función puramente visual> (does not have anything to do with the sense of hearing, and, on the contrary is a purely visual act) (Braslavsky, 1962, p. 71). In addition, Decroly believed that readers read ideas and not graphic symbols and that those ideas were related to something beyond the symbols themselves. Thus, the global method was also called at times the ideovisual method. Decroly especially believed that children need sensorimotor, intellectual, and affective preparation before they begin to read. He stressed the idea that children are at different stages of maturity at age six when most reading instruction is begun, and for that reason, reading should be individualized. His entire ideovisual approach stresses readiness to read.

Hendrix (1952) wrote enthusiastically about *el método global* explaining how the students he taught reading to found this method so much more interesting than the synthetic methods that were normally used:

> En el transcurso de mi enseñanza de la lectura mediante el método global, siempre me llamó la atención el interés que suscitaba en mis alumnos y, me atrevo decirlo, en todos mis alumnos (p. 2).

Translation:

> In the course of my teaching of reading using the global method, I was always impressed by the interest that it provoked in my students, and I dare to say it, in all my students.

Hendrix explains that the global method does not ignore analysis of the parts, and he describes the stages of learning with this method as moving from the sentence to the word to the syllables. However, for those who believe strongly in a synthetic approach to reading, this method has been critiqued because students fail to acquire ". . . a system for unlocking unfamiliar words beyond visual clues and visual patterns" (Thonis, 1976, p. 31).

Moreno (1982), drawing on Braslavksy (1962), has summarized four basic principles of the Global or Visual Concept Method:

1. Conceptualization is global. Thought is constructed not from part to whole, but beginning with chunks. Children get concepts <en bloque sin análisis previo> (in a block without previous analysis) (p. 74).

2. Reading is a purely visual process. Reading has nothing to do with sounds, but instead, is purely visual. The visual images are understood by the brain as wholes.

3. Reading is ideovisual, which implies a reading of ideas, not of symbols.

4. The global method is a natural method. The acquisition of reading is natural, just like the acquisition of spoken language is natural in a child.

El *método global* is an analytic method that starts with wholes and breaks them into parts. However, in practice, the method can look very different in different classrooms. Below we describe two reading lessons that could be classified as *el método global*. The first shows a lesson that does quite a bit of analysis even though the students start with a whole sentence. In the second, no analysis—in the more traditional sense—occurs. These two lessons represent two very different versions of this method.

Scenario #1 for el método global o ideovisual
The teacher begins by showing the children a picture of a father sitting in a chair reading the newspaper. The class discusses the picture. After the discussion, the children read a sentence about the picture, copy the sentence, and analyze its parts.

MAESTRA: Niños, miren el dibujo que tengo aquí. ¿Qué ven ustedes?	TEACHER: Children, look at the picture I have here. What do you see?
NIÑO: Es un hombre.	BOY: It is a man.
MAESTRA: Si, es un hombre. ¿Qué está haciendo?	TEACHER: Yes, it is a man. What is he doing?
NIÑO: Está leyendo.	GIRL: He is reading.
MAESTRA: ¿Qué está leyendo?	TEACHER: What is he reading?
NIÑA: Un periódico.	GIRL: A newspaper.
MAESTRA: Sí. ¿Quién es el hombre?	TEACHER: Yes. Who is the man?
(Silencio. Nadie contesta.)	(Silence. No one answers.)

MAESTRA: ¿Puede ser un papá?

NIÑOS: Sí.

MAESTRA: Bueno. Vamos a leer juntos una oración acerca de este dibujo. <El papá lee.> (La maestra escribe la oración en el pizarrón.) Lean conmigo. <El papá lee.>

NIÑOS: <El papá lee.>

MAESTRA: Copien la oración en sus cuadernos. Ahora vamos a dividir la oración en partes. Lean y escriban

<El papá>
<El papá lee>

¿Todos copiaron en sus cuadernos? Bien. Ahora voy a escribir la oración dejando por fuera algunas palabras. Ustedes deben llenar los espacios con las palabras que faltan.

(La maestra escribe lo siguiente.)

El _____ lee.
El papá _____.
_____ papá lee.

TEACHER: Could it be a father?

CHILDREN: Yes.

TEACHER: Good. We are going to read a sentence together about this picture. "The father reads." (The teacher writes the sentence on the blackboard.) Read with me. "The father reads."

CHILDREN: "The father reads."

TEACHER: Copy the sentence in your notebooks. Now, we are going to divide the sentence into parts. Read and write

"The father"
"The father reads"

Did everyone copy that down in their notebooks? Good. Now, I am going to write the sentence leaving out some words. You should fill in the spaces with the words that are missing.

(The teacher writes the following.)

The _____ reads.
The father _____.
_____ father reads.

Analysis of el método global #1

In this lesson the children are given some opportunity to see that reading is a meaning-making process. The teacher shows them a picture and discusses it with them. Then they read the sentence about the picture. Students can make a meaning connection between the text and the picture. However, there is no choice and little variety in what students are given to read. There is no emphasis here on graphophonics, and it could be argued that this method draws on syntax. In the follow-up exercise students are asked to put words with different functions in the sentence slots. The subject, *papá* (father), is to be filled into the first blank. The verb, *lee* (reads), should fill the second. The article, El (the), completes the third.

The teacher does make an attempt to connect the picture to the children's lives by proposing that the man might be a father. Though the children do not make this connection, there is the possibility that they might after the teacher's suggestion. The students do some writing related to the reading, but the writing is so tightly controlled that it becomes just a copying exercise. Although this analytic method does include more possibilities for emergent readers to view reading as meaning making, it still is quite structured and meets few of the requirements that we identified earlier for effective reading instruction. With this method children aren't given opportunities to read engaging stories and articles. They don't learn to value reading as an enjoyable or useful activity.

At the other end of the global or visual concept method spectrum, students are taught to read and write either whole words or complete sentences without ever analyzing the parts (Thonis, 1976). Elements of both language experience and sight-word reading are evident in this version of the method. Often, students get many readiness-for-reading activities before they are ever given any texts to read. Eventually, students are involved in an activity in which they talk about a picture. The teacher writes down what the children say, and then they read it together. We describe both the readiness activities and the language experience lesson for this version of *el método global*.

Scenario #2 for el método global o ideovisual
The students are looking at their workbooks (see Figure 4–1) while the teacher gives them directions for some reading-readiness activities.

FIGURE 4–1: Reading Readiness Activity (Four Bears and Four Houses)

MAESTRA: Abran sus libros en la página veinte. Miren la página. Noten que hay varios dibujos que son iguales o casi iguales. En cada fila hay un dibujo que es un poco diferente a los demás. Dibujen un círculo alrededor del dibujo que ustedes crean que es diferente. Vamos a hacer el número uno juntos. ¿Qué ven ustedes en el número uno?

TEACHER: Open your books to page twenty. Look at the page. Notice that there are several pictures that are the same or almost the same. In each row there is one picture that is a little different from the others. Draw a circle around the picture that you think is different. We are going to do number one together. What do you see in number one?

NIÑO: Veo cuatro ositos.

BOY: I see four teddy bears.

MAESTRA: Bien. ¿Son todos iguales?

TEACHER: OK. Are they all the same?

NIÑA: No, uno es diferente.

GIRL: No, one is different.

MAESTRA: Muy bien. Dibujen un círculo alrededor del osito que es diferente. Ahora ustedes pueden continuar con las casas en el segundo ejemplo haciendo el resto del ejercicio.

TEACHER: Very good. Draw a circle around the bear that is different. Now you can continue with the houses in the second example and do the rest of the exercise.

After the students finish this page, the teacher gives directions for the following page which shows pictures of children holding different shaped rectangular boxes and two words repeated in Spanish, *papá* (father) and *lima* (lemon). At the bottom of the page, words are listed next to different shaped rectangles (see Figure 4–2).

MAESTRA: Ahora, vean la página veinte y uno. ¿Qué están haciendo los niños en el número dos de esta página?

TEACHER: Now, look at page twenty-one. What are the children doing in number two on this page?

JUAN: Están cargando unas cajas.

JUAN: They are holding some boxes.

MAESTRA: ¿Qué ven en el dibujo del número tres?

TEACHER: What do you see in the drawing of number three?

FRANCISCA: Veo una niña cargando una caja.

FRANCISCA: I see a little girl holding a box.

MAESTRA: ¿Hay algo dentro de la caja?

TEACHER: Is there something inside the box?

FIGURE 4-2: Reading Readiness Activity (Boxes)

MAGDALENA: Sí, hay una palabra dentro de la caja.

MAGDALENA: Yes, there is a word inside the box.

MAESTRA: Muy bien. ¿Cabe bien la palabra dentro de la caja?

TEACHER: Very good. Does the word fit inside the box?

NIÑOS: Sí.

CHILDREN: Yes.

MAESTRA: Ahora, en el último dibujo, hay unas cajas vacías y unas palabras. Dibujen una línea desde la palabra hasta la caja donde ustedes piensan que cabe la palabra.

TEACHER: Now, in the last picture, there are some empty boxes and some words. Draw a line from the word to the box where you think the word fits.

Next, the teacher shows the children a picture of a boy in a classroom painting a picture.

MAESTRA: ¿A quién ven ustedes en el salón de clases?

TEACHER: Who do you see in the classroom?

FELIPE: A un niño.

FELIPE: A boy.

MAESTRA: ¿Qué está haciendo el niño?

TEACHER: What is the boy doing?

ANGÉLICA: Está pintando.

ANGÉLICA: He is painting.

MAESTRA: Ahora, vamos a escribir un cuento juntos sobre este dibujo. Ustedes me van a decir el cuento y yo voy a escribir lo que ustedes me dicen. ¿Quién quiere empezar?

ROBERTO: Yo, maestra. Yo sé lo que debemos escribir.

MAESTRA: Está bien, Roberto. ¿Qué debo escribir?

ROBERTO: El niño está pintando en la escuela.

MAESTRA: (al escribir) <El niño está pintando en la escuela.> Bien. Ahora, ¿Qué más?

ANA: El niño está pintando un árbol y un sol.

MAESTRA: Ok, Ana. (al escribir) ¿Algo más para nuestro cuento?

ALBERTO: Su camisa está sucia. Tiene pintura.

MAESTRA: Bien, Alberto. (Ella escribe y lee en voz alta.) <Su camisa está sucia. Tiene pintura.> Ahora, tenemos un cuento. Lean conmigo mientras yo señalo las palabras con mi dedo.

NIÑOS Y MAESTRA: El niño está pintando en la escuela. El niño está pintando un árbol y un sol. Su camisa está sucia. Tiene pintura.

MAESTRA: Muy bien. ¿Quién quiere señalar las palabras mientras leemos otra vez?

FAUSTO: Yo, maestra. Yo.

TEACHER: Now, we are going to write a story together about this picture. You are going to tell me the story and I am going to write what you tell me. Who wants to start?

ROBERTO: I do, teacher. I know what we should write.

TEACHER: OK, Roberto. What should I write?

ROBERTO: The boy is painting at school.

TEACHER: (while writing) "The boy is painting at school." Good. Now, what else?

ANA: The boy is painting a tree and a sun.

TEACHER: OK, Ana. (while writing) Something else for our story?

ALBERTO: His shirt is dirty. It has paint on it.

TEACHER: Good, Alberto. (She writes and then reads aloud.) "His shirt is dirty. It has paint on it." Now, we have a story. Read with me while I point to the words with my finger.

CHILDREN AND TEACHER: The boy is painting at school. The boy is painting a tree and a sun. His shirt is dirty. It has paint on it.

TEACHER: Very good. Who wants to point to the words while we read again?

FAUSTO: I do, teacher. I do.

MAESTRA: Está bien, Fausto, ven acá. Ahora, vamos a leer mientras Fausto nos señala las palabras.

TEACHER: OK, Fausto, come here. Now, we are going to read while Fausto shows us the words.

NIÑOS: El niño está pintando en la escuela.
El niño está pintando un árbol y un sol.
Su camisa está sucia. Tiene pintura.

CHILDREN: The boy is painting at school.
The boy is painting a tree and a sun.
His shirt is dirty. It has paint on it.

MAESTRA: Muy bien. ¿Quién quiere leer solo?

TEACHER: Very good. Who wants to read alone?

JORGE: Yo, maestra.

JORGE: I do, teacher.

MAESTRA: Ok, Jorge. Tú puedes leer mientras Fausto señala las palabras con su dedo.

TEACHER: OK, Jorge. You can read while Fausto points to the words with his finger.

Analysis of el método global o ideovisual #2

This lesson really has two distinct parts. In the first part, students are focused on reading-readiness activities that are intended to check how children visualize *wholes*. Decroly believed that students beginning to read are at different stages of maturity and that reading-readiness materials help teachers determine if their students are indeed ready for reading. First, the students are asked to pick out the picture that is different from a series of pictures. Then they are asked to match words to boxes that represent the shapes of those words.

Both of the readiness activities tie into the first two principles Moreno listed for the global or visual concept method. The two exercises reflect both that conceptualization is global and that reading is a purely visual process, unrelated to the sounds of language. Although readiness activities fit the principles of this method, they do not fit with a socio-psycholinguistic view of reading, and they do not appear on the Checklist for Effective Reading Instruction. Teachers who take a socio-psycholinguistic view of reading assume that all children are ready to read. Any prereading activity is designed to build background for a particular reading or to create interest in a book or article. These prereading activities, then, are very different from readiness activities that are designed to help students develop better visual discrimination abilities.

The second part of the lesson, the language experience activity, reflects the second two principles of the method: reading is ideovisual, or is the reading of ideas, and the global method is a natural method. The teacher has the students discuss the drawing of the child painting a picture in his classroom. Then, the picture is used as the basis for the story the children dictate to the teacher and then read with the teacher's help.

Language experience is certainly a valid way for emergent readers to begin to construct meaning from text. When children *write* the text, it has meaning for them. The text of a language experience story is usually interesting, predictable, and reflective of students' background interests and experiences. Students do value themselves as readers when they read stories they have helped to construct. However, student-dictated stories shouldn't comprise the entire reading curriculum. Students also need to be exposed to a rich variety of children's books with colorful illustrations if they are to develop an interest in reading. Even though the language experience aspect of *el método global* comes closer to reflecting a socio-psycholinguistic view of reading than the other methods we have described, the complete method has severe limitations if our goal is to help students value reading and to value themselves as readers.

A Positive Alternative to el método global o ideovisual

Doing a language experience activity can be very beneficial for emergent readers, especially when they are also excited about the activity. While working with elementary schools in Venezuela during a sabbatical year, Yvonne did the following activity which included language experience. The teachers had been working with their students on the theme of *¿Cómo podemos comer sano?* (How can we eat healthfully?). Because most cultures have some kind of bread or rice staple, Yvonne thought bread could be a starting point to discuss both nutrition and the rich diversity in eating practices around the world. She began by bringing in a small loaf of *pan francés* (French bread), a hot dog bun, and a Venezuelan *arepa* which is a kind of thick tortilla made with processed corn flour or wheat flour and cooked on a hot griddle. She asked the children to compare the three kinds of bread by asking: <¿En qué se parecen?> and <¿En qué se diferencian?> (How are they the same? How are they different?). During brainstorming the children listed differences in how and when the breads are eaten, what people put on, or in, the breads, and what different ingredients are used to make the breads.

Next, Yvonne showed a Scholastic poster entitled, *Los panes del mundo* (The Breads of the World) (1993). The poster shows people around the world eating, making, or selling bread. The students were fascinated with the poster and commented on the different things they saw. Reading the big book, *Pan, pan, gran pan* (Bread, Bread, Huge Bread) (Cumpiano, 1990), after these discussions pulled the students further into the topic, and reinforced the idea of bread making and the importance of yeast.

After reading the story, Yvonne suggested that the students write a group report on what they knew about bread. She wrote on a large piece of butcher paper while the students told her what they knew and what they had learned. When they had finished, they had written two long paragraphs.

This group report then became the basis for the students' reading lesson. The whole group read what they had written about bread in their country and around the world. Finally, the students copied the sentences onto separate sheets of paper and each student illustrated his or her own book of facts about *Los panes del mundo* (The Breads of the World). This lesson helped students build background, but it did not include readiness activities. It also involved students in reading and writing in ways that move beyond a language experience approach.

El método léxico (The Lexical Method)

According to Moreno (1982), this method was developed over two hundred years ago in Germany. It included a series of steps:

1. Present the object or a picture of the word that is to be taught.

2. Say the name of the word.

3. Write and read the word.

4. Divide the word into syllables and letters.

5. Form new words with the now known elements of the original word (p. 83).

This method has been referred to in English as the whole word method and is often confused with whole language. The idea behind this method is that every word has its own form and is remembered individually by the reader. The goal of this method is to make the reading of individual words automatic.

More recently, this method has included the first three of the above steps though not usually the last two. In the whole word method, flash cards are often used to introduce the words. The words are then put into sentences to provide some context and are repeated by the emergent reader. Once the words are learned they can be used to construct new sentences.

Scenario for el método léxico

The teacher is going to read a story with the children about some children in school who paint a picture of the sun. The three words the teacher is teaching are *¿quién?* (who?), *sol* (sun), and *amarillo* (yellow). The teacher has flash cards of the words and has written a sentence with each word on the chalkboard.

MAESTRA: (enseñándoles a los niños una tarjeta con la palabra <quién> escrita sobre ella) Repitan la palabra después de mí: <quién>.

TEACHER: (showing the children a card with the word *quien* written on it) Repeat the word after me: *quién* (who).

NIÑOS: <quién>

CHILDREN: *quién* (who)

MAESTRA: Ahora, miren la primera oración en el pizarrón y léanla en silencio.

TEACHER: Now, look at the first sentence on the chalk board and read it silently.

MAESTRA: Lean la oración después de mí: <¿Quién pinta?>

TEACHER: Read the sentence after me: "*¿Quién pinta?*" (Who paints?)

NIÑOS: <¿Quién pinta?>

CHILDREN: "*¿Quién pinta?*" (Who paints?)

MAESTRA: (enseñándoles a los niños una tarjeta con la palabra <sol> escrita sobre ella) Repitan la palabra después de mí: <sol>.

TEACHER: (showing the children a card with the word, "*sol*" written on it) Repeat the word after me: "*sol*" (sun).

NIÑOS: <sol>

CHILDREN: "*sol*" (sun)

MAESTRA: Ahora, miren la segunda oración en el pizarrón y léanla en silencio.

Teacher: Now, look at the second sentence on the chalkboard and read it in silence.

MAESTRA: Lean la oración después de mí. <María pinta un sol grande.>

TEACHER: Read the sentence after me: "*María pinta un sol grande.*" (María paints a big sun.)

NIÑOS: <María pinta un sol grande.>

CHILDREN: "*María pinta un sol grande.*" (María paints a big sun.)

MAESTRA: (enseñándoles a los niños una tarjeta con la palabra *amarillo* escrita sobre ella) Repitan la palabra después de mí: <amarillo>.

TEACHER: (showing the children a card with the word, *amarillo* (yellow) written on it) Repeat the word after me: "*amarillo*" (yellow).

NIÑOS: \<amarillo>	CHILDREN: "*amarillo*" (yellow)
MAESTRA: Ahora, miren la tercera oración en el pizarrón y léanla en silencio.	TEACHER: Now, look at the third sentence on the chalkboard and read it in silence.
MAESTRA: Lean la oración después de mí. \<Ella pinta un sol amarillo.>	TEACHER: Read the sentence after me: "*Ella pinta un sol amarillo.*" (She paints a yellow sun.)
NIÑOS: \<Ella pinta un sol amarillo.>	CHILDREN: "*Ella pinta un sol amarillo.*" (She paints a yellow sun.)

Next, the teacher has the students look at the first page of their story which shows María painting a sun and two boys watching her.

MAESTRA: Miren la página veinti-nueve. ¿Quién pinta?	TEACHER: Look at page twenty-nine. Who paints?
FELIPE: María está pintando.	FELIPE: María is painting.
MAESTRA: Sí, Felipe. María pinta. ¿Qué pinta María?	TEACHER: Yes, Felipe. María paints. What does María paint?
ANITA: Un sol.	ANITA: A sun.
MAESTRA: Sí, María pinta un sol. Y ¿De qué color es el sol?	TEACHER: Yes, María paints a sun. And, what color is the sun?
NIÑOS: Amarillo.	CHILDREN: Yellow.
MAESTRA: Ahora, escriban las tres palabras nuevas en sus cuadernos y escriban tres oraciones nuevas usando las tres palabras.	TEACHER: Now, write the three new words in your notebooks and write three new sentences using the three words.

Analysis of el método léxico

Few of the elements critical for effective reading instruction are present in *el método léxico*. What students read is very carefully controlled. The words they read are first presented in isolation and then put in sentences. These sentences seldom provide enough context to make the meaning of the words very clear. The sentences are not really even good examples of natural language. When the students answer the teacher in a more natural way as in "María is painting," the teacher has to restate the unnatural text sentence, "María paints." In the first sentence above, for example, \<¿Quién pinta?> (Who paints?), there is not any real context provided by the word *paints* to help a reader infer the meaning of *quien*.

The main emphasis of instruction is on recognizing individual words. Students are not encouraged to use the three cueing systems to construct meaning. Instead, they memorize words and then use them to decode sentences. Students connect the words to pictures and this helps them construct sentence meaning, but the meanings are seldom related to their own background experiences or interests. This method presents reading as a rather mechanical process of word identification through visual cues. It does not involve students in using all the cueing systems to construct meaning from text. Since students are not exposed to real stories or articles, they don't come to value reading as a meaningful or enjoyable activity.

A Positive Alternative to el método léxico

When students are just beginning to read, they do need to have some access to books with limited text so that they can start to construct meaning from the text. Several years ago, kindergarten and first-grade whole language bilingual teachers approached Yvonne because they did not have enough materials to support their Spanish-speaking emergent readers. The teachers explained that they did have an abundant supply of quality children's literature to read to their students, but very few books with limited enough text that their young students could read independently.

Since that time, many books have been published that do support very beginning Spanish readers. The small emergent literacy series mentioned earlier include some books that show pictures or drawings and simply label the objects. Others have very limited vocabulary. In *¿Quién quiere helado?* (*Who Wants Ice Cream?*) (Cappellini, 1994) several pages show animals simply answering <yo> (I do), and the final page shows all the animals who say, <Todos queremos> (We all want it.). In another book, *En mi escuela* (*In My School*) (Kratky, 1995), the pictures show a child's hand with a pencil that is labeled, <mi lápiz> (my pencil), a child's hand with a pair of scissors labeled, <mis tijeras> (my pair of scissors), and a teacher labeled, <mi maestra> (my teacher).

Even most of these small emergent literacy books have more than single words, however. Most books have at least a repetitive short sentence to accompany the pictures or drawings. In *El ranchito* (*The Little Ranch*)

(Charpenel, 1995), pictures of toy animals accompany each page of text, and the number of animals pictured corresponds to a number written in the top corner of the page. The pages read as follow:

Tengo un burro.	I have a donkey.
Tengo dos chivos.	I have two goats.
Tengo tres conejos.	I have three bunnies.
Tengo cuatro caballos.	I have four horses.
Tengo cinco cochinitos.	I have five little pigs.
Tengo seis gallos.	I have six roosters.
Tengo un ranchito.	I have a little farm.

On the final page, a young Hispanic boy dressed like a cowboy is playing on the floor with his model farm and the animals pictured on the previous pages.

Another type of text that supports early readers is literature that has a repetitive pattern. For example, in *Olmo y la mariposa azul* (*Olmo and the Blue Butterfly*) (Ada, 1993), a young boy sees a beautiful butterfly and chases it. The text, beautifully represented in colorful and artistic illustrations, follows a pattern that includes the boy's name, Olmo, and verbs of action followed by the sentence, <Quiere la mariposa azul.> (He wants the blue butterfly.). So the first pages of the text read:

Olmo salta.	Olmo jumps.
Quiere la mariposa azul.	He wants the blue butterfly.
Olmo corre.	Olmo runs.
Quiere la mariposa azul.	He wants the blue butterfly.

This lovely story ends imaginatively with Olmo in a spaceship and an airplane and finally in his bed dreaming the whole adventure. Relevant emergent literacy books, as well as limited text literature, can support reading for beginning Spanish readers in a way consistent with current reading theory. The texts are limited, but unlike *el método léxico*, the focus is on the meaning of the story, not on the individual words (see Table 4-2).

El método ecléctico o mixto (The Eclectic or Mixed Method)

This method contains features of several other methods. For that reason, it has also often been called *el método ecléctico mixto* (Bellenger, 1979). As in the visual concept method, students are often given readiness activities to promote skills in spatial organization or visual-motor coordination. In addition, they may be given exercises to develop auditory discrimination, attention, memory, or oral language. Next, letter sounds are introduced and

ALTERNATIVES TO METODO LEXICO

Ada, Alma Flor. *Olmo y la mariposa azul, HBJ Estrellas de la Literatura*. Orlando: Harcourt Brace Javanovich (1993).

Cappellini, Mary. *¿Quién quiere helado?*, *Literatura 2000*. Crystal Lake: Rigby (1994).

Cappellini, Mary, and Almada, Patricia. *Literatura 2000*. Crystal Lake: Rigby (1994).

Charpenel, Mauricio. *El ranchito, Pan y Canela, Colección* A. Carmel: Hampton-Brown Books (1995).

Kratky, Lada Josefa. *En mi escuela, Pan y Canela, Colección* A. Carmel: Hampton-Brown (1995).

Kratky, Lada Josefa. *Pan y Canela*. Carmel: Hampton-Brown Books (1995).

TABLE 4–2: Alternatives to método léxico

students are encouraged to learn the sound, the letter name, and the written symbol in order to produce the letters. Often after learning the letters, students practice syllable sounds and relate them to sentences they read. Students are also taught to take dictation, to copy, to create new words, to visualize the shapes of letters, to identify sounds represented by letters, and to practice penmanship. Eclecticism characterizes many of the approaches to *lecto-escritura* (literacy) that have been used in Latin America. A mixed approach has also characterized much literacy instruction in Spanish in the United States.

Scenario #1 for el método ecléctico o mixto
The lesson here is based on pages from a beginning reading text, *Chiquilín* (Cabrera, text not dated), used in Venezuela in primary school. It is interesting to note that none of the mandatory workbooks that are sold to the children in Venezuela for reading instruction are dated. This practice might have been developed to extend the use of the books for a longer period of time.

The lesson presented below is imaginary, but the text is real. The children and the teacher are looking in their reading book at the page labeled, <pre-lección> (pre-reading) which shows the vowels and pictures of words that begin with each vowel.

MAESTRA: Miren la página tres. Aquí miren los dibujos y las letras. Estas letras son las vocales. Cada letra está en mayúscula y en minúscula. Cada dibujo comienza con una de las vocales. Primero, pongan su dedo sobre la primera vocal, A, y repitan, <A, avión>.

TEACHER: Look at page three. Here you see the pictures and the letters. These letters are vowels. Each letter is in uppercase or lowercase. Each picture begins with one of the vowels. First, put you finger on the first vowel, A, and repeat, "A, *avión*" (airplane).

NIÑOS: <A, avión>.

CHILDREN: "A, *avión*" (airplane).

MAESTRA: Bien, ahora, pongan su dedo en la segunda letra, E, y repitan, <E, elefante>.

TEACHER: Good, now put your finger on the second letter, E, and repeat, "E, *elefante*" (elephant).

NIÑOS: <E, elefante>.

CHILDREN: "E, *elefante*" (elephant).

MAESTRA: Bien, ahora, pongan su dedo en la tercera letra, I, y repitan, <I, imán>.

TEACHER: Good, now put your finger on the third letter, I, and repeat, "I, *imán*" (magnet).

NIÑOS: <I, imán>.

STUDENTS: "I, *imán*" (magnet).

MAESTRA: Bien, ahora, pongan su dedo en la cuarta letra, O, y repitan, <O, ola>.

TEACHER: Good, now put your finger on the fourth letter, O, and repeat, "O, *ola*" (wave).

NIÑOS: <O, ola>.

CHILDREN: "O, *ola*" (wave).

MAESTRA: Bien, ahora, pongan su dedo en la quinta vocal, U, y repitan, <U, uno>.

TEACHER: Good, now put your finger on the fifth vowel, U, and repeat, "U, *uno*" (one).

NIÑOS: <U, uno>.

CHILDREN: "U, *uno*" (one).

The teacher and the children then turn to the next page and repeat the same kind of exercise with another set of pictures that represent the vowels, this time with the vowel letters in a different order, so the pictures begin with *E* for *enano* (dwarf), *O* for *oso* (bear), *I* for *iglesia* (church), *U* for *uña* (fingernail), and *A* for *asa* (cup handle). After the repetition of the vowel practice with new words and pictures, the students and the teacher move on to the next page which has a picture of a mother and a child and introduces the syllables <*ma, me, mi, mo, mu*>.

MAESTRA: Miren ustedes la página cinco. ¿Qué ven ustedes en el dibujo?

TEACHER: Look at page five. What do you see in the picture?

MARTA: Una mamá y su hija.

MARTA: A mother and her daughter.

MAESTRA: Sí, Marta. Es una mamá y su hija. Debajo del dibujo ustedes pueden ver la palabra, <mamá>. Vamos a aprender a leer esta palabra y otras. Ahora, miren las sílabas junto al dibujo, y repitan después de mí, <ma, me, mi, mo, mu>.

TEACHER: Yes, Marta. It is a mother and her daughter. Under the picture you can see the word, "*mama*" (mother). We are going to learn to read that word and others. Now, look at the syllables next to the picture and repeat after me: "*ma, me, mi, mo, mu.*"

NIÑOS: <ma, me, mi, mo, mu>

CHILDREN: "*ma, me, mi, mo, mu*"

MAESTRA: Bien. Ahora, lean después de mí las palabras que están en la primera línea: <ama, mima, amo>.

TEACHER: OK. Now, read the words under the first row after me: "*ama*" (he/she loves), "*mima*" (he/she spoils), "*amo*" (I love).

NIÑOS: <ama, mima, amo>.

STUDENTS: "*ama*" (he/she loves), "*mima*" (he/she spoils), "*amo*" (I love).

MAESTRA: En la segunda línea, <eme, mimo, mía>. Repitan.

TEACHER: In the second row, "*eme*" (m), "*mimo*" (I spoil), "*mía*" (my). Repeat.

NIÑOS: <eme, mimo, mía>.

CHILDREN: "*eme*" (m), "*mimo*" (I spoil), "*mía*" (my).

MAESTRA: En la tercera línea, <eme, mimí, eme>.

TEACHER: In the third row, eme, mimí, eme.

NIÑOS: <eme, mimí, eme>.

CHILDREN: "*eme*" (m), "*mimí*" (I spoiled), "*eme*" (m).

MAESTRA: Muy bien. Ahora vamos a leer una oración completa. Lean conmigo, <Mi mamá me ama.>

TEACHER: Very good. You are now ready to read a complete sentence. Read with me: "Mi mamá me ama." (My mother loves me.)

NIÑOS: <Mi mamá me ama.>

CHILDREN: "Mi mamá me ama." (My mother loves me.)

Analysis of el método ecléctico o mixto #1

In this method one can see elements of several other methods we have already described. The lesson begins, like *el método alfabético*, by teaching letters. It continues, like *el método fónico*, by relating the beginning sounds to the words beginning with those sounds. Like *el método silábico*, this lesson uses syllables to teach words. In addition, there are elements of *el método global* since the students' attention is directed to the picture of the mother and the child, and then students read a sentence related to the picture.

In the opening pages of this basic reading textbook, *Chiquilín*, the philosophy of teaching reading is laid out for teachers. The first two points of this explanation clearly show that this approach to teaching reading is a combination of the analytic and synthetic methods described previously:

> La metodología de la enseñanza para la lectura del libro, *Chiquilín* debe de seguir los siguientes pasos:
>
> 1. El niño debe leer y pronunciar los fonemas vocales asociándolos con la imagen que los origina. Ejemplo: *a* de *aro*, de *avión*. Debe pronunciar cada sonido silábico, relacionándolo rápidamente con la palabra que lo contiene y la imagen que lo representa.
>
> 2. El niño debe leer frases, oraciones y pequeños párrafos, dentro de un contexto relacionado con una escena en particular. Luego el docente reforzará la lectura realizada con preguntas sencillas que permitan fijar el aprendizaje adquirido (p. 2).

Translation:

> The teaching methodology for reading in the book, *Chiquilín* should follow these steps:
>
> 1. The child should read and pronounce the vowel sounds, associating them with the image of the word they come from. Example: *a* for aro or for avión. He (the child) should pronounce each syllabic sound, relating it rapidly with the word that contains the syllable sound and the image it represents.
>
> 2. The child should read phrases, sentences, and small paragraphs, within a context related to a particular scene. Then the teacher will reinforce the reading by asking simple questions that allow the learning to be retained.

Although the eclectic method may appear to combine the best of all other methods, it does not help students come to value reading or to value themselves as readers. A mixed method includes both part-to-whole and whole-to-part exercises whose goal is to have students identify words. The exercises seldom involve the reading of complete, authentic texts, so readers are not engaged in a process of using all the cueing systems to construct meaning. Students are given little choice in what they read, and teachers seldom read real literature to children.

Scenario #2 for el método ecléctico o mixto

A number of different methods fall into the general category of *el método ecléctico o mixto*. One that is currently in use in the United States is Ada's *el método de temas generadores* (method of generative themes) (Ada, 1988). Pérez and Torres-Guzmán (1992) explain that this method brings together both analytic and synthetic methods by combining a syllabic method for emergent readers with a theme-based approach for students with some proficiency.

This method begins with a very controlled syllabic approach to print in early literacy. In a basal reading program Ada and Olave authored for Addison-Wesley, *Hagamos Caminos* (1986), exercises in the beginning readers all focus on the subword level, the syllable (Freeman, 1987). In fact, as Freeman points out, the teacher's guide clearly states that "The structure of the Spanish language rests on the syllable" (p. 249).

The method also involves students in more global themes. The *temas* (theme) part of Ada's approach to literacy draws on Freire (1970) and his work teaching literacy to peasants in Brazil. Freire wanted to create conditions in which the peasants could empower themselves. Through his critical literacy approach, he helped his students realize they needed literacy to improve their lives. Freire's problem-posing approach to curriculum engages students in investigating topics that directly affect their lives and leads them from study to direct actions once they have *posed* and analyzed a problem.

Following Freire's model, Ada identifies four phases in the creative reading act that she believes are important for literacy: the descriptive phase, the personal interpretive phase, the critical phase, and the creative phase. In the descriptive phase, the reader receives information or learns what the text says. Teachers ask comprehension questions to see if students understand the literal meaning of the text. In the next phase, the personal interpretive phase, students are invited to relate ideas in the text to their own experiences and emotions in order to make the text more meaningful. In the critical phase, students move on to further reflection and are asked to decide if the information presented in texts is real and valid in light of their knowledge and experiences. Finally, in the creative phase, students are asked to apply what they have read and reflected upon to their lives. At this stage, students do what is called for in problem posing. They make decisions and take actions that might improve and enrich their lives. *Temas generadores*, then, is an approach that has both synthetic and analytic elements and represents *el método ecléctico o mixto*.

Analysis of el método ecléctico o mixto #2

Ada's approach to critical literacy following a Freirian model has much to commend it. Students read authentic literature. They apply what they read to their lives. They move from reading and discussion to meaningful actions designed to improve conditions in their lives and in their communities. Once students learn to read, they use literacy for important purposes. We would strongly support this aspect of Ada's method.

The approach is mixed, however, since it is based on the idea that a syllabic approach is necessary for learning to read in Spanish. The syllabic method, as we discussed earlier, is a word recognition method. For those students who learn to read in classes where this method is used, the *temas* that Ada suggests are wonderful. Our concern is with the students who fail to learn to read because of the early focus on syllables. Constructing meaning should be the goal of any reading instruction from the beginning. It shouldn't only come into play at the advanced stages.

A Special Case: Basal Readers

Before giving an alternative to *el método ecléctico o mixto*, we believe it is important to make a few comments about Spanish-language basal reading programs published for schools in the United States. Schools often use state funds to purchase these materials, and once they are adopted they become *the* reading program in many classrooms. Before the 1980s Spanish basals were carefully controlled programs based on a combination of phonetic, whole word, and syllabic approaches to teaching reading in Spanish. Freeman's studies (1987, 1988) of seven contemporary Spanish language basal programs concluded that the materials reflected an eclectic approach to reading and were really more alike than different. She critiqued the adapted—and sometimes poorly translated—literature, the skill-based worksheets, the long lists of comprehension questions, and the teacher-centered approach to reading that the programs contained.

More recently, several publishers of Spanish language basal programs have responded to the earlier critiques (Freeman, 1993). Some now reflect an understanding of current reading theory by including collections of quality children's literature organized around themes. Many of the selections were originally written in Spanish. They are accompanied by an appealing collection of expository support readings, either carefully translated or originally published in Spanish.

These same basal publishers who produce materials that reflect a socio-psycholinguistic approach to reading must still remain competitive in a market that is more and more influenced by politics and the demands of a conservative public calling for a move back toward the basics. As a result, support activities in teachers' guides still reflect a more eclectic approach to the teaching of reading. Often, these come in response to state approval guidelines. In California, for example, these guidelines for adopted materials call for explicit attention to spelling, phonics, and grammar instruction.

Some publishers, of course, still produce support materials based on a synthetic, part-to-whole approach to reading to go along with their stories. In fact, the materials they produce are often popular with some teachers who seem grateful when reading programs include worksheets and scripted plans for every minute of their teaching time. These are often the same teachers who prefer simplified reading texts because they are not sure their students are ready to read real literature or respond in writing without the support of lots of controlled writing activities first. This holds true whether they are teaching in Spanish or English.

In summary, the principal focus for some basal programs is on reading as constructing meaning. These programs are more consistent with a socio-psycholinguistic perspective. They include authentic literature organized around themes. Other programs take a word-recognition view of reading and contain fewer stories and more controlled vocabulary. However, market forces ensure that basals remain essentially eclectic. In both kinds of programs teachers' guides include interesting activities that help students build background concepts and relate the selections to their lives. But they also include phonics lessons lists of sight words, and exercises in grammar and spelling.

Principled Eclecticism   It is difficult to analyze *el método ecléctico o mixto* as represented in basals because the programs vary so widely. Generally, an eclectic method could be considered an attempt by educators to blend new understandings about learning and teaching with the old. It might be seen as a movement toward a methodology that is more consistent with a socio-psycholinguistic view of reading. While many educators today maintain that eclecticism is the best approach to teaching reading, we hold that it is important for educators to examine their beliefs about the reading process and learning and match those beliefs to their practice. We agree with Harste (1992) that, "Eclecticism is a disease, not an educational philosophy . . . it is curable by taking a position" (p. 5).

Generally, eclectic methods combine some elements of synthetic and analytic approaches, and they focus on various levels of analysis or synthesis—the sentence, the word, or the syllable. Some attention is usually given to constructing meaning, but often with very limited texts. The basic problem with an eclectic approach is that teachers may combine techniques that reflect different views of how people learn to read. This sends a mixed message to kids, and often they become confused about just what reading is supposed to be. Is it fluent oral reading? Is it completing exercises? Is it making sense of text?

An alternative to a grab bag of techniques approach is what some educators call a *principled* eclecticism. They argue that teachers can use a variety of techniques, but should check to be sure that the different techniques reflect a consistent view of how people learn to read. Whole language teachers attempt to be principled in the choices they make as they support their students' literacy development.

We have already suggested positive alternatives to many of the methods that *el método ecléctico o mixto* combines. Rather than give additional ideas here, we describe and present a scenario for Spanish literacy development that follows a principled, whole language approach.

El lenguaje integral (Whole Language)

This learner-centered approach is based on the theory of socio-psycholinguistics that has been discussed in previous chapters. It draws on the immediate interests of students. Teachers who take a whole language approach believe that children first develop global understandings and gradually come to understand the parts. Reading and writing are developed during meaningful activities that are centered around units of interest to the students. Reading is seen as an enriching experience, not a process of skills mastery. Whole language teachers generally use trade books of interest to their students, and they encourage authentic student writing. Reading and writing become integral parts of all the learning that goes on in school.

Scenario for el lenguaje integral
In bilingual programs in non-Spanish speaking countries like the United States, it is especially important that Spanish-speaking students be given lots of reading and writing in their primary language. Since these students are often living in both English- and Spanish-speaking worlds, it is natural for them to make connections in both English and Spanish. The following lesson incorporates books in both Spanish and English to develop a theme centered on the questions, "What is a seed?" and "How do seeds grow?"

The teacher begins the lesson by bringing in a jar full of different kinds of seeds, including pumpkin seeds, lettuce seeds, watermelon seeds, beans, and corn. The teacher sits down on a chair and the children sit on the floor around her. She hands the children the jar to look at and pass around.

MAESTRA: ¿Qué ven ustedes en este frasco?

TEACHER: What do you see in this jar?

ROBERTO: Pepitas, yo veo pepitas de maíz.

ROBERTO: Little grains, little grains of corn.

MAESTRA: Sí, Roberto. Hay unas pepitas de maíz y de otras cosas. ¿Qué más hay?

TEACHER: Yes, Roberto. There are little grains of corn and other things. What other things are there?

INGRID: Son pepitas . . . son semillas, muchas semillas.

INGRID: They are little grains . . . they are seeds, many seeds.

MAESTRA: Son semillas. También llamamos pepitas a las semillas. Ustedes saben ¿qué tipos de semillas hay aquí? Roberto ya identificó las semillas de maíz. ¿Qué otras semillas reconocen ustedes?

TEACHER: They are seeds. Also, we call little grains seeds. You know what kinds of seeds there are here? Roberto has already identified corn seeds. What else do you recognize?

ESTEBAN: Las de calabaza y frijol.

ESTEBAN: Squash and beans.

SUZANA: Las de sandía pero no sé de qué son estas semillitas pequeñas y negras.

SUZANA: Watermelon, but I don't know what these little black seeds are.

PACO: Yo sé, maestra. Son semillas de lechuga. Mi papá siempre siembra lechuga.

PACO: I know, teacher. They are lettuce seeds. My father always plants lettuce.

MAESTRA: Ustedes saben mucho de las semillas. Hoy vamos a leer algunos libros sobre las semillas y lo que pasa después que sembramos unas semillas. Al principio de este año yo les leí un cuento en inglés sobre un niño que sembró una semilla de zanahoria que tardó mucho en crecer. ¿Recuerdan ustedes ese cuento?

TEACHER: You know a lot about seeds. Today we are going to read some books about seeds and what happens after planting some seeds. At the beginning of the year I read you a story in English about a little boy who planted a carrot seed that took a long time to grow. Do you remember that story?

INGRID: Sí, *The Carrot Seed*. Está allí en la mesa.

MAESTRA: Muy bien, Ingrid. Tienes muy buena memoria. Hoy les voy a leer el mismo cuento en español, *La semilla de zanahoria*. (Lee el cuento a la clase.)

MAESTRA: ¿Qué opinan ustedes?

ANITA: El niño tenía mucha paciencia.

MARÍA: La zanahoria era muy grande.

FELIPE: A mí me gustaría comérmela.

JESÚS: Sus papás no le ayudaban.

PACO: Ni su hermano tampoco.

MANOLO: Yo le ayudaría si estuviera allá.

MAESTRA: Estoy segura que ustedes le hubieran ayudado. Hoy tengo un libro nuevo que no hemos leído antes. (Les enseña un libro grande, *Una semilla nada más*.) ¿Ustedes pueden leerme el título?

NIÑOS: <*Una semilla nada más.*>

MAESTRA: y, ¿Quién es la autora?

NIÑOS: Alma Flor Ada.

MAESTRA: Sí. Este cuento es parecido a *La semilla de zanahoria*. Voy a leerlo y después ustedes van a ayudarme a comparar los dos cuentos. Es un libro grande y ustedes pueden leer conmigo lo que dice el niño.

INGRID: Yes, *The Carrot Seed*. It is here on the table.

TEACHER: Very good, Ingrid. You have a good memory. Today I am going to read the same story in Spanish, *La semilla de zanahoria* (*The Carrot Seed*). (She reads the story to the class.)

TEACHER: What do you think?

ANITA: The little boy had a lot of patience.

MARY: The carrot was very big.

FELIPE: I would like to eat it.

JESÚS: His parents didn't help him.

PACO: His brother didn't either.

MANOLO: I would have helped him if I had been there.

TEACHER: I am sure you all would have helped him. Today I have a new book that we have not read before. (She shows them the big book, *Una semilla nada más*) (*Just One Seed*). Can you read me the title?

CHILDREN: *Una semilla nada más.*

TEACHER: And, who is the author?

CHILDREN: Alma Flor Ada.

TEACHER: Yes, Alma Flor Ada. This story is like *La semilla de zanahoria*. I am going to read it and afterward you are going to help me compare the two stories. This is a big book and you can read with me what the boy in the story says.

The teacher reads the story. The children read the words the boy repeats with her, <Espérate y lo verás.> (Just wait, and you'll see.). After reading the story, the teacher draws a Venn Diagram of two large intersecting circles on the board. She puts the names of the two stories under the pictures. Then she writes *Semejanzas* (Similarities) in the area where the two circles intersect and *Diferencias* (Differences) over the two circles (see Figure 4–3).

MAESTRA: Ahora, ¿Me pueden decir cuáles son las semejanzas y cuáles son las diferencias entre los dos cuentos? Yo voy escribiendo mientras ustedes me dicen lo que piensan.

TEACHER: Now, can you tell me what the similarities and what the differences are between the two stories? I'll write while you tell me what you think.

ESTEBAN: Los niños en los dos cuentos tienen una semilla que siembran.

ESTEBAN: The children in the two stories have one seed they plant.

MARÍA: En los dos cuentos hay una mamá, un papá, y un hermano.

MARÍA: In both stories there is a mother, a father, and a brother.

SILVIA: No ayudan a los niños.

SILVIA: They don't help the children.

FELIPE: Pero en uno de los cuentos hay una hermana también.

FELIPE: But in one of the stories there is a sister, too.

PACO: Sí, y en el segundo el pájaro ayuda al niño.

PACO: Yes, and in the second story the bird helps the boy.

MAESTRA: ¿Dónde escribo lo de la hermana y del pájaro?

TEACHER: Where do I write about the sister and the bird?

JESÚS: Abajo de <Diferencias-*Una semilla nada más.*>

JESÚS: Underneath where it says, "Differences-*Una semilla nada más.*"

ROBERTO: Yo sé otra diferencia, maestra. Una planta es una zanahoria y la otra es un girasol.

ROBERTO: I know another difference, teacher. One plant is a carrot and the other is a sunflower.

MARTA: Sí, y el girasol tiene muchas semillas más.

MARTA: Yes, and the sunflower has a lot of seeds.

MANOLO: El girasol crece alto, pero la zanahoria crece debajo de la tierra.

MANOLO: The sunflower grows tall, but the carrot grows under the ground.

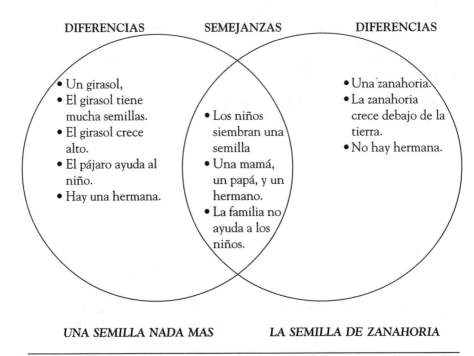

DIFERENCIAS	SEMEJANZAS	DIFERENCIAS

- Un girasol,
- El girasol tiene mucha semillas.
- El girasol crece alto.
- El pájaro ayuda al niño.
- Hay una hermana.

- Los niños siembran una semilla
- Una mamá, un papá, y un hermano.
- La familia no ayuda a los niños.

- Una zanahoria.
- La zanahoria crece debajo de la tierra.
- No hay hermana.

UNA SEMILLA NADA MAS   **LA SEMILLA DE ZANAHORIA**

FIGURE 4–3: Venn Diagram Seeds Stories

ANITA: Las semillas son diferentes también.

MAESTRA: Ustedes recuerdan mucho de los cuentos. Ahora Felipe y Jesús nos van a leer dos libros más sobre semillas, *Semillas y más semillas* y *Plantas y semillas*. Después, ustedes van a investigar sobre algunas semillas. Tengo aquí una bolsa de plástico llena de varios tipos de semillas. Voy a poner una bolsa en cada una de las mesas redondas. Quiero que ustedes observen las semillas. Las pueden abrir, tocar, y comparar. Pero, ¡Por favor no se las coman! También pueden buscar más información en algunos libros que tenemos aquí. (La maestra lee los títulos.) *Los secretos de las*

ANITA: The seeds are different also.

TEACHER: You all remember a lot about the stories. Now Felipe and Jesús are going to read two more books about seeds, *Seeds and More Seeds* and *Plants and Seeds*. Afterwards, you are going to study some seeds. I have here a plastic bag full of several kinds of seeds. I am going to put one bag on each of the round tables. I want you to look at the seeds. You can open them, touch them, and compare them. But, please do not eat them. Also, you can look for information about the seeds in some books that we have here. (The teacher reads the titles.) *The Secrets of Plants,*

plantas, El autobús mágico planta una semilla, La vida de las plantas, Diviértete con una lupa, Pon una semilla a germinar, Cómo crece una semilla, Quiero conocer la vida de las plantas, Las plantas, Un jardín en su dormitorio, Explorando el bosque, Plantas, Las semillas crecen y Experimenta con las plantas. Estos libros les pueden ayudar a identificar algunas. También voy a poner estas dos hojas de papel en cada mesa. ¿Pueden leer lo que está escrito en los papeles?

The Magic Bus Plants a Seed, Plant Life, Enjoy Yourself with a Magnifying Glass, Plant a Seed, How a Seed Grows, I Want to Know About the Life of Plants, The Plants, A Garden in Your Bedroom, Exploring the Woods, Plants, Seeds Grow and Experimenting with Plants. These books can help you to identify some of the seeds. Also, I am going to put two sheets of paper on each table. Can you read what is written on the papers?

NIÑOS: <preguntas>, <observaciones>.

CHILDREN: "Questions", "Observations".

MAESTRA: Sí, un papel dice, <preguntas> y el otro dice <observaciones>. En el papel donde dice <preguntas>, ustedes van a escribir todas las preguntas y dudas que tengan sobre las semillas que tienen sobre la mesa. En el papel donde dice <observaciones>, ustedes van a escribir todo lo que están observando y aprendiendo con las semillas y con los libros que están leyendo.

TEACHER: Yes, one paper says "questions", and the other says, "observations". On the paper where it says "questions", you are going to write all the questions that you have about the seeds that are on the table. On the paper where it says, "observations", you are going to write all that you are noticing and learning from the seeds and the books that you are reading.

The children work busily for forty minutes. They handle the seeds, open some of the bigger ones, look in resource books for information about the names of parts of seeds, and try to identify some unusual ones. At the end of the time, the teacher is again at the chalkboard.

MAESTRA: Ahora, ustedes han escrito sus observaciones y sus preguntas en los papeles. Voy a escribir lo que ustedes piensan aquí en el pizarrón. <¿Qué aprendieron?> <¿Qué más quieren aprender?>

TEACHER: Now, you have written your observations and your questions on the papers. I am going to write what you think here on the board. "What did you learn?" "What else do you want to learn?"

FELIPE: Las semillas vienen en muchos tamaños. La piña del pino es muy grande y tiene muchas semillas. Las semillas de la lechuga son muy chiquitas.

FELIPE: The seeds come in many sizes. The pine cone is very big and has a lot of seeds. The lettuce seeds are very small.

MARTA: Algunas son muy duras, otras son blanditas.

MARTA: Some are hard, others are soft.

FRANCISCO: Algunas semillas tienen cáscaras y las semillas están adentro.

FRANCISCO: Some seeds have shells and the seeds are inside.

SILVIA: Las semillas tienen muchas formas y colores.

SILVIA: The seeds have many forms and colors.

ROBERTO: No pudimos reconocer todas las semillas.

ROBERTO: We could not identify all the seeds.

PACO: ¿Qué pasaría si las comiéramos todas?

PACO: What would happen if we ate all of them?

The children continue listing what they learned and their questions, and then discuss ways they can find out even more about seeds and plants. The teacher then asks Francisco and Marta to read two books about how plants grow, *Las semillas crecen* (*Seeds Grow*) (Walker, 1995) and *Cómo crece una semilla* (*How Does a Seed Grow?*) (Jordan, 1996). With that base in the students' first language, the teacher then reads the children two books in English, *Growing Radishes and Carrots* (Bolton and Snowball, 1985) and *I'm a Seed* (Marzollo, 1996). The first book is a small pop-up book which tells how to sow and grow radishes and carrots and highlights the difference in the length of germination for the seeds of radishes in comparison to carrots. The second book tells the story of a marigold plant and a pumpkin plant growing from the seed through all the stages until they bear flowers and pumpkins. Then the teacher discusses the stories with the students in Spanish.

MAESTRA: ¿Qué recuerdan de lo que leí?

TEACHER: What do you remember of what I read?

SILVIA: Hay que trabajar mucho para cuidar las plantas.

SILVIA: It's necessary to work hard to take care of plants.

FRANCISCO: Hay que regar las plantas.

FRANCISCO: It is necessary to water the plants.

MEMO: Los rábanos están listos en cinco semanas pero las zanahorias tardan mucho más.

MEMO: The radishes are ready in five weeks, but the carrots take much longer.

PACO: Sí, las zanahorias tardan quince semanas.

PACO: Yes, carrots take fifteen weeks.

ESTÉBAN: Las plantas dan flores y frutas y también semillas.

ESTÉBAN: Plants produce flowers, fruit, and also seeds.

SUSANA: Yo recuerdo cuando mi mamá sembró zanahorias y calabazas. Tardaron mucho tiempo para crecer.

SUSANA: I remember when my mother planted carrots and pumpkins. They took a long time to grow.

MAESTRA: Tienes razón, Susana.

TEACHER: You are right, Susana.

Next the teacher reads another book in English, *Growing Colors* (McMillan, 1988). In this book colorful photographs of fruits and vegetables are associated with the basic color words. After reading the book the teacher solicits more discussion.

MAESTRA: ¿Qué opinan ustedes del libro?

TEACHER: What do you think about the book?

PACO: Maestra, nosotros tenemos semillas de algunas de las plantas que están en las fotos. Mira, aquí tenemos semillas de maiz, de calabaza, y de frijol.

PACO: Teacher, we have seeds for some of the plants in the pictures. Look, here I have corn, squash, and bean seeds.

MEMO: Sí, pero habían fotos de papas y de cebollas también. ¿Cómo son las semillas de la papa y de la cebolla?

MEMO: Yes, but there were potatoes and onions in the pictures too. What are potato and onion seeds like?

MAESTRA: Ustedes saben mucho de las semillas pero también tienen algunas preguntas sobre las semillas. Una manera de contestar a esas preguntas es sembrando algunas semillas y observando qué pasa con ellas. Vamos a hacer un jardín en un bolsillo de plástico.

TEACHER: You know a lot about seeds but you have some questions about them, too. One way to answer our questions is to plant some seeds and observe what happens to them. We are going to make a garden in a plastic pocket.

On a long table in the classroom there is a box of small plastic bags, several packages of seeds, paper towels, and a bowl with water. In small groups, the children go to the table to make their pocket gardens. Each child picks out five different seeds and places the seeds in a dampened paper towel. The towel is then folded and placed inside the plastic bag.

MAESTRA: Ahora, ustedes van a observar lo que pasa con sus semillas. Vamos a hacer un librito especial en el que vamos a escribir nuestras observaciones cada día. También vamos a leer más sobre las semillas en algunos de nuestros libros. Antes de ir a casa hoy, les voy a leer otro libro más en inglés sobre este tema. Mañana vamos a hablar de todo lo que sembraron en el libro y de todas las herramientas necesarias para sembrar. En sus casas esta noche, hablen con sus papás sobre lo que ustedes han estudiado hoy de las semillas y hablen con ellos sobre lo que ellos siembran y cosechan en sus patios.	TEACHER: Now, you are going to observe what happens with your seeds. We are going to make a special little book in which we are going to write our observations down each day. Also, we are going to read more about seeds in some of our books. Before going home today, I am going to read you one more book in English about this theme. Tomorrow we are going to talk about what they planted in the book and about all the tools needed to plant. At home tonight, talk to your parents about what you have studied today about seeds and talk to them about what they plant and harvest in their yards.

The teacher reads *Growing Vegetable Soup* (Ehlert, 1987). The children then make science logs with construction paper, putting lined paper inside. They illustrate the covers for the logs and put their names on them. They also put their names on their pocket gardens and place them on the windowsills before they leave class for the day (see Table 4-3).

Analysis of el lenguaje integral
Throughout the lesson, the teacher tries to involve her students in the theme through readings to which they respond and by building on their past experiences. The children are exposed to a variety of books as they listen to the teacher read and read with the teacher. The teacher continually asks the students to tell her what they know and what they have learned from the readings and explorations. The writing students do uses vocabulary that has already been introduced. Repeatedly in the lesson, there is opportunity for the students to predict what the readings will be about, to construct meaning together about the stories, and to compare and contrast the stories. The stories and content books are made more relevant and interesting by using real seeds and hands-on experiences with seeds. This not only connects to the students' past knowledge, but helps them construct new knowledge as well. The stories are interesting and visually attractive. In fact, *Una semilla nada más* (Ada, 1990) is even a pop-up big book. When the plant finally flowers, two large pages open up to make a huge pop-up sunflower.

LITERATURE FOR EL LENGUAJE INTEGRAL

Ada, Alma Flor. *Una semilla nada mas*. Carmel: Hampton-Brown (1990).

Bolton, Fay, and Snowball, Diane. *Growing radishes and carrots*. New York: Scholastic Inc. (1985).

Burnie, David. *Los secretos de las plantas*. Madrid: ALTEA (1990).

Cole, Joanna. *El autobús mágico: Planta una semilla*. New York: Scholastic (1995).

Costa-Pau, Rosa. *La vida de las plantas, Mundo invisible*. Bogotá: Editorial Norma (1993).

Cutting, Brian, and Cutting, Jillian. *Semillas y más semillas*. (Andujar, G., Trans., Pye, W., ed., *Sunshine science series*). Bothell: Wright Group (1995).

Darlington, Arnold. *Diviértete con una lupa, El niño quiere saber*. Barcelona: Ediciones Toray (1984).

Ehlert, Lois. *Growing vegetable soup*. San Diego: Harcourt Brace & Company (1987).

Flores, Guillermo Solano. *Pon una semilla a germinar, Niño científico*. México, D.F.: Editorial Trillas (1985).

Jordan, Helene J. *Cómo crece una semilla*. (Fiol, María A., Trans., *Harper Arco Iris*.) New York: Harper Collins (1996).

Krauss, R. *The carrot seed*. New York: Scholastic, Inc. (1945).

TABLE 4–3, Part 1: Literature for el Lenguaje Integral

In addition, the teacher reads to the students in their second language, English. The reading and discussions done in Spanish before reading in English provide a preview in the students' first language so that they can predict and construct meaning from the English text. In addition, the students are allowed to discuss the books in Spanish after they are read in English. As the students become familiar with the theme, many will be comfortable to read and write and discuss in both Spanish and English.

Conclusion

El lenguaje integral is actually an approach to reading rather than a method. It may take different forms, but it is distinguished from the analytic and synthetic methods we have described in this and the previous chapter by its

le zanahoria. (Palacios, A., Trans.) New York: Scholastic, Inc.

Quiero conocer la vida de las plantas, Quiero conocer. México, cnicos de Edición (1987).

I'm a seed. New York: Scholastic (1996).

ice. *Growing colors.* New York: William Morrow & Co. (1988).

en, and Evans, Joy. *Las plantas.* (Ficklin, Dora, and Liz Wolfe, Trans.) A: EVAN-MOOR CORP (1992).

Murphy, Barnes. *Un jardín en tu dormitorio, El niño quiere saber.* Barcelona: Ediciones Torray (1983).

Saville, Malcolm. *Explorando el bosque, El niño quiere saber.* Barcelona: Ediciones Toray (1982).

Sealey, Leonard. *Plantas.* (Sealey, L., ed., *Colección nuestro mundo.*) Barcelona: Editorial Juventud (1979).

Walker, Colin. *Las semillas crecen.* (Andujar, G., Trans., Pye, W., ed., *Sunshine science series.*) Bothell: Wright Group (1995).

Walker, Colin. *Plantas y semillas.* Andujar, G., Trans., Pye, W., ed., *Sunshine science series.*) Bothell: Wright Group (1995).

Watts, Claire, and Parsons, Alexandra. *Experimenta con las plantas.* (Rodríguez, B., Trans.) Madrid: CESMA (1993).

TABLE 4–3, Part 2: Literature for el Lenguaje Integral

view of reading as constructing meaning. Lessons, such as the seed lesson described above, based on *El lenguaje integral*, are consistent with current reading theory and meet all the criteria of the Checklist for Effective Reading Instruction. When teachers take this approach, they increase the possibility of success for their Spanish readers.

The teacher read with the children several times during the lesson. She had collected a number of interesting books related to the theme. As students examined the seeds, they also had access to reference books. Throughout the lesson they were involved with reading and writing. These kinds of experiences promote the development of literacy. The results of miscue studies described in an earlier chapter support the claim that the reading process involves more than word recognition. Readers use cues from all three systems as well as their knowledge of the world to become effective and efficient readers. They use this knowledge to construct meaning in their transactions with texts. They come to value themselves as readers and to value the activity of reading. What they write also reflects the structures and the vocabulary present in what they read or what the teacher reads to them.

It is important for teachers to reflect on the approach they take when they teach literacy. As this scenario shows, literacy also includes writing. In the next two chapters, we will turn our attention to writing. We will describe how writing develops in classes where students are engaged in authentic literacy activities throughout the day. We will outline the natural development of spelling in both Spanish and English. In addition, we will discuss the importance of encouraging students to use writing in many different ways and for different functions as they learn.

5

Writing Development

The writing samples that follow were produced by one child who is becoming bilingual and biliterate. Pablo is a fourth-grade student in a two-way bilingual school where he receives part of his day's instruction in Spanish and part in English. Pablo does lots of reading and writing in both Spanish and English in a wide variety of genres. In Figure 5–1 we see one section of Pablo's long report entitled, "My Grandfather and Me." For this report Pablo interviewed his grandfather and then wrote up both what he found out and how he felt about his grandfather's life. Pablo describes his grandfather's adult life and records details that seem especially interesting, including killing a pig for his wedding celebration. In his conclusion (see Figure 5–3), Pablo shows his respect for his grandfather.

Pablo's writing sample in Spanish (see Figure 5–2) is the first chapter of a four chapter story about the adventures of King Cobra. In this opening chapter we see that Pablo has imagination and an understanding of how to set up a plot. In his story there is an evil character who must be overcome, a favorite theme of fourth-grade boys. His story's ending is also quite predictable. The last line shows that the heroes win in the end (see Figure 5–4).

Pablo's writing contains errors. However, he expresses himself clearly in both English and Spanish. In addition, he writes comfortably both nonfiction and fiction. At fourth grade Pablo is well on his way to becoming a

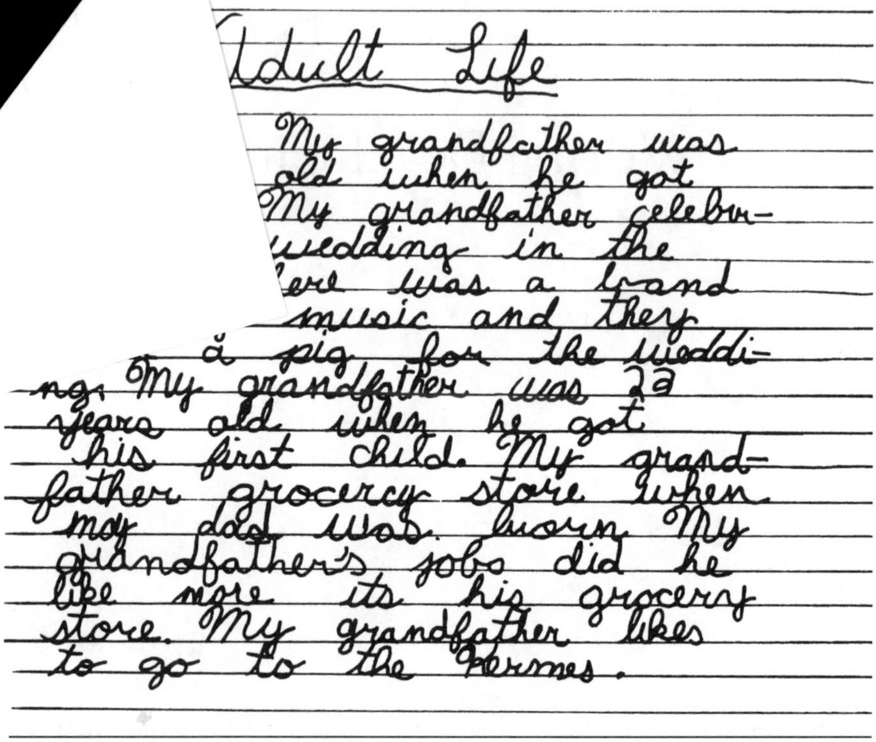

Adult Life

My grandfather was
old when he got
My grandfather celebra-
wedding in the
'ere was a brand
music and they
a pig for the weddi-
ng. My grandfather was 22
years old when he got
his first child. My grandfather grocercy store when
may dad was born My
grandfather's jobs did he
like more its his grocery
store. My grandfather likes
to go to the Hermes.

FIGURE 5–1: Pablo's Grandfather Story

confident writer in two languages. How did Pablo arrive at this stage? It is
important that bilingual teachers understand how to support student writing in their classrooms. This includes providing a variety of rich writing experiences and knowing how to evaluate and support emergent writing.

In the first four chapters we have focused primarily on reading. In this
chapter we turn to writing development. Even though we discuss reading
and writing development in different chapters, we recognize that they are
interrelated processes. As we have discussed views of reading and methods
of teaching reading, we have described lessons in which reading and writing
are linked. As we discuss writing development, we will give examples that
come from classrooms rich in opportunities for meaningful reading as well
as for writing. The teachers in these classrooms understand that a good program of literacy development connects reading and writing. These teachers
have theoretical knowledge of both the reading and writing processes, and
they can transform that theory into practice in their classrooms.

Below we begin by contrasting two views of writing that we refer to as a
traditional approach and a process approach. We review the checklist from
Chapter One that lists the elements of an effective process writing class-

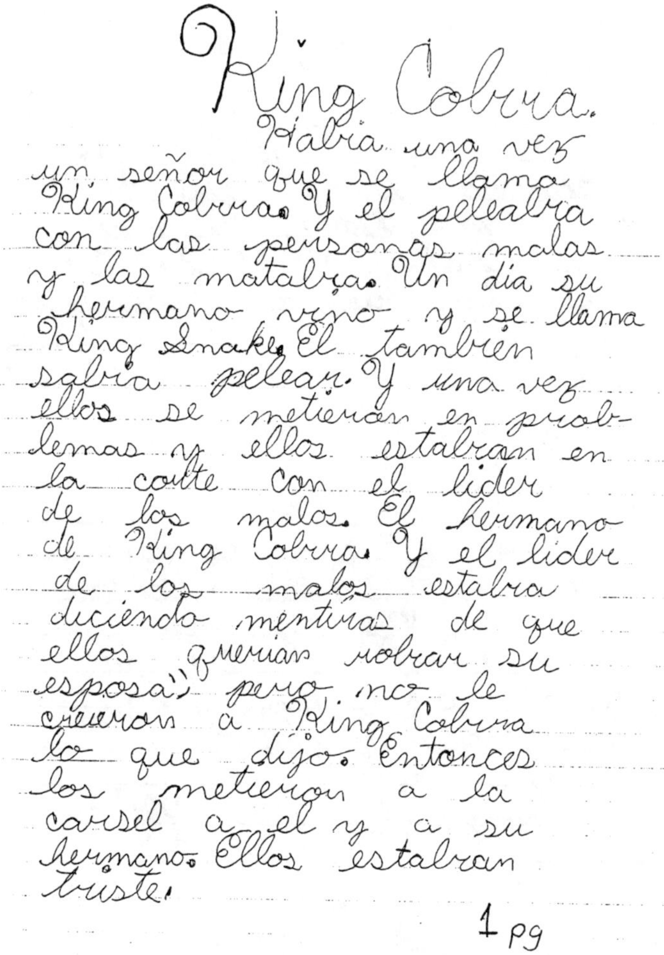

King Cobra.
Había una vez
un señor que se llama
King Cobra. Y el peleaba
con las personas malas.
y las mataba. Un día su
hermano vino y se llama
King Snake. El también
sabía pelear. Y una vez
ellos se metieron en problemas y ellos estaban en
la corte con el líder
de los malos. El hermano
de King Cobra. Y el líder
de los malos estaba
diciendo mentiras de que
ellos querían robrar su
esposa" pero no le
creieron a King Cobra
lo que dijo. Entonces
los metieron a la
carsel a el y a su
hermano. Ellos estaban
triste.

1 pg

FIGURE 5–2: Pablo's King Cobra Story

King Cobra
Once there was
a man who was called
King Cobra. And he fought
the bad guys
and they treated him badly. One
day his
brother came and his name was
King Snake. He also
knew how to fight. And one time
they had some problems
and they were in
court with the leader
of the bad guys. The brother
of King Cobra and the leader
of the bad guys were
saying lies that
they wanted to steal his
wife, but they didn't
believe what King Cobra
said. Then
they put them in jail,
him and his brother.
They were sad.

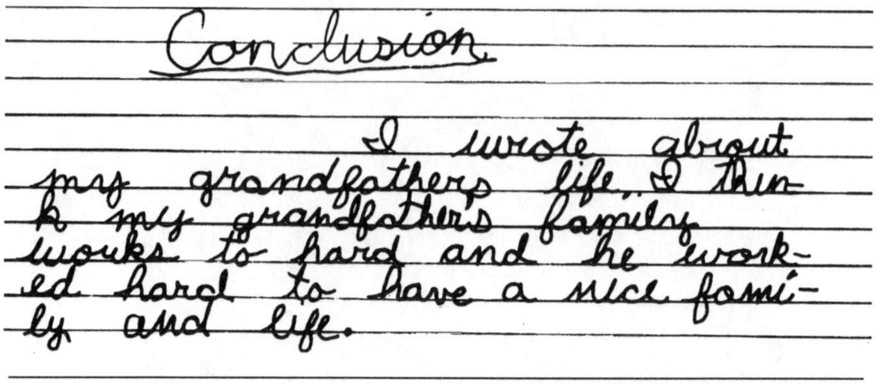

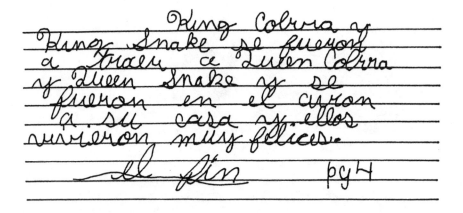

Conclusion

I wrote about my grandfathers life. I think my grandfather's family works to hard and he worked hard to have a nice family and life.

FIGURE 5–3: Conclusion to Grandfather Story

King Cobra y King Snake se fueron a traer a Quen Cobra y Queen Snake y se fueron en el avion a su casa y ellos vivieron muy felices. El fin. pg 4

FIGURE 5–4: Conclusion to King Cobra Story

King Cobra and King Snake went
to get Queen Cobra and Queen Snake and
they went by plane
to their house and they
lived very happily.
The end.

room. After describing the elements of a successful writing program in general, we turn to the details of writing development. We focus on the natural development of writing in both English and Spanish in classrooms where teachers take a process approach. Children have to develop control over the writing system itself, so we begin by explaining how alphabetic writing systems work. We then look at spelling development in English. In the following chapter, we consider spelling development in Spanish.

Two Views of Writing

When we discussed theories of reading, we contrasted two views. The first we called a word recognition view. This view holds that learning to read involves learning to recognize words. The traditional methods of teaching reading in Spanish all consist of different ways of getting the words. The assumption is that once students can recognize words, they can put the word meanings together to make sense of a text. The second view of reading, the socio-psycholinguistic view, holds that reading is a process of constructing meaning. Readers use cues from different systems, not to recognize words, but to construct meaning from texts.

In the same way, we might consider two views of writing. In traditional approaches, teachers often start by having students copy letters or words. Then young writers might put words together to create sentences. Finally, they build up to complete stories or messages. This traditional approach can be contrasted with a process approach. A process approach begins by helping students understand that writing involves communicating messages across time and space. Young writers start by having something to say; then they discover how to represent ideas in written form. Traditional approaches, then, begin with the parts of writing and build up to whole messages. In contrast, process approaches start with the whole message, and then teachers help students with the parts they need to communicate their message.

Another contrast between traditional approaches to writing instruction and more current process approaches has to do with the role of the teacher. In traditional approaches, the teacher instructs students directly. She might show students how to form the letters of the alphabet and then direct them to copy those letters. Later, once students have mastered letters, she shows them how to combine them into words and sentences. The assumption is that students come to writing with no useful knowledge, and the teacher's job is to transmit that knowledge to them.

On the other hand, teachers who follow a process approach assume that children come to school with a good deal of knowledge about written language. This knowledge continues to develop with experience, and the teacher's job is to create situations in which writing is a natural response. For example, after hearing many stories read to them, children want to write their own stories. Or, after a class party, children might want to write a thank you note to parent volunteers who helped organize the party. The teacher not only provides experiences that lead naturally to writing, she also helps students with the different aspects of the writing process itself.

Elements of an Effective Process Writing Program

Teaching writing in a process classroom means following the lead of individual children. But it also involves a thorough understanding of normal developmental patterns. In Chapter One we listed the characteristics of an effective program in the form of a writing checklist. We reproduce the Checklist for Effective Writing Instruction here (see Figure 5–5) and comment briefly on each of the points. We encourage teachers to use this checklist as they set up and then refine their own writing program.

The checklist reflects the three general components of good process writing classes: prewriting activities, writing activities, and postwriting activities. A great deal has been written about process writing for students writing in English as their first language (Calkins, 1986, 1991; Graves, 1983). Additional books and articles focus on process approaches for students writing in a second language (Hudelson, 1989; Rigg and Enright, 1986). We encourage readers to consult these books for a more complete discussion of process writing. Here we only comment briefly on the checklist questions. Then we examine in detail the nature of writing systems and the normal developmental patterns teachers may expect when working with young writers.

In traditional approaches to writing, teachers usually give students their topics. They may do this by making a specific assignment, providing a list of topics to choose from, or putting a story starter on the board. When teachers give students the topic, they miss an essential component of writing: writers choosing their own topics. Good writers make good choices of what to write about. When students choose their own topics, they are more concerned with developing and expressing their ideas. They take ownership of the writing and write for authentic purposes. That is, they write to express ideas that are important to them, rather than simply writing in response to an assignment.

Teachers help students make good topic choices by modeling the process of deciding what to write about and what not to write about. For example, a teacher might think aloud for the class: "Today I thought about three things I might write about." Then the teacher could list all three and discuss why one is better than the other two. Some teachers brainstorm with students how to choose topics, and they keep a list of possible topics up in the room.

The best writing comes when students choose topics that tap into their own experiences and interests. Many teachers have students keep a personal list of possible topics. Students can keep an updated list of things they have written about and things they want to write about. Teachers discuss these topics with students in whole class settings and in individual conferences, and they have students share possible topics with one another. Students also get

CHECKLIST FOR EFFECTIVE WRITING INSTRUCTION

1. Do teachers model the steps they go through to choose topics? Do they help students go through these same steps as they choose topics to write about?
2. Are students encouraged to draw upon their own experiences when they choose topics? Do they write for authentic purposes?
3. Do students make connections between their reading and writing? Do they see that reading provides ideas for writing?
4. Do students keep and update a list of topics that they have written about and that they plan to write about?
5. Do students see writing as a process, and do they understand the various activities they should engage in as they move a piece of writing toward its final form?
6. Does the classroom have ample accessible literature, content, and resource books for students to reference as they write?
7. Are students allowed to invent spelling, drawing on their internal phonics hypotheses and their pictures of words derived from their reading experiences as they write?
8. Do students have opportunities to share their writing with others? Is there authentic response which is both critical and sensitive to the writer's needs?

Translation:

LISTA DE PREGUNTAS PARA VERIFICAR SI LA ENSENANZA DE LA ESCRITURA ES EFECTIVA

1. ¿Ejemplifican los maestros los pasos que ellos siguen para escoger los tópicos? ¿Ayudan ellos a sus estudiantes a seguir estos mismos pasos cuando escogen los tópicos sobre los que quieren escribir?
2. ¿Se estimula a los estudiantes que escriben a tomar en cuenta sus propias experiencias cuando escogen los tópicos acerca de los cuales van a escribir? ¿Escriben ellos con fines verdaderamente auténticos y comunicativos?
3. ¿Establecen ellos relaciones entre lo que leen y lo que escriben? ¿Pueden percibir que la lectura les proporciona ideas para la escritura?
4. ¿Mantienen permanentemente los estudiantes una lista de los tópicos sobre los cuales ya han escrito y de aquellos otros sobre los que están planificando escribir?
5. ¿Perciben ellos que la escritura es un proceso? ¿Entienden ellos que deben desarrollar una serie de actividades antes de poder llegar a la escritura final de un texto?
6. ¿Disponen ellos en el aula de una amplia variedad de libros de literatura y otros materiales de consulta que les puedan servir de referencia cuando van a escribir?
7. Cuando ellos escriben, ¿se les permite inventar su propia ortografía partiendo de sus hipótesis fónicas internas y de las imágenes que se han formado de las palabras a partir de sus experiencias previas con la lectura?
8. ¿Tienen ellos oportunidades de compartir con otras personas lo que escriben? ¿Reciben de estas personas respuestas auténticas que les servirán de apoyo a su sensibilidad y necesidades como escritores?

FIGURE 5–5: Writing Checklist

s for writing from their reading (Hansen, 1987) or write to report on topics y have investigated in social studies, math, science, or other subjects.

Besides helping students learn how to choose topics, teachers in process writing classrooms also give students ample time for researching topics and for writing drafts, rather than assigning topics and giving a definite time period for the writing to be completed. In a process writing classroom most teachers create a kind of workshop setting, a large block of time each day devoted to reading and writing. Of course, teachers also have to help children understand how to use their time well. Not only do students have to start to see writing as a process, but they have to come to understand the process itself by being immersed in it during the workshop time.

Good writers don't start with all their ideas in their heads. Instead, they learn as they write. For this reason, writers need to know how to use a variety of resources. Teachers discuss with students possible resources for developing ideas and often encourage students to read more to get ideas, and to look at other resources such as video or computer data banks to research topics. They also encourage students to talk to classmates, parents, and others as they plan their writing. In traditional classrooms, writing is private and individual, while in process classrooms, writing is shared and social.

Often, young writers have good ideas, but they become frustrated by their lack of control over writing conventions when they try to put their ideas on paper. They may have trouble forming letters, spelling words, or punctuating their messages. Teachers encourage these emergent writers to invent spellings and punctuation to represent their thoughts. However, these teachers also monitor student development and nudge them gradually toward more conventional forms. In addition, they help students edit their work for publication when appropriate.

In classrooms where students share their writing with others in a supportive environment, they become more aware of the need for using conventional writing forms that classmates, parents, and the teacher can understand. Control over standard forms takes time, but when students write for authentic purposes—when they have a real message and a real audience—they gradually refine their inventions and move toward writing that others can read. Below we summarize the differences between traditional approaches and process approaches to the teaching of writing (see Figure 5–6).

In the next sections, we focus more specifically on the natural development of writing as children move from invention to convention. First, we look at how alphabetic writing systems are organized, since these are the systems that English or Spanish writers have to gain control over. Following

Traditional Writing Classrooms	Process Writing Classrooms
Focus on the product.	Focus on the process and product.
Begin with parts and build to whole messages.	Begin with the messages and then focus on the parts.
Teacher directly instructs on how to form letters, then words, and combine words into sentences.	Teacher creates conditions for authentic written responses.
Teacher gives topics.	Teachers help students learn to choose good topics.
Topics may or may not relate to students' lives.	Topics come from students' backgrounds and interests.
Time for writing is restricted and inflexible.	Time for writing is open and flexible.
Few resources are available for writers.	Many resources are available for writers.
Writing product must be conventional.	Writing moves naturally from invention to convention.
Students write for the teacher.	Students write for a real audience.
The teacher corrects.	Classmates and others respond.
Writing is private and individual.	Writing is shared and social.

FIGURE 5–6, Part 1: Two Views of Teaching Writing (English)

that, we turn to a discussion of normal developmental patterns for children writing in English. Teachers who understand these patterns can better help students become effective writers.

Nonalphabetic Writing Systems

Children learning to write in Spanish or English must gain control over an alphabetic writing system. In this section, we provide some background on the nature of such systems. Young students don't need to know these technical details in order to write, but teachers should know them in order to help children as they move into literacy.

Various writing systems have been developed throughout history. The three principal systems currently used are logographic, syllabic, and

Aulas donde se enseña la escritura de una manera tradicional	Aulas donde se enseña la escritura como un proceso
Enfasis en el producto.	Enfasis tanto en el proceso como el producto.
Los estudiantes comienzan con las partes para poder llegar a la construcción de mensajes completos.	Comienzan con los mensajes completos para después analizar las partes.
El docente enseña directamente la formación de las letras, después las palabras y finalmente la combinación de palabras para formar oraciones.	El docente crea condiciones para que los estudiantes respondan ante la escritura de una manera auténtica.
El docente escoge los tópicos sobre los cuales van a escribir los estudiantes.	El docente ayuda a los estudiantes a escoger tópicos apropiados.
Los tópicos no siempre se relacionan con la vida y experiencias de los estudiantes.	Los tópicos surgen de las experiencias e intereses de los estudiantes.
El tiempo destinado para la escritura es restringido e inflexible.	El tiempo destinado para la escritura es abierto y flexible.
Existen pocos recursos disponibles para ser utilizados por los estudiantes en su escritura.	Los escritores disponen de muchos recursos que les estimulan a escribir.
Lo que escriben los estudiantes debe ser sin errores (escritura convencional).	La escritura surge de manera natural y procede de la invención hacia la escritura convencional.
Los estudiantes escriben sólo para el docente.	Los estudiantes escriben para una audiencia real y auténtica.
El docente corrige la escritura.	Otros estudiantes y otras personas responden a la escritura.
La escritura es algo privado e individual.	La escritura es algo compartido y social.

FIGURE 5–6, Part 2: Two Views of Teaching Writing (Spanish)

alphabetic. Chinese is a good example of a logographic writing system. Japanese uses a combination of logographs and a syllabic system. English and Spanish are alphabetic writing systems. What is important is that in each case the kind of writing system that has developed meets the needs of the people who use it. As Goodman (1993) points out, "Alphabetic writing did evolve from nonalphabetic, and in general it works well for its users. However, nonalphabetic systems are better suited for some specific purposes" (p. 9). One system is not better than the other two. Each system represents a set of conventions that a particular social group has adopted.

In logographic systems like Chinese, each written symbol represents a word. For example, the symbol 日 stands for *sun*. Chinese characters do have a phonetic element, and the system is more complex than simply having a different symbol for each word, but we may say that in languages like Chinese, the characters generally represent words rather than sounds. This is an advantage for Chinese, because speakers of the main spoken varieties of the language (Cantonese and Mandarin, principally) can not understand each other when they talk, but both groups share the same written language.

In other widely-used systems, the characters represent sounds. Syllabic writing systems consist of marks that represent syllables. In Japanese, for example, grammatical function words are represented by having a character for each syllable. For example, the character カ stands for /ka/ and マ represents /ma/. To a great extent, it would be possible to develop a similar system for Spanish, and syllabic reading methods reflect that fact. Rather than writing two letters for *ma* or *pi*, Spanish could have used just one symbol that stood for the sound made by the combination of the consonant and vowel.

Alphabetic Writing Systems

English and Spanish are both alphabetic writing systems. Such systems also employ characters that represent sounds. The difference between syllabic and alphabetic systems is that in alphabetic systems each character represents just one sound—either a vowel or a consonant—instead of a whole syllable.

Of course, the correspondence between the sounds and the letters is not perfect, as anyone who has tried to spell English or Spanish knows. For example, both languages have silent letters as in *knows* or *hijo* (son). Both languages can represent a single sound with more than one letter. In English, the sound of *s* can be represented by *s*, *ss*, *se*, or *ce* among others. And in Spanish the *s* sound could be written with an *s*, *c*, or *z*. In addition, one letter can represent more than one sound. The English letter *g* has a hard sound in *gate* and a soft sound in *gentle*. In Spanish the letter *g* also has different sounds. Before *e* or *i* as in *gente* (people) or *girasol* (sunflower) the *g* is like a strongly aspirated *h*. In other cases, it sounds like the hard *g* of English.

Often, people have focused on the lack of correspondence between sounds and letters and suggested that spelling should be reformed. However, even though alphabetic systems do not represent a perfect match between sounds and letters, they are not deficient. People who want to reform spelling to make the correspondences more regular fail to understand that writing systems are just that: systems. Like other complex systems, writing has developed in response to different demands. In particular, we need to recognize the demands put on spelling systems by readers as well as those demands imposed by writers.

Most plans for spelling reform would make life easier for writers by having one letter for each sound. Such a system would make it easier to write, but all of us spend more time reading than we do writing, and a system designed exclusively for writers would make reading much more difficult. Smith (1971) offers a good example of the potential problems in the following sentence: "The none tolled hymn she head scene a pare of bear feat inn hour rheum" (p. 125). Most readers are confused when they first look at this sentence. If they read the words aloud, they can make sense of them, but it is a good example that alphabetic writing systems must do more than represent sounds.

The problem with a system that only represents sounds is that every language uses the same sound combinations to represent more than one meaning. As Smith's sentence shows, we can write one collection of sounds as *nun* or as *none*. And we can spell another combination as *told* or *tolled*. A spelling system that only relied on sound would not allow us to signal that two words that sound the same have different meanings. Of course, context helps us decide on the right meaning, but with written language we have an additional cue by how the word looks. Since writing systems are visible marks on a page, it makes sense to use both sound cues and visual cues. This puts a greater burden on the writer, but it's a real help to the reader.

Our present system helps readers with meaning cues by using different spellings like *nun* and *none* to represent different meanings. C. Chomsky (1970) has pointed out that these spellings show that words that look different have different meanings. Further, words that look the same have similar or related meanings. We add a silent *b* to *bomb* so that we can more easily recognize it as the base in a word like *bombard*. If *sign* didn't have a silent *g* we would have difficulty in making the meaning connection between *sign* and *signal*. To take one more example, both *medicine* and *medical* are spelled with a *c* even though the *c* represents different sounds in the two words.

In English, spellings even help us with syntax. Linguists divide English words into two types: content and function. Content words include nouns, verbs, adjectives, and adverbs. These words essentially carry the meaning content of the sentence. Prepositions, conjunctions, pronouns, and so on, are called grammatical function words. They serve to show relations and connections among the concepts represented by the content words. Readers use various syntactic cues, but one important cue is whether a word is a function word or a content word. In part, readers predict these words by their position in a sentence. However, they also rely on word length. For the most part, function words are short. They are the little words like *it* or *and*. There are exceptions, of course, such as *throughout*, but most function words are short.

Content words, on the other hand, are longer. Since they represent content, they should have some content themselves, and the general rule seems to be that they have to have at least three letters. For that reason, if a content word only has two letters, we either double the final letter or add a final *e*. This increased length cues the reader that the word is a content word and thus carries some of the essential meaning of the sentence. For example *in* is a function word, but *inn* is a content word. Similarly, *be* is a function word (an auxiliary verb), and *bee* is a content word. These variations in spelling, which violate the demand that words be spelled like they sound, actually help readers by giving them syntactic cues.

In Spanish the accent mark serves a similar function to that of doubling letters in English. The accent actually distinguishes the meaning of the words, though the pronunciations are the same. For example, when two words are spelled exactly alike, the more emphatic one receives an accent (Ramsey and Spaulding, 1963). Generally, the words without the accent serve more as function words and the words with the accent are more often content words. So *dé* means *give* in the command or subjunctive form and *de* is the preposition meaning *of* or *from*; *sé* is the verb meaning *I know* while *se* is the reflexive pronoun in a phrase like *se mira en el espejo*; *sí* means *yes* while *si* means *if*.

Alphabetic writing systems, then, represent both sounds and meanings.

When we realize this, it helps us understand that writing really is systematic. Some variations, though, don't seem to reflect either sound or meaning. For example, why do we spell *avalanche* with a silent *e* at the end? We don't need the *e* to make the vowel long as in *hope* (compared with *hop*). Adding the *e* doesn't help us distinguish *avalanche* from some other word, like *avalanch* either. So why is it there? Does it just go to prove that English spelling really doesn't have rhyme or reason?

D.W. Cummings (1988) has pointed out that three forces work on alphabetic writing systems. Each of these forces makes certain demands. We have already seen two of the demands. We try to spell words the way they sound. If we did that perfectly, writing would be easier. But we also try to spell words to reflect what they mean. That makes reading easier. The third force working on our spelling system is history, or what linguists refer to as etymology. The demand here is to spell words in a way that reflects where they came from.

People's names often give us a clue as to their origins. Many people who came to live in the United States had their name changed to sound more like English. That's why a *Juan* might end up as *John*. Words also have a history, and when they are borrowed from another language, they may be changed to reflect the rules of the new language, or they may retain their identity. This shows up in how they are spelled. A word like *avalanche* has an *e* because it was borrowed from French, and even though we don't really need the *e* in English, we didn't change the spelling. Another example would be the word *yacht*. We borrowed the word from Dutch, where the *ch* is pronounced. Even though those letters are not pronounced in English, we kept the original spelling.

An example in Spanish of spelling being influenced by word derivation comes from some words in Spanish that begin with *hie*, such as *hiena* and *hierro*. These words are spelled that way because of their word history and their relationship to the original words in Greek. *El déficit* and *el ultimátum* are a couple of other interesting examples of borrowed words which do not follow normal Spanish spelling patterns.

It's important, then, to see that alphabetic writing systems are really systematic. There isn't something wrong with the system, and it doesn't need reform. Alphabetic systems have developed over time in response to different needs. Like political systems, writing systems are a compromise that balance the competing needs of readers and writers. But since alphabetic systems are complex, it takes children a while to figure out how they work.

Writing Development

Goodman and Goodman (1990) have described learning to read and write as finding a balance between invention and convention. Young writers invent spellings to express their ideas. They also invent words and punctuation marks. As they read, they become aware that the community of readers and writers has established certain conventional forms for writing. Different communities have established different conventions. In Spanish punctuation, for example, questions are signaled by a mark at the beginning of the sentence as well as one at the end. In English, on the other hand, the only cue comes at the end of the sentence. In Spanish, proper adjectives (like *español*) are not capitalized, but in English, they are. Children need to learn these conventions.

In order to facilitate the writing development of emergent writers, teachers need to understand the normal patterns of writing development. With that knowledge, teachers can interpret and support students' written inventions, while at the same time moving them toward conventional forms. If invention goes unchecked, nobody can read a child's message. However, if too much convention is imposed too early, children may lose the sense of writing as a process of constructing their own meanings. Bilingual teachers, as always, have even more to learn. They need to understand patterns of writing development that occur in English and Spanish, as well as what might be expected of Spanish speakers growing up in an environment dominated by print in English.

Early research by Read (1971), Chomsky (1970), and others has provided important insights into the natural process children go through as they move from invention to convention. Continued investigations into children's spelling development (Goodman and Wilde, 1992; Wilde, 1992) suggest more specific ways that teachers can help foster children's writing development.

Before discussing this research, we wish to point out two things. First, the researchers we are relying on have looked at spelling development in settings where children wrote for a variety of authentic purposes. The researchers were not asking children to complete tasks divorced from real reading and writing. Second, while we use the term *stage* to describe different points of students' progress in writing, we wish to emphasize that this is just a convenient way of discussing behaviors that really fall along a continuum. Kids move in and out of stages. There is no neat, linear progression. However, the categories we refer to as stages reflect our understanding of the major insights that children generally achieve as their writing becomes progressively conventional. The following discussion draws on work done by Buchanan (1989) in her excellent book, *Spelling for Whole Language Classrooms*.

Buchanan divides children's spelling development into four major stages: prephonetic, phonetic, phonic, and syntactic-semantic. For each stage she discusses the major concept that the child has developed, and she suggests ways teachers can help children progress and move toward the next stage. Buchanan encourages teachers to keep samples of student writing so that the teacher can identify patterns in student writing and keep track of their progress.

The Prephonetic Stage

Blanca asked her students to write about their Thanksgiving celebrations. Anthony drew a picture. Then he wrote under it (see Figure 5–7). He told Blanca that his writing said, "I went to my grandma's on Thanksgiving." Anthony's writing is a good example of the prephonetic stage. The major concept that children in the prephonetic stage develop is that "things can be represented on paper by symbols that are not pictures" (Buchanan, 1989, p. 134). It is easy to distinguish Anthony's drawing from his writing. His letters are not yet well formed, but they are clearly intended to represent writing, not drawing. In fact, the writing of young children from different first language backgrounds will generally correspond to the kinds of symbols used by adults who write that language.

This stage is referred to as prephonetic because children are using symbols to represent things, not the names of things. A mark on the paper might represent a stuffed bear, not the name of the bear. As children in this early stage move from scribble writing to recognizable letters, they frequently mix letters and numbers. They often rely on the letters of their own name as they write. And they may not understand the difference between being asked to write or to draw even though their marks on paper show that they can do both.

The most important thing teachers can do for children at the prephonetic stage is to encourage them to continue writing. At the same time, teachers should ensure that children are surrounded by meaningful print. Many teachers label children's desks or pictures with their names. They put alphabet letters up around the room. They read to children frequently using alphabet books and big books so that children can see the print easily. Many teachers also have children dictate stories. The teacher writes, and then the teacher and students read them.

FIGURE 5–7: Anthony's Thanksgiving Picture

The Phonetic Stage

Over time, children move into the phonetic stage. The major concept for students in this stage is that "there is a connection between the physical aspects of producing a word and the spelling of a word" (Buchanan, 1989, p. 135). Children in the phonetic stage are not yet connecting sounds to spellings. Instead, they are linking sound production with

FIGURE 5–8: Rosalinda's *Rainbow* and *House*

spelling. This may seem like a strange distinction, but spelling development moves gradually from concrete to abstract, and the physical actions involved in producing a sound are more concrete than qualities of the sound itself.

Young children are good phoneticians. They are very aware of how and where sounds are produced in their mouths. Read (1971), for example, showed that what appeared to be very odd spellings simply reflected children's reliance on sound production mechanisms. For example, one young child spelled *truck* with the letters *chrak*. Substituting *ch* for *t* seems strange to many adults, but it you say *truck* and then *chruck*, you'll notice that the actions you use and the movement of your tongue are nearly the same. The convention in English is to use a *t* before *r* to represent this sound rather than a *ch*, but from the point of view of sound production, a linguist (or a small child) could justify either choice equally well.

In the early phonetic stage, children usually use one letter for each word. Later in the phonetic stage they use one letter for each syllable. Two samples of Rosalinda's writing (see Figures 5–8 and 5–9) show her use of initial and final consonants. In the first sample she writes *house* as *hs* and *rainbow*

FIGURE 5–9: Rosalinda's *Ladybug*

as *rbl*. The *l* may be the result of her pronouncing the word more like *rain-bowl*. Children often sound out words as they write, and sometimes they overenunciate. In the second example, Rosalinda spells *ladybug* as *ldbg* reversing the *g*. Here she puts the initial consonant of each syllable plus the final consonant. As she writes, Rosalinda is aware of how she is producing the sounds, and the initial consonants of each syllable along with the final consonant are the ones she notices most.

Like Rosalinda, children writing in English most often represent the syllables with consonants. That's because consonants are more consistent in English than vowels are. We usually use the same consonant to represent a sound, especially at the beginning or end of a word. There are exceptions, of course. The sound of /k/ can be written with either a *c* or *k*. Nevertheless, consonants work more consistently than vowels in English. Our alphabet has only five vowel letters for about fifteen distinct sounds. Many of these vowel sounds are reduced to a schwa, and that sound can be spelled with any vowel. That's why even advanced students spell *grammar* as *grammer*.

In contrast, children writing in Spanish often represent syllables with vowels. Spanish has just five vowel sounds, and they match up consistently with the five vowel letters. As we shall see in the next chapter, Spanish-speaking children learning to write in Spanish respond to that regular pattern by beginning to write with vowels.

Children at an early phonetic stage benefit from the same strategies as those in the prephonetic stage. Teachers should read to them, do language experience activities, and ensure that there is lots of print up around the room. In addition, teachers can begin to use alphabet books and songs more. Children can also play with alphabet cards or magnetic letters. In many classes, teachers work with children to create a large-format class alphabet book. Above all, children in this stage should be encouraged to continue writing.

Buchanan divides the phonetic stage into an earlier and a later phase. The early stage is characterized by students' using one letter for each word or syllable. At the advanced phonetic stage they begin to connect the production of each sound with a letter. They move from a syllabic hypothesis to an alphabetic hypothesis. Their inventions still don't match conventional spelling since our spelling system isn't based solely on sound production. But now they begin to use vowels as well as consonants.

A third example from Rosalinda (see Figure 5–10) shows her progression toward the advanced phonetic stage. She reverses the order of *l* and *f* in *butterfly*. This is not a cause for concern. Rather, it simply illustrates that writing is a difficult physical activity at first for children, and sometimes

FIGURE 5–10: Rosalinda's *Butterfly*

they have difficulty representing the sounds they are producing with letters they are just learning to write. What is more significant is that Rosalinda adds a final *i* here. This shows that she may be moving into the later phonetic stage where children begin to use both consonants and vowels. A fourth sample from Rosalinda's writing (see Figure 5–11) shows this progression more clearly. Her spelling of *star* as *stor* shows her awareness of the vowel production along with the consonants.

Students at the advanced phonetic stage will often assume that the name of a letter is the same as the sound it makes. Norma, for example, writes, "My favorite ting is a shine dress." Here she assumes that the *e* in *shine* says its own name.

Students whose first language is not English may also rely on letter names during spelling, but they may think that the names for letters in English are the same as their sounds in their first language. A good example comes from a bilingual kindergartner writing to her friend, Dolly (see Figure 5–12). She writes *take* as *tec*, *me* as *mi*, and *please* as *plis*. In each word, the vowel she uses has the right name in Spanish for the sound she wants to represent.

FIGURE 5–11: Rosalinda's *Star*

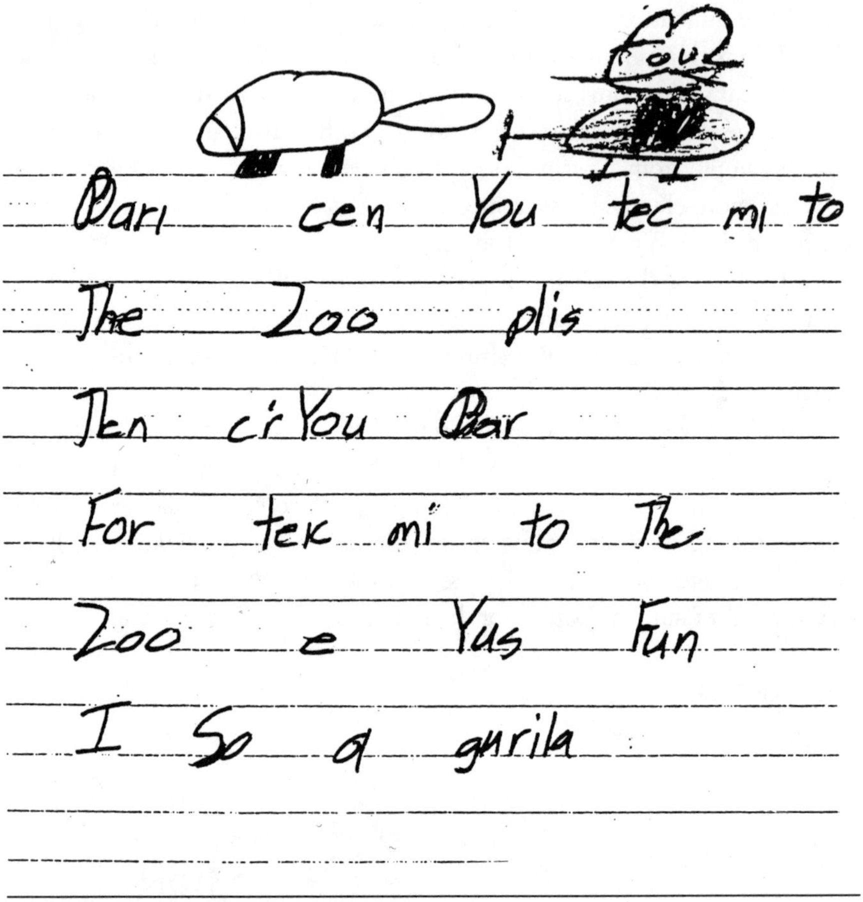

Dari cen You tec mi to

The Zoo plis

Ikn cr You Dar

For tek mi to The

Zoo e Yus Fun

I So a gurila

FIGURE 5–12: Bilingual Student's Note to Dolly

Bilingual children have two spelling systems to sort out, but they do this very well if they are given many chances to read and write. Of course, the task is easier for them if they first develop literacy fully in their primary language, but they are not confused by being exposed to two languages. Teachers, though, should be aware of first language influences when they analyze the English writing of bilingual children.

The same activities that are helpful in earlier stages continue to aid children in the advanced phonetic stage. They need to be read to, to be read with, and to write. Using poem charts or big books, teachers can start to point out different ways to represent sounds, but as long as children continue to read and write every day, they will continue to move toward conventional spelling. It is important for teachers to keep track of students' progress and then to work with individuals or small groups who don't seem to notice that their spellings are irregular. In general, though, more reading and writing is the key, especially if children are writing for real purposes. They will move toward conventional spelling if they have a message they really want a classmate to read and that classmate is confused by the spelling.

The Phonic Stage

Buchanan calls the next stage in spelling development the phonic stage. It is at this point that children realize the importance of the sounds themselves. In the phonetic stage they are concerned with the physical actions involved in producing the sounds, and in the phonic stage they are more focused on the sounds that result. They may also begin to use syntactic and semantic cues to some degree. Many of their misspellings at this stage show they are overgeneralizing about relations between sounds and spellings. For example, they might spell all /s/ sounds with an s and use c to represent the /k/ sound.

Benita's writing (see Figure 5–13) has many of the characteristics of the phonic stage. For example, she writes *phone* as *fon*. Both *ph* and *f* can represent the /f/ sound, and Benita hasn't sorted out when to use which spelling. She also writes *so* as *sow*. Again, she knows that the sound of /ow/ can be spelled either way, and she hasn't yet figured out which spelling she should

FIGURE 5–13: Benita's Note to Teacher

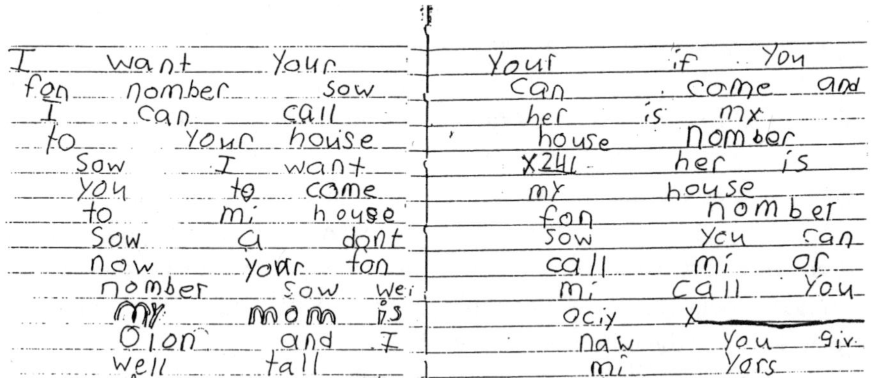

use for this word. In the same way, she spells *know* as *now*. She is also beginning to be aware of final silent *e* and adds one to *can* to produce *cane*. Benita's writing still shows some features of the advanced phonetic stage. She hasn't worked all the vowels out, and she uses letter name spelling, as in *mi* for *my*.

Another good example of the phonic stage comes from Kelly, a first grader who is our one example from a native English speaker (see Figure 5–14). Her story contains many conventional spellings, but she still needs to work out how to represent certain vowels. For example, *town* is spelled *tone*, and Kelly spells *they* as *thea*. In addition, she assumes that *little* will be spelled as it sounds, *littel*, with the vowel before the final consonant. Her spelling of *decided* as *desideit* shows that she is still working out the correct way to represent the /s/ sound in this word. Like other children, she assumes that the past tense should be spelled differently on different words to reflect the different sounds of the past tense. With continued writing, Kelly will begin to control some of these conventions, and, like the little girl in her story, live *haplee aver after*.

Teachers can help children who have moved to the phonic stage by having them find words that follow a certain pattern that they are having trouble with. A child might make a list of words where *ea* makes the long sound of *e* as in *tea*. A good way to make children more aware of a pattern is to put a key word up on butcher paper and then have children add other words that follow the same pattern. For example, a teacher could begin with *night*, and children could add other words as they notice them during class reading and writing activities.

It is especially helpful to talk with students about the idea that one sound can be represented by more than one letter or letter combination, and one letter or letter combination can represent different sounds. Teachers can have children make hypotheses and then collect and categorize words to test their hypotheses out. For instance, a teacher could ask children to collect words with *ea*, and categorize their words by the different sounds associated with the digraph. Then students could try to form a rule to account for the patterns they see.

The best way to help students who are in this stage advance is to give them time to read and write. Word games, playing with words and sounds, and activities like those described above can help bring spelling patterns to conscious awareness, but many of the insights children gain are subconscious and come from their reading and writing. However, the more interest teachers show in words and spellings, the more children are apt to take a similar interest, especially if the teacher takes the approach that this is a

Once thar was a littel girl and her Mother. Thae lived in a littel tone. In U.S.A. The tone was frasno. One day thea desideit to go to the ZOO. So thea whint to the ZOO. Thea had a grat time. Thea sooe all the animles. The littel girl liked the hippo the best. Her MoM liked the appies the best. But son it was time to go home. "All Rade" said the girl. "Yes All Rade" said her MoM. "It is time for lanch new," said her MoM. "What are we haveing for lanch MoM!" We are going to Mikedonillds Today. O Boy! and thea lived hapiee aver after.

the end

FIGURE 5–14: Kelly's Story

topic worth investigating rather than information that should be memorized. In process writing classrooms, language is always an intriguing topic for investigation.

A Short Detour—Phonemic Awareness   Some calls for reform in reading instruction, such as the Report of the California Reading Task Force (California, 1995), have claimed that readers need to develop something called phonemic awareness. When we consider how writing develops, it seems to us that phonemic awareness is at least part of what children in the phonic stage are demonstrating. Certainly Kelly is well on her way to figuring out the connections between sound patterns and spelling patterns.

Even though this chapter is primarily about how writing develops, we would like to take a short detour back toward reading. We wish to show that these calls for reading reform are misguided because they fail to recognize that what they call phonemic awareness is something that develops naturally when children write frequently in process classrooms. Phonemic awareness is not a skill that must be explicitly taught as a prerequisite to effective phonics instruction. An insistence that all children develop phonemic awareness early presents a potential detour on their road to literacy development.

To understand this confusion, we need to look again at different views of reading. Even though many researchers (Goodman, 1986a; Goodman, 1990; Smith, 1985; Weaver, 1994) argue that reading is a process of constructing meaning by using different kinds of cues, another group claims that learning to read involves identifying words. The latter see reading as a two step process. First readers identify words. Then they combine word meanings to get at sentence meanings. And the best way to identify words is to use phonics cues. So it's phonics first and meaning later. This leads to such statements as "Children need to learn to read, and then they can read to learn."

The two step theory is logical, but it doesn't reflect several decades of research in socio-psycholinguistics. Still, an approach to teaching reading that begins with phonics has popular appeal, and phonics approaches continue to surface. The usual argument of phonics advocates is that phonics itself is the right way to go, and if it didn't work in the past, it's just because it wasn't done correctly. A good example is Honig's (1996) influential new book, *How Should We Teach Our Children to Read?* Drawing on research by Juel (1994) and others, he claims that students need to know letter names and sounds, and they need to develop phonemic awareness. Only then can they benefit from the systematic instruction in phonics rules needed to identify words as a first step in learning to read.

What is phonemic awareness? Clearly, all children who come to school speaking a language can use sounds (phonemes) to comprehend and produce meaningful sentences. Bilingual children actually control two phonological systems. However, the argument is that children need to have an *awareness*, or conscious control of this system. In her study of children learning to read, Juel used a phonemic awareness test developed by Roper/Schneider (1984) that measures students' ability to segment words, blend sounds, delete the first phoneme, delete the last phoneme, substitute the first phoneme, and substitute the last phoneme of a word. She links scores on this test of phonemic awareness with reading ability.

In the phonemic awareness test Juel used, students are given a word like *cat* and asked how many sounds there are. They should be able to say each sound. Also, if they are given sounds, they should be able to blend them to form words. Children are also expected to be able to take off the first sound or the last sound (*cat* becomes *ca* or *at*) and to substitute a new sound at the beginning or the end (*cat* becomes *rat* or *car*). This sort of manipulation is fairly abstract, but teachers can prepare students, advocates claim, by using songs, chants, poems, and so forth. It is only when children have developed this phonemic awareness, along with knowledge of letter names and sounds, that phonics rules can be taught effectively.

When we look at the kinds of writing samples we have presented in this chapter what we see is phonemic awareness developing naturally. As children move toward conventional writing, they become increasingly aware of how the sound system relates to the spelling system. It is in trying to write down messages they want to convey that children really grapple with what is now being called phonemic awareness. Perhaps one reason that our perspective here is different from the view of researchers like Juel, is that we are looking at what kids do in classes where teachers read frequently and children write for real purposes every day. We are not looking at tests where children are asked to manipulate parts of language out of context.

Because many children can not demonstrate phonemic awareness as measured by tests, books like Honig's call for early intervention. As he says, all "students need to be assessed early for their phonemic awareness level and then an organized support program should be provided for those who score below the levels necessary to profit by phonics instruction" (p. 50). Honig asserts that if children do not develop phonics knowledge by mid-first grade, then they should be put into a special program that emphasizes skills. This early intervention ignores developmental differences among children. Many children just need more time to become proficient readers and writers. Early intervention programs also ignore differences in the kinds of language proficiencies children have when they enter school.

Many language minority children are expected to learn to read and write in English. It's asking a great deal that they read on grade level by mid-first grade if they are expected to develop both literacy and English in that short time. Early intervention will harm many bilingual children who will have to spend time on decontextualized skills, rather than engaging in authentic reading and writing. An insistence on all children developing phonemic awareness can constitute more than just a detour in their educational progress, it can turn into a real roadblock.

The focus of the reading reformers is on developing phonemic awareness for reading. We believe that phonemic awareness develops naturally as children write, but Honig seems to view writing exercises primarily as a way to get better at reading. He advises, "Another strategy essential to helping students learn phonic and phonemic awareness is to provide daily practice encoding the letter/sound correspondences being taught. These include assigned writing activities or writing as part of the guided reading sessions with children, and writing the words being read for examples of the phonics principles being taught" (p. 58). Writing that is only intended to help students practice letter/sound correspondences is very different from the kind of writing students do in process classes.

Writers like Juel and Honig, who emphasize the need for phonemic awareness as a prerequisite for reading, don't really understand how reading (or writing) works. Their goal is to prepare children for phonics. In the past, basal readers included readiness books to get kids ready to actually read. This new approach takes the process back a step and claims we have to get kids ready to do phonics first. It's true that if children can manipulate phonemes, they are more apt to be able to follow phonics exercises. But is this all really necessary?

Goodman (1993) defines phonics as "the set of complex relationships between phonology (the sound system of an oral language) and orthography (the system of spellings and punctuation of the written language)" (p. 8). As we discussed above, neither English nor Spanish orthography is based solely on the sound system of the language, so there is not a neat one-to-one relationship between the sounds and the writing. What we do find is that patterns of spelling generally correspond to patterns of sounds. For example, in English the consonant-vowel-consonant pattern of three letter words, as in *rat*, signals to readers that the vowel has a short sound. When we add another vowel at the end, usually a silent *e*, we change the pattern and create a new pattern in which the vowel is long, as in *rate*. Phonics is knowledge, usually subconscious, of these kinds of patterns.

Goodman further claims that readers and writers construct meaning by using graphophonics as one of three cueing systems. Graphophonics is a combination of cues from phonology, orthography, *and* phonics. Students don't need just phonemic awareness and knowledge of letters to write. They also need phonics. It's a combination of knowledge of sounds, letters, and the complex patterns that relate them that young readers and writers develop. Any approach to teaching reading based on phonics alone misses the

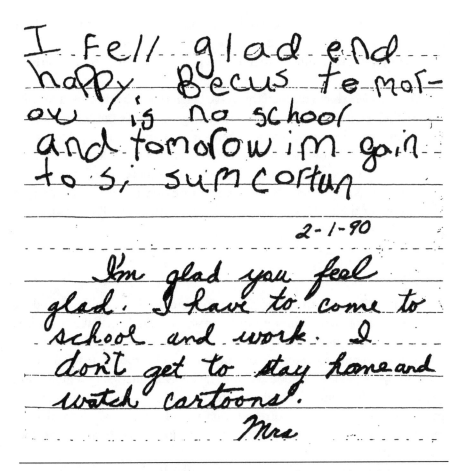

I Fell glad end
happy, Becus temor-
ow is no school
and tomorow im goin
to s, sum cortun

2-1-90

I'm glad you feel
glad. I have to come to
school and work. I
don't get to stay home and
watch cartoons.
Mrs

FIGURE 5–15: Carmen's Journal Entry

point that phonics is only one element in one of the three cueing systems. Readers and writers also use syntactic and semantic cues as they construct meaning. We can observe this development in samples of their writing. Children begin to use cues from all three systems in the phonic stage, and they continue to develop them in the final stage.

The Syntactic-Semantic Stage
In the syntactic-semantic stage children become increasingly aware that spelling systems reflect more than sounds. Spelling is also shaped by syntax and meaning. Students at this stage spell most words correctly, but they may have trouble with homophones or homographs. An example of a student who is entering the syntactic-semantic stage is Carmen (see Figure 5–15). She still is having some difficulty with segmentation in a word like *tomorrow* and not all her vowels are spelled conventionally, but many of

her misspellings are actually words. She substitutes *fell* for *feel, end* for *and*, and *sum* for *some*. She may have seen these words in her reading. She simply can't remember which of the possible spellings to use in these contexts.

Students who have reached this stage benefit most by increased reading and writing. However, they can also become more aware of spellings by investigating word histories. Many students also enjoy word play. Most puns are based on the use of homophones or homographs. If students maintain a lively interest in words, they begin to spell words more conventionally. In addition, at this stage students are often writing for wider audiences and are more aware of the need to move toward conventional spelling in order to communicate effectively.

Conclusion

We began this chapter by sharing writing samples from Pablo, a student becoming a proficient biliterate in Spanish and English. Pablo's work is the result of experiences in a process writing classroom in contrast to a traditional writing classroom. In traditional classrooms teachers offer their students models of good writing, make assignments, and give them feedback on their efforts, usually in the form of grammatical corrections. Instruction is focused on correct formation of letters, words, and then sentences. The form of student writing is considered more important than the content.

In contrast, in process writing classes like Pablo's, teachers help students develop and express their ideas through writing. The focus is on the actual process that writers go through to collect ideas, write drafts, conference and revise, and finally edit their work. Students write for real purposes and for audiences that extend beyond just the teacher. Pablo's writing about his grandfather and his story about King Cobra both show his understanding that writing should communicate important or entertaining messages.

The Checklist for Effective Writing calls for the kinds of experiences with writing that Pablo has had. In such classes, students have many opportunities for meaningful reading and writing, and in that context their control over the conventions of written language develop naturally. In order for Pablo's teacher to respond appropriately to Pablo's writing, she needs to understand the developmental stages children normally go through as their inventions gradually move toward conventional forms. She also needs to understand that what has been called phonemic awareness develops naturally as Pablo writes. He doesn't need to be taught phonemic awareness explicitly as a prerequisite for reading.

In this chapter we have looked at how spelling develops for Hispanic students, like Pablo, learning to write in English. In the following chapter, we turn to Spanish writing development and consider some of the differences between writing development in English and in Spanish.

6

Spanish Writing Development

The following three pieces were written by second graders in a Spanish/English bilingual classroom in a rural school. Many of the students in this school are migrant children, and most families work in agriculture. Since the class had been studying about dinosaurs, Carolina, their teacher, asked the children to write what they had learned as one of the selections for their school-required portfolio. Although all three children are in the same classroom, their writing samples show that they are at very different stages of writing development in Spanish.

FIGURE 6–1: Alejandra's Dinosaurio Piece

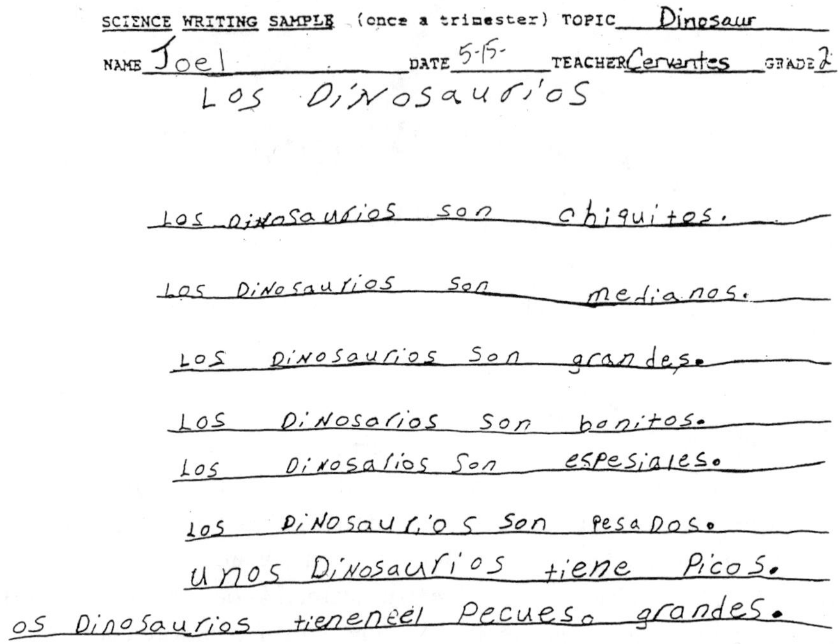

SCIENCE WRITING SAMPLE (once a trimester) TOPIC Dinosaur

NAME Joel DATE 5-15- TEACHER Cervantes GRADE 2

Los Dinosaurios

Los dinosaurios son chiquitos.
Los Dinosaurios son medianos.
Los Dinosaurios son grandes.
Los Dinosarios son bonitos.
Los Dinosalios Son espesiales.
Los Dinosaurios son pesaDos.
unos Dinosaurios tiene Picos.
os Dinosaurios tieneneel Pecueso grandes.

FIGURE 6–2: Joel's Dinosaurio Piece

Dinosaurs
Dinosaurs are small.
Dinosaurs are medium sized.
Dinosaurs are big.
Dinosaurs are pretty.
Dinosaurs are special.
Dinosaurs are heavy.
Dinosaurs have beaks.
Dinosaurs have big necks.

Alejandra's piece is at an earlier stage of development than the writing of her peers. She does form letters into words, and some of the words can be understood. For example, Alejandra told Carolina that the title was *Los dinosaurios comen mucho* (Dinosaurs eat a lot) and the first sentence read <Unos comen hojas.> (Some eat leaves.). Few words beyond *los* and *y* appear to be spelled conventionally. Alejandra does not use capital letters and only puts a period after the first sentence. In addition, she draws pictures and numbers her sentences rather than using paragraph form. She circles the parts of her paper (title, body, and conclusion)

SCIENCE WRITING SAMPLE (once a trimester) TOPIC Dinosaur

NAME José DATE 5-13- TEACHER Cervantes GRADE 2

Los dinesaurios.

ase mucho Tiempo
cuado La Tiera era
mas Caliete quela de
nosotros avia muchos
dinosourios avia unos
gordos, otros Flacos
oTros Largos oTkos chico
oTros grandes ai unos
en Forma de dinoser
Te oTros Forma de
cocodriLo.

FIGURE 6–3: José's Dinosaurio Piece

Dinosaurs
A long time ago
when the earth was
hotter than
ours there were many
dinosaurs there were some
fat ones, others thin
others long others small
others big there are some
in the shape of a dinosaur
and others in the shape of a crocodile.

rather than indenting. This convention is one that many writers use in the early stages. At this stage, however, Alejandra's writing is characterized more by her inventions than by her awareness of the standard conventions for writing.

By contrast, Joel's piece has only three errors. He spells *especiales* (special) without the *c* in the fifth sentence, and he does not add the *n* to the verb in the seventh. In the last sentence, he misspells *pescuezo* (neck), a difficult word. Sentences start with a capital letter and end with a period. The piece lists characteristics of dinosaurs using the same sentence structure for each of the first six sentences and then only changing the verb from *son* (are) to *tienen* (have) in the last two. While this piece is almost completely correct, it lacks variety and imagination. Joel is not taking risks with his writing. Rather than inventing new ways of expressing his ideas, Joel is following a conventional pattern carefully.

The third piece shows a writer who is experimenting with more complex sentence structure, vocabulary, and ideas. José begins by relating the time and setting in which dinosaurs lived and making a comparison with the present. He then goes on to describe different kinds of dinosaurs. Although there are examples of unconventional spelling, orthography, and punctuation, José does a good job of not only demonstrating his command of the structure and vocabulary of Spanish, but also of showing what he has learned about dinosaurs.

All three writers attempt to express what they learned from readings and discussions in Carolina's classroom. Their pieces show that they know some important things about the conventions of writing. They are at different stages in their development, and they show varying degrees of willingness to risk inventing new forms to express their meanings. It is only through the process of inventing written forms and receiving meaningful feedback in a community of learners that writers develop. It is important for teachers to understand normal developmental patterns of writing conventions for Spanish-speaking students. This knowledge can help teachers validate what children do know. It can also guide teachers in providing the kinds of encouragement and instruction that will help their students become more effective writers.

In the last chapter we considered the nature of alphabetic writing systems, and we traced the developmental stages that children writing in English generally follow. In this chapter we focus more specifically on children writing in Spanish. Although there are similarities in English and Spanish writing development, there are differences as well. Teachers in bilingual Spanish/English classes should be aware of both the similarities and the differences.

Writing Development in Spanish

Ferreiro and Teberosky (1979, 1982) in their classic study of the literacy development of Spanish-speaking children in Argentina, identified several stages of writing for children whose first language is Spanish. As we discuss these stages, we will draw parallels with the developmental stages for English spelling that we outlined in the last chapter.

We should note that Ferreiro and Teberosky are Piagetian scholars, so the methods and the theoretical framework they use for analyzing spelling is somewhat different from Buchanan's approach, which we described in the last chapter. There are also differences in spelling development between students writing in English and students writing in Spanish. Nevertheless, there are many more similarities than differences. As we discuss Ferreiro and Teberosky, we will point out similarities with the model we presented earlier. Taken together, these two frameworks for analyzing children's writing development complement one another and provide teachers added insights into the normal developmental patterns of young writers.

Depending on their exposure to print in both English and Spanish, Spanish-speaking children in the United States follow similar patterns as those in the Argentine study. One conclusion that seems to be universal, and which will be evident throughout our discussion, is that the child's name is extremely important in early writing development. The chart in Figure 6–4 provides a summary in both Spanish and English of the Ferreiro and Teberosky conclusions

In this section we will lay out the stages of writing identified by Ferreiro and Teberosky, showing writing samples that follow those stages taken from children in both Argentina and the United States. In addition, we will comment on the evidences of the influences of English print that appear in the writing of students in the United States. It should also be pointed out that the writing samples from the Ferreiro and Teberosky study were the results of words and sentences dictated to the children while the United States samples were written by children who generally chose the words they would write as they wrote in journals or responded to class activities or to literature.

DESARROLLO DE LA ESCRITURA EN ESPANOL

Ferreiro y Teberosky, *Los sistemas de escritura en el desarrollo del niño*, 1979. preparado por Yvonne S. Freeman. Traducido por Marisela B. Serra.

Nivel Uno
 a. Egocéntrico—La escritura no sirve para transmitir información.
 b. Figurativo—Correspondencia entre la escritura y el objeto de la escritura.
  pato . . . oso   hermano . . . papá
  Veronica . . . (la *b* grande)
 c. No hay diferenciación entre el dibujo y la escritura.

Nivel Dos
 a. Número fijo y variedad de los grafismos.
 b. En esta etapa es interesante observar cómo los niños utilizan primero las letras de su nombre.
  A r o n = sapo
  A o r n = pato
  I a o n = casa
  r A o I = Mamá sale de casa.

Nivel Tres
 a. Cada letra corresponde a una sílaba.
 b. Las vocales son estables y convencionales.
  I E A O A O = Mi nena toma sol.

Nivel Quatro
 a. Los niños van del nivel silábico al nivel alfabético.
 b. Las hipótesis que hacen los niños en el nivel silábico no se corresponden con lo que ellos ven impreso en el ambiente. Por eso, comienzan a añadir más consonantes.
  PAO = palo   MCA = mesa   MAP = mapa
  MINENATOMCSO = Mi nena toma sol

Nivel Cinqo
 a. En este nivel los niños comienzan a prestar atención a los grafismos que están dentro de las sílabas.
 b. Los problemas son ortográficos y no de escritura.
  mesa— ¿s? o ¿z?
  casa— ¿c? o ¿k?
  cielo— ¿c? o ¿s?
  queso—¿k? o ¿c? o ¿qu?
  yo— ¿ll? o ¿y?
 c. Los niños comienzan a segmentar el sujeto del predicado.
  MINENA TOMASOL

FIGURE 6–4, Part 1: Ferreiro and Teberosky Spelling Stages

WRITING DEVELOPMENT IN SPANISH

(summarized from Ferreiro and Teberosky, *Literacy Before Schooling, 1982*)

Level One
  a. Egocentric—writing does not serve to transmit information.
  b. Figurative—correspondence between the writing and the object of the writing.
     pato . . . oso   hermano . . . papá
     Veronica . . . (la *b* grande)
  c. Nondistinction between drawing and writing.

Level Two
  a. Fixed number and variety of characters.
  b. At this stage it is interesting to observe how children first use the letters of their name.
     A r o n = sapo
     A o r n = pato
     I a o n = casa
     r A o I = Mamá sale de casa.

Level Three
  a. Each letter stands for one syllable.
  b. Vowels are stable and conventional.
     I E A O A O = Mi nena toma sol.

Level Four
  a. Children move from syllabic to alphabetic hypotheses.
  b. The hypotheses that the children make conflict with print in the environment. Because of this, they begin to add more consonants.
     PAO = palo   MCA = mesa   MAP = mapa
     MINENATOMCSO = Mi nena toma sol.

Level Five
  a. At this level, children begin to notice characters that are within syllables.
  b. Problems are orthographic not writing problems.
     mesa = s   or z?
     casa = c   or k?
     cielo = c   or s?
     queso = k   or c   or qu?
     yo =   llo or yo??
  c. Children begin to segment subjects and predicates.
     MINENA TOMASOL

FIGURE 6–4, Part 2: Ferreiro and Teberosky Spelling Stages

Level One Writing

Level One in Ferreiro and Teberosky's chart corresponds to Buchanan's prephonetic stage because at this level children do not associate writing and sounds. Ferreiro and Teberosky expand our understanding of this stage. They found three characteristics of children's writing at Level One: First, the writing is egocentric. That is, children do not realize that they have a responsibility for writing something that others might be able to read. Sometimes they know what they are writing, but they do not expect others to read it, nor do they expect to be able to read what others write. Even within Level One, though, children begin to develop a sense of audience and start to expect that others can read what they write.

Second, children believe the size of the written word should correspond to the size of the object the word represents. For example, children at this level would expect the word *papá* (father) to be bigger than the word *hermano* (brother) because for most young children, their fathers are bigger than their brothers.

When Ferreiro and Teberosky (1979) asked four-year-old Gustavo to write *pato* (duck), he drew some wavy lines. The dialogue between Gustavo and the researcher that follows shows Gustavo's thinking:

RESEARCHER:	GUSTAVO:
¿Podés escribir \<oso>?	
¿Será más largo o más corto?	Más grande.
¿Por qué?	(Gustavo comienza a hacer una escritura enteramente similar, pero que resulta más larga que la anterior, mientras silabea.)
	O-so. ¿Viste que sale más grande?
Sí, pero ¿por qué?	Porque es un nombre más grande que el pato. (p. 242)

Translation:

Can you write "bear"?	
Will it be longer or shorter?	Bigger
	(Gustavo begins to write something similar but longer than what he wrote before while he sounds out.)
	O-so. Do you see that it comes out bigger?
Yes, but why?	Because it is a bigger name than duck.

Gustavo reasons that since bears are bigger than ducks, the written representation for bear should also be bigger. Two other examples from Ferreiro and Teberosky (1979) clarify how children relate quantifiable aspects of words to quantifiable aspects of meaning. A five year old in Mexico visiting her doctor told him to write her name longer for this visit because her birthday had been the previous day.

An additional example from Ferreiro and Teberosky shows another way that Level One children connect writing and size:

una niña mexicana de 5 años, llamada Verónica, escribe su nombre así: VERO; pero piensa que cuando sea grande lo va a esribir <con la be grande> (es decir, BERO, ya que en México la V es llamada <be chica> y la B es la <be grande>) (p. 243).

Translation:

A five year old Mexican girl named Verónica writes her name like this: VERO; but thinks that when she is older she is going to write it "with the big B" (that is BERO, because in Mexico the V is called *small b* and the B is the *big b*).

A third characteristic of writers at Level One is that they do not distinguish clearly between what we call writing and drawing. For example, if a parent tells a child to "write mother," she might, instead, draw a mother. On the other hand, a child might say they will *draw* something and then write letters. In a study that replicated parts of Ferreiro and Teberosky's research, Freeman and Whitesell (1985) found this same confusion of terms among preschool children in Tucson, Arizona. Children appear to distinguish writing from drawing, but they may not consistently use the words *write* and *draw* to describe what they are doing. They also frequently mix numbers and letters.

The Argentine researchers also point out that young writers often reverse characters, both letters and numbers, and that <en este nivel y en niveles subsiguientes, señalemos que no puede ser tomada como índice patológico (preanuncio de dislexia o disgrafia), sino como algo totalmente normal> (p. 248). (At this level, and in subsequent levels, we wish to point out that this (reversal of letters and numbers) cannot be taken as a pathological indication of a problem (announcing dyslexia or dysgraphia) but instead as something totally normal.)

Vicente, for example, drew a picture of the sun and some playground toys (see Figure 6–5). Then he wrote on his picture.

Vicente told his teachers that his writing said, <Había mucho sol y

A O R ⅄ M N E F ℓ t S ρ ∧ o ᵇ H ⌐ ⌐ I \ R R
M R N L _ c   n ∘ A   ∘ R r
H R A M ⅄ X e t o ≥ 9 ℛ r ∧ ⌐ I \ R R

Había mucho sol y jugué afuera
muchos días.

FIGURE 6–5: Vicente's Picture of the Sun

jugué afuera muchos días.> (There was a lot of sun, and I played outside many days.). He appears to have reversed the number 4 and the letters *n*, *S*, and *R* though small *r* and both the *n* and the *R* were also written conventionally. He also inverts *v* in two places. It is important to realize that reversals like these are a natural part of writing development.

It's not that children *see* the letters backward. Instead, they are making hypotheses about the directionality of letters and numbers. They have to decide which way they face. Most letters of the alphabet can be thought of as facing toward the right. However, letters like *d* face to the left. Other letters, such as *g* may face either way, depending on the font, although capital G faces right. Numbers, on the other hand, face left except for 5 and 6. Young children usually look for consistency and overgeneralize as they make their hypotheses. Unfortunately, the system isn't completely consistent. Children are constructing an underlying rule, not simply imitating surface forms. Since the rule they need is complex, this takes time. Unfortunately, some young children are not given the time they need. They are labeled as dyslexic early in their schooling even though their reversals are a natural part of development.

Level Two Writing

In Level Two Ferreiro and Teberosky found that the graphic forms children made were more defined and more conventional. Most of their letters were recognizable, although some reversals still occurred. The researchers also found that children at this level operate on the hypothesis that words must have a certain, fixed number of characters and that words require a variety of characters. Although the writing in Level Two shows certain advances over Level One writing, it still falls into Buchanan's prephonetic stage because children are not yet associating sound production with letters. Instead, the letters simply represent the thing or idea itself, not the sounds of the words.

For example, when Ferreiro and Teberosky asked Romina to write three words and a sentence, she wrote the following, using letters from her name:

R I O A
O A I R
A R O I
O I R A (p. 251)

Like many other children that Ferreiro and Teberosky studied, Romina believes that words must have at least four letters. She also knows that different words have different sequences of letters. Romina mixes the letters from her name to accomplish this. It's interesting to note that for Romina, there is no difference between the number of characters in a word and the number in a sentence. Terms like *word* and *sentence* are quite abstract for young writers, and they may not distinguish between the two at first.

Writing samples from bilingual kindergarten children in the United States help confirm Ferreiro and Teberosky's conclusions. José is a kindergartner in Blanca's classroom where children are encouraged to write daily. They read their writing to Blanca who writes their words with conventional spelling. His writing (see Figure 6–6) shows that he also believes that words or sentences must have a minimum number of letters and also must have a variety of letters. He writes ten letters per line and, although letters are repeated, the order of the letters is varied. It is interesting to note that he is beginning to rely on letters that are not in his name, and he is beginning to experiment with the use of double letters, which he may have noticed in environmental print.

SK PABRPEAB
SSAVVBPPBA

Yo fui ha la biblioteca y saque un
libro. Y alguin tiro una piedra.

FIGURE 6–6: José's Writing

I went to the library and I
took out a book. And someone threw a rock.

Looking at José's writing, it is more difficult to decide what he thinks is a minimum number of letters for a word. He writes strings of letters that represent his ideas. Ferreiro and Teberosky controlled the writing they collected by asking children to write a *word* or a *sentence* that they dictated. In contrast, the samples we have collected come from classrooms where children choose what they write. Since words or sentences are not dictated to them, they often write in letter strings, usually without spacing between words at this early stage. This makes it more difficult to decide what the children think represents a word, but we can see that children expect words to have several letters, and they expect that words will contain different letters.

These insights into children's writing development have implications for teaching them to read. When children notice print, they focus on the bigger, more salient, words. Most signs for stores or names of products, like breakfast cereals, have several letters. Children often ignore short words. In both English and Spanish writing, the content words—the nouns, verbs, adjectives, and adverbs—are generally longer than the function words—the articles, conjunctions, prepositions, and so on. If we write a telegram, it's the function words we leave out because the content words carry the essential message. So it is natural for children to focus on those bigger, more important words.

Even though children come to school more aware of long words than short words, and even though their own writing shows that they think words should have a minimum number of letters and should have a variety of letters, books for beginning readers often feature short words with repeated letters (*ball*, *is*, *oso*, *la*). The idea is that if we use short, simple words with only a few letters, we make reading easier for children. However, children may not believe that these short words are really for reading since they come to school already having made hypotheses about words based on the words they see around them every day. At first, children notice these bigger chunks, or wholes, and only later do they attend to the smaller parts. If reading materials start with the parts, this makes reading harder for children, not easier.

One difference we have noticed in comparing the writing samples from the United States and those from the Argentina study is that many of the Argentinean children have a few words fixed in their repertoire. They seem to have learned the words from a family member, or they may have often seen the word. Laura, for example, could write four words: *mamá*, *papá*, *oso*, and *Laura*. Ferreiro and Teberosky report Laura's explanation, <*Laura* me enseñó mi mamá, y *papá*, *oso* y *mamá* aprendí yo de un librito para empezar a leer.> (*Laura* my mom taught me and *papá*, *oso*, and *mamá* I learned myself from a little beginning reading book.).

The memorization of certain words to write seems less common in the samples we have from classrooms. However, beginning writers often copy down words they see in classroom environmental print, including the covers of books the class has read. As a language experience activity, Rhonda had her students choose a favorite story, illustrate it, and then tell her what was happening. Figure 6–7 shows Anita's drawing and labeling of *La bella durmiente*, as well as Rhonda's writing of her summary. Even though Anita is at an early stage of writing, she does recognize the story title and is able to copy it quite accurately. Anita has a bit of trouble writing the article straight on the title. She first writes a crooked *L* and then erases it. When she showed her paper to Rhonda, together they decided the *a* was missing from her straightened *L*, and Rhonda added an *a*.

A final example of Level Two writing comes from Ramón, a five year old in Pricila's kindergarten (see Figure 6–8). This sample shows the hypotheses that young writers at this level generally make. Ramón drew a picture and then wrote using many letters of his name. He repeats letters and appears to mix in some numbers. Several of his letters are still reversed.

bebe la Durmiente Anita

No invitaron a la hada mala a la fiesta de la princesita. Se enojó la hada olvidada y su regalo que le dió fue que se picara el dedo y morirá.

FIGURE 6–7: Anita's Drawing

They didn't invite the bad fairy to the party
of the little princess. The forgotten fairy got mad
and her gift that she gave was that she would prick
her finger and die.

Nevertheless, he has at least seven letters on each line, and he varies the order of the letters. Ramón knows the difference between drawing and writing, and he is beginning to use conventional representations of the letters of the alphabet to convey his meanings to others.

Level Three Writing
In Level Three, Ferreiro and Teberosky noticed that children begin to assign a sound value to letters and sound out words for themselves. Up to this point, children think that letters represent objects directly. Now, they realize that the letters connect to the sounds of the words we use to name the objects. Actually, children focus more on the physical actions required to produce the sounds than on the sounds themselves. Level Three corresponds to Buchanan's early phonetic stage in which there is "a correspondence between the physical aspects of producing a word and the spelling of a word" (Buchanan, 1989, p. 135).

Children at Level Three begin to sound words out. As children write,

FIGURE 6–8: Ramon's Writing

teachers can observe this process. At this stage, young writers make a syllabic hypothesis. They use one letter to represent each syllable in a word. This step is a major one for young writers because for the first time they make the connection between sound segments of speech and the letters in a text.

For Spanish-speaking children becoming biliterate in Spanish and English, this stage is especially interesting, because emergent Spanish writers in Spanish-speaking countries generally write vowels first. The appearance of vowels in Spanish writing can be attributed to the fact that in Spanish, the five vowel sounds correspond to the five letters for vowels. In contrast, emergent English writers in English-speaking countries generally write consonants first. Spanish speakers raised in an environment dominated by English print may show a mixture of vowels and consonants. Below we will share examples that show young Spanish-speaking writers in the United States developing in a similar way to those of the Argentine study, where vowels are definitely most used as well as an example that differs.

In the Argentinean study, the children were asked to write words and sentences dictated by the researchers. Mariano first wrote his name correctly. Like many children, he had learned to write his own name, and he used the letters from his name to represent other words. When asked to write *sapo* (toad), he wrote AO. He was able to use letters from his name to write the vowels from the two syllables of *sapo*. Then, when the researchers asked him to write *Mi nena toma sol.* (My baby girl sunbathes.), he wrote every vowel in the sentence IEAOAO. He also wrote PO when asked to write *pato* (duck), showing that consonants are not always deleted. This finding that Spanish writers frequently begin with vowels is especially important information for bilingual teachers who encourage inventive spelling with their Spanish writers. While in the past, strings of vowels on a child's paper may have been interpreted as random letter practice, teachers can now recognize that those vowels could relate directly to a message the child intended to write.

Efraín's writing provides a good example of a child using vowels to represent the syllables in his words (see Figure 6–9). Carolina, his teacher, wrote the words when he read his story back to her, matching them to his writing. This type of record keeping is an excellent practice because it provides teachers with valuable information they can use as they chart students' progress in writing. Unless a teacher listens to a child and writes down what he or she says, it is very difficult to figure out the writing later. When a teacher listens to a child in this way, it also helps the child understand the communicative nature of writing.

The first line of Efraín's writing includes all the vowels from the words in order. The only exception is that the letters *d* and *a* appear after the *ea* for *está*. He may have repeated the last syllable of the word to himself as he wrote and added the consonant and repeated the final vowel. He writes the consonant as *d*. Both *d* and *t* are produced in the same place in the mouth, and children at this stage rely on such features of physical production. In the second line, Carolina wrote only the first two words. Efraín adds an extra *o* after the *e* for *el* and then includes two consonants in *submarino*. He also includes three additional consonants in the remaining letter string. This shows that he is beginning to become aware that writing contains both consonants and vowels. However, in most of his writing he still uses one vowel for each syllable.

Another student in Carolina's class, Rosa, showed Carolina her picture and told her, <La niña está en la casa. Tiene mucho frío.> (The girl is in the house. She's cold.). Carolina wrote on Rosa's paper a question for her to write the answer to: <Por qué tiene frío?> (Why is she cold?). Carolina read the question, and Rosa wrote back OEAELO to represent <porque hay hielo> (because there is frost) (see Figure 6–10). Here she represents each

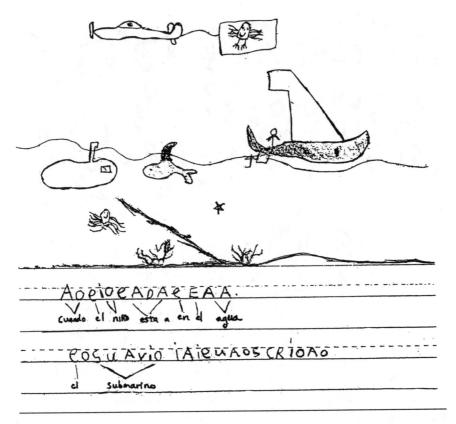

FIGURE 6–9: Efraín's Writing

*When the boy was in the water
the submarine . . .*

syllable with one vowel consistently for the first two words. She uses *e* for *ie*. Like Efraín, she shows a beginning awareness of consonants by including the *l* in *hielo*.

Spanish-speaking children are exposed to environmental print in English at school, on the streets, and on television: their early writing often shows this influence as well. Ana, who is in kindergarten, showed an awareness of both English and Spanish in her writing (see Figure 6–11). The letters she used to label two drawings include several vowels, but they also contain *K* and letter combinations *PH* and *SH*, which are not common to Spanish.

Whether they use vowels, consonants, or some combination, writers at Level Three operate on a syllabic hypothesis. They generally write one letter for each syllable in a string of words. It is more difficult for teachers to read children's writing when it consists entirely of vowels. However, Spanish-

FIGURE 6–10: Rosa's Writing

speaking children usually begin with vowels, and if teachers ask students to read what they have written (as soon as possible after they complete the writing), they will note the close correspondence between the letters the children write and the vowels in the words of their message. Children at this level have made an important conceptual leap: They have begun to connect letters and sounds, and it is important for teachers to recognize and support this advance.

Level Four Writing

According to Ferreiro and Teberosky, the children who have reached Level Four are those who move from a syllabic hypothesis to an alphabetic hypothesis. Buchanan refers to Level Four as the advanced phonetic stage. Children at Level Four begin to realize that "Each element of sound production of a word should be represented in the spelling of a word" (Buchanan, 1989, p. 136).

Spanish writers begin with vowels. However, they begin to notice that both vowels and consonants are used in environmental print. If teachers read them big books, children also start to notice that the words have more

FIGURE 6–11: Ana's Earlier Writing

than vowels. This leads them to the alphabetic hypothesis that each sound in the word should be represented by a letter. They realize that the writing only reflected by the vowels for the syllables is not enough and begin to add the consonants.

In Rhonda's kindergarten other children were still only writing their names or strings of vowels, but Susi drew a picture of the ugly duckling hatching and labeled it on her own using both vowels and consonants (see Figure 6–12). In this example, Susi seems to be moving into Level Four. However, these stages are not fixed. Sometimes children move back and forth between the syllabic and the alphabetic hypothesis.

Ariana, a first grader in Sam's bilingual class, had seen the words *Valentine* and *San Valentín* written all around the classroom. When she went to make her valentine card, she wrote *sanvavenn*, using both consonants and vowels (see Figure 6–13). She represented the eleven sounds in the words with nine letters. She substituted *v* for *l* and omitted *ti*. Here she appears to

FIGURE 6–12: Susi's Drawing

The Ugly Duckling

be operating on the alphabetic hypothesis. However, she then carefully sounded out the syllables of <¿Cómo está su familia?> (How is your family?) and wrote the words using only the vowels. For *familia* she reversed the last two vowels and then added the initial *f*.

Ariana's writing is a good example of a student moving from Level Three to Level Four. She is beginning to add consonants she sees in the environment. She has begun to notice the print around the classroom, as well as the environmental print outside the classroom; her writing reflects her new awareness. Her invented spelling is becoming more conventional. This example also shows the importance of teachers ensuring that students are exposed to as much print as possible.

FIGURE 6–13: Ariana's Valentine

Level Five Writing

The final stage that Ferreiro and Teberosky identify is Level Five. At this stage children refine their alphabetic hypothesis. They use both consonants and vowels to represent all the sounds in each word more consistently. This is equivalent to Buchanan's phonic stage. At this level, children's spelling continues be more conventional, and many of their errors show confusions among different ways of representing a particular sound. For example, they might not be sure whether to use *s* or *z* in *mesa*.

Figure 6–14 is an extremely interesting example from a kindergartner in Blanca's class. At first glance, Daniel's work might cause a teacher concern. He writes his name backward, and his other letters have reversals and do not appear to be well-formed. However, Daniel read back what he had written, and a comparison of his writing with his intended message shows that even in kindergarten Daniel is already breaking code and writing words that have both vowels and consonants.

Students at this level must solve orthographic problems, but they now have an underlying understanding of how the writing system works. In

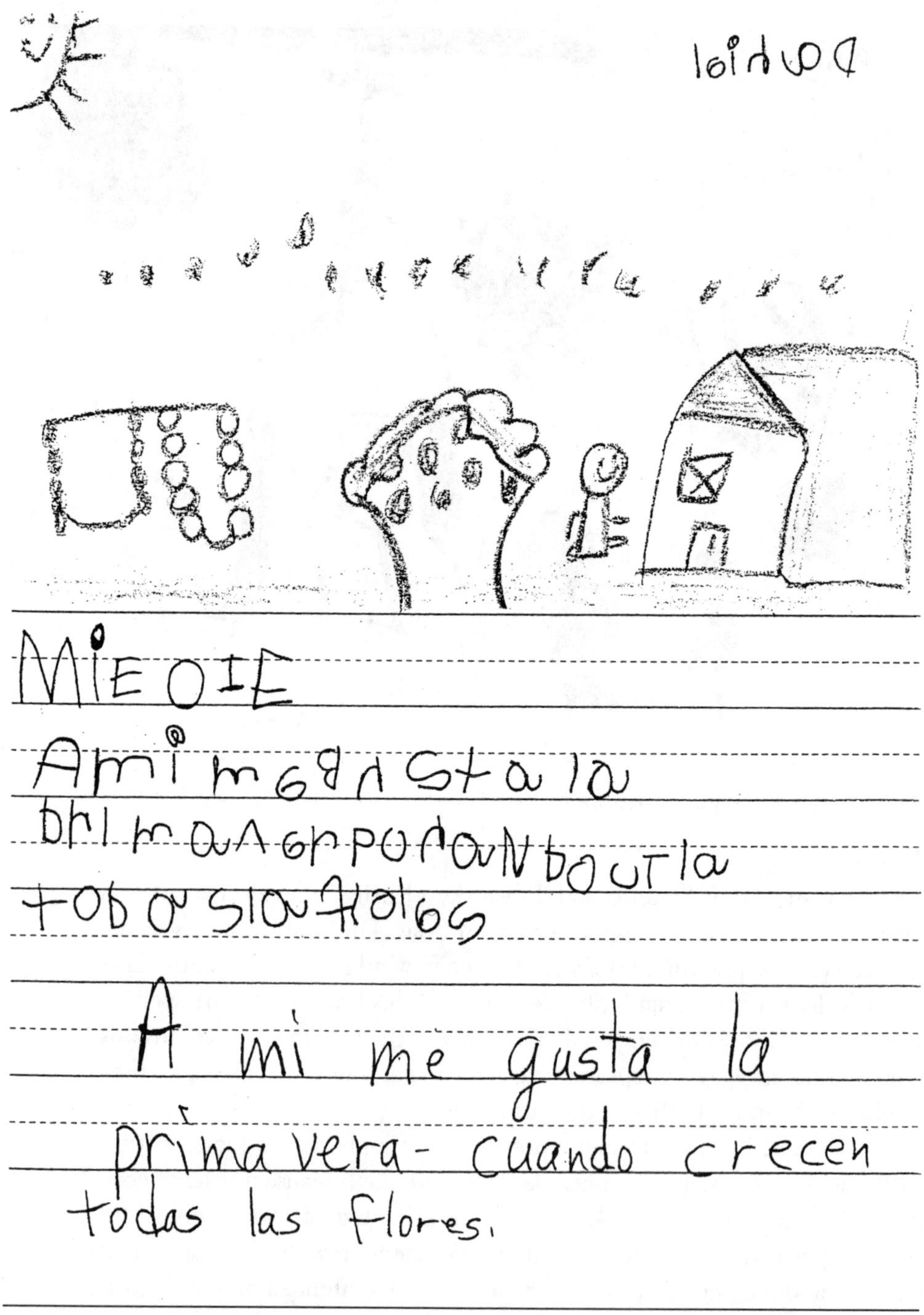

Daniel

MIEOIE
AmI m68nStala
brimaGrpononboutla
Tobo'SlontoI6S

A mi me gusta la
primavera- cuando crecen
todas las flores.

FIGURE 6–14: Daniel's Writing

I like spring when all the flowers grow.

Spanish, young writers struggle with sounds where alternate spellings are possible, such as the choice between *ll* and *y*, or between *s*, *c*, or *z*. A good example comes from the writing of another kindergartner in Blanca's class. Angélica is moving toward conventional spelling as she writes about Martin Luther King (see Figure 6–15). She writes CEiA CE lA EDE no BElE for <Quería que la gente no peleara.> (He wanted that people not fight.).

Angélica still omits some consonants, but she uses both consonants and vowels. She also clearly separates her words. Though it might at first seem she is only writing random letters, she is actually quite close to conventional spelling and is certainly using the sounds and letter correspondences when she attempts to write *quería* and *que* with a *c*. She probably

FIGURE 6–15: Angélica's Writing

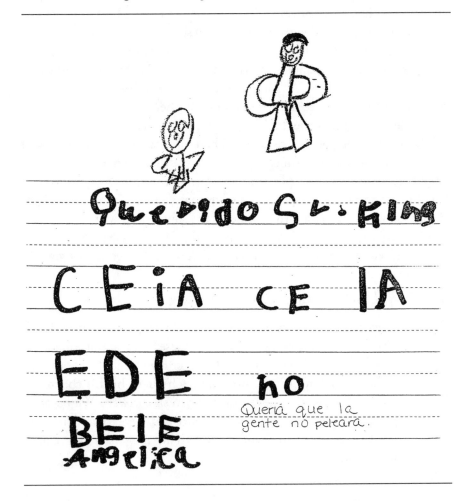

knows that c can have a /k/ sound, as in *cada*. In these words, the /k/ sound is represented by *qu*. Angélica has simply made the wrong choice.

It is not surprising that she omits the *g* in *gente* since the consonant only makes a minimal sound. She substitutes *d* for *t*, a common error since the two sounds are produced at the same place in the mouth. Her omission of *n* is also predictable. Nasals like *n* are often omitted before consonants because they are produced at the same place in the mouth. In actual speech production, the *n* spelling actually represents a nasal sound of the preceding vowel. Finally, she writes *b* instead of *p*, another predictable error for a Spanish writer. These two sounds only differ in voicing. They are both produced in the same place in the mouth. Angélica leaves off the final sounds, which receive little stress when the sentence is spoken. In sum, the spellings here show an attempt to represent the salient sounds in the words. The misspellings are cases of making the wrong choice among the alternatives that the Spanish spelling system offers. Students at Level Five are primarily concerned with sorting out these options.

A delightful example of Level Five characteristics comes from Ana, whose earlier writing samples we saw in Figure 6–11. Her later writing is shown in Figure 6–16. A comparison of the two samples shows real progress. In the last piece she wrote for her teacher in kindergarten, Ana is telling her teacher that she is ready now for first grade.

Note that her piece is readable. There are still some problems with spacing, and, at the same time, a good sense of syllable boundaries. For example, she writes <megus ta bi nira> for <me gusta venir a> (I like to come to). Almost all of her misspellings are alternative representations of a particular sound. She consistently represents the sound of /y/ with *ll* when convention requires a *y*. She also substitutes *b* for *v* in *venir* and *s* for *c* in *cien*. Ana is indeed "preparada para ir a primero" (prepared to go to first grade).

Summary: Levels or Stages of Writing Development

Young writers move through a series of developmental stages or levels. Their writing at each stage reflects the hypotheses they are making about how to represent their ideas in print. In Chapter Five we looked at the typical writing development of English-speaking children. In this chapter we have considered how writing develops for Spanish speakers. We began by presenting the five level analysis of Ferreiro and Teberosky. These researchers worked in Argentina, where children are immersed in a Spanish print environment.

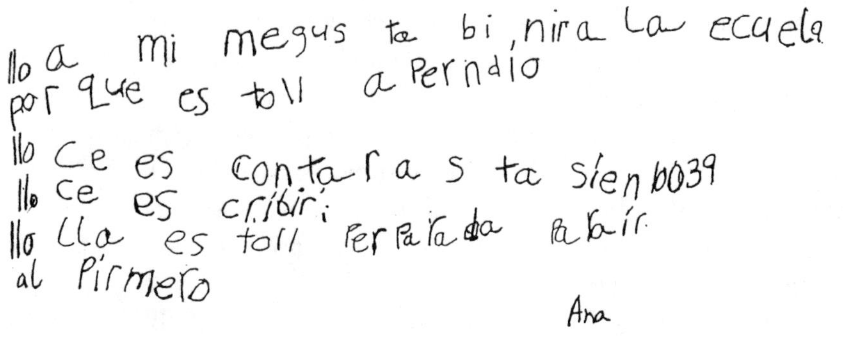

llo a mi megus ta bi,nira La ecuela
por que es toll a Perndio
llo Ce es conta r a s ta sien b039
llo ce es cribiri
llo Lla es toll rerrarada a bir
al Pirmero

Ana

FIGURE 6–16: Ana's Later Writing

Conventional Spanish
Yo a mí me gusta venir a la escuela
porque estoy aprendiendo
Yo sé es contar hasta cien
Yo sé escribir
Yo ya estoy preparada para ir al primero

Translation:

I like to come to school
because I am learning
(What) I know is to count to one hundred
I know how to write
I am now ready for first grade

We then considered how their model might apply to children in bilingual classes in the United States, where teachers encourage writing through a process approach. Our samples show many of the characteristics of writing development discussed by Ferreiro and Teberosky. However, we also note important differences. Those differences are probably due to two main reasons: Students in the classroom examples we provide are also exposed to a great deal of environmental print in English, and are, in fact, becoming literate in English while they are developing their literacy in their first language. In addition, the writing in the Ferreiro and Teberosky study was very carefully controlled. Words and sentences that children wrote were dictated in a one-on-one setting. The writing samples from the bilingual classes were complete texts produced in classrooms where students are given choices and write frequently for a variety of purposes.

The examples we have provided show how children's writing develops in Spanish. The bilingual teachers who provided these samples have seen the benefits of primary language writing development for their students. However, in many schools, debates rage over whether Spanish-speaking children should learn to write in Spanish or whether they should be immersed in English. Therefore, before leaving our discussion of writing development, we wish to briefly summarize one important study of the early writing of bilingual children.

Edelsky (1989, 1986) conducted an extensive study of children's writing in Spanish. She analyzed the writing of twenty-six first-, second-, and third-grade bilingual children in a settled, semirural, migrant school. Edelsky (1989) described the purpose of the study:

> The study was an effort of qualitative research in which a team of researchers analyzed more than 500 written pieces from three different classrooms for code switching, invented spelling, nonspelling conventions (punctuation, segmentation), stylistic devices, structural features (e.g. beginnings, ending, links between clauses), and quality of content, in order to note changes over time as well as to make cross-sectional comparisons (p. 166).

Edelsky's data led her to several important conclusions. Her writing has helped dispel myths about biliteracy and bilingual education, myths about learning to write, and myths about the teaching of writing. Perhaps the most important myth that the study dispelled was the myth that "to begin literacy acquisition in Spanish and then to add English leads to interference with English literacy" (1986, p. 73). Instead Edelsky concluded that first language literacy supported the acquisition of literacy in English. When the students Edelsky studied wrote in English, they used what they knew about literacy in their first language, but Spanish did not interfere with their acquisition of English.

Edelsky's study, like the samples we have shown, also demonstrated that Spanish-speaking children in bilingual classrooms do invent spelling in Spanish, even though Spanish orthography matches fairly closely with Spanish phonology, and even when students are given Spanish phonics instruction. In fact, many features of the students' writing reflected the kinds of developmental patterns we have outlined here, but the writing did not show noticeable effects of the direct instruction some of the students received. It appears that instruction can help students move from one stage to the next or help students progress within a stage, but instruction doesn't provide a quick shortcut. Children still have to invent spelling, punctuation, and so on and then test their inventions against social conventions as they read.

In addition, the study showed that students need extensive exposure to a wide variety of literature and other texts in Spanish to reach conventional spelling. Students produced their best writing when they wrote for authentic reasons to respond to real audiences. Edelsky's study confirms many of the practices of effective bilingual teachers, and it provides important research support for teachers who are helping their bilingual students write in their first language.

Functions of Writing

In the last two chapters we have focused primarily on how writing develops when children are given frequent opportunities to read and write in a supportive classroom community. We are convinced that teachers need to understand these normal developmental patterns so they can provide the support young writers need. This knowledge is essential for establishing an effective writing program.

In addition, in effective programs teachers engage students in writing for a variety of purposes. An important feature of Edelsky's study was that the students whose writing she examined wrote for a variety of purposes. In many classes teachers only ask children to write personal responses in journals or to write stories. However, people write for many other reasons, and these other functions of writing should also be developed. For teachers who wish to engage their students in writing for different purposes, one useful list of the functions of language has been compiled by Halliday (1975) (see Figure 6–17). In the sections that follow, we discuss how each of these functions apply to written language and provide examples of student writing for each. It might be noted that many pieces of writing serve more than one function.

Instrumental Writing

The first function of written language that Halliday identifies is the instrumental function. People use writing as an instrument to get things they want. The instrumental function is often expressed through a note asking for something. Letters to Santa Claus are a common *I want* kind of writing. Roberto, aged three, asked his mother to write a letter for him and then dictated a long list of <yo quiero . . . y quiero . . . y quiero . . .> (I want . . . I want . . . I want . . .) Edelsky (1986) provided an example of a letter to Santa Claus in which the writer not only made a request for a motorcycle, but also explained how to get the gift into the house without trying

HALLIDAY'S FUNCTIONS OF LANGUAGE

1. Instrumental: Using language to get things—"I want."
2. Regulatory: Using language to control the behavior of others—"Do as I tell you."
3. Interactional: Using language to create interaction with others—create social relationships—"You and me."
4. Personal: Using language to express personal feelings and meanings—"Here I am."
5. Heuristic: Using language to learn and to discover—"Tell me why."
6. Representational: Using language to communicate information—"I've got something to tell you."
7. Imaginative: Using language to create a world of the imagination—"Let's pretend."

Translation:

FUNCIONES DEL LENGUAJE DE HALLIDAY

1. Instrumental: Uso del lenguaje para obtener cosas—<Yo quiero>.
2. Reguladora: Uso del lenguaje para controlar la conducta de los demás—<Haz lo que te digo>.
3. Interactiva: Uso del lenguaje para crear interacción con los demás—<Tú y yo>.
4. Personal: Uso del lenguaje para expresar significados y sentimientos personales—<Estoy aquí>.
5. Heurística: Uso del lenguaje para aprender y descubrir—<Dime por qué>.
6. Representativa: Uso del lenguaje para comunicar información—<Tengo algo que decirte>.
7. Imaginativa: Uso del lenguaje para crear un mundo de imaginación—<Vamos a hacer como si . . .>.

FIGURE 6–17: Halliday's Functions of Language

to get it in through the window. In case Santa did not know, the writer also gave Santa the address:

> Yo le voy a llevar esta carta a usted, Santa Clos, para que me de una moto. Y la casa tiene un cuartito y allí puede meter la moto para que no batalle mucho metiéndolo por una ventana. Y mi casa es 13574. Gracias (p. 62).

Translation:

I am going to send this letter to you, Santa Claus, so that you give me a motorcycle. And our house has a little room and there you can put the motorcycle so that you don't have to go to a lot of the trouble getting it in the house through a window. My house is number 13574. Thank you.

FIGURE 6–18: Example of Instrumental Writing by María Elena

Another example of instrumental writing comes from María Elena, a kindergartner who was excited about the graduation party her class was going to have (see Figure 6–18). She and the other children talked about the party, and then she drew a face and wrote in invented spelling, <Vamos a bailar.> (We are going to dance.). Her message clearly expresses one feature of the party that she wants.

Regulatory Writing
A second function of language is regulatory. This kind of writing is designed to regulate the behavior of others. Children see a great deal of regulatory writing around them in the form of signs. It is natural for young writers to use this function. Children have different ways to regulate others' behavior. In Cristina's classroom, Marisa was annoyed when the children around her borrowed her pencils and crayons. To solve this problem she made several small signs with her name on them. She then carefully taped her name onto her pencils, her crayon box, and several of

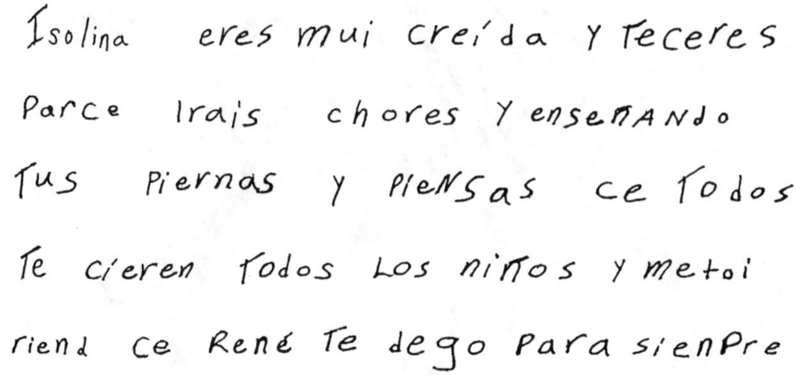

Isolina eres mui creída y feceres
Parce lrais chores y enseñando
Tus Piernas y Piensas ce Todos
Te cieren Todos Los niños y metoi
riend ce René Te dego Para sienPre

FIGURE 6–19: Example of Regulatory Writing

Isolina, you are very conceited and you love yourself because you go around in shorts and showing your legs and you think that everyone loves you all the boys and I are laughing that René left you forever.

---

her books, <para que no toquen lo mío> (so they won't touch my things).

Another example of regulatory writing comes from one of Carolina's second graders (see Figure 6–19). The writer was angry with Isolina because she thought she was showing off to the boys. She is very happy that René broke up with Isolina. While the writer does not tell Isolina what to do, the message is clearly an attempt to regulate her behavior. Her teacher, Caro, speculated that this type of note and language might come from students watching "lots of soap operas."

Interactional Writing
A third function of writing is interactional. This is writing that helps establish or maintain a social relationship. Things like friendly letters or thank you notes are examples of interactional writing. The note to Isolina could be regarded as interactional since it promotes a negative relationship. Some more positive examples come from three different grade levels. Rhonda received a note from one of her kindergartners at the end of the year telling her to take care of herself and that she loved her very much. She used Rhonda's last name, Dutton, for the note, probably because she called her Sra. Dutton (see Figure 6–20).

A second example of interactional writing may be seen in a response from Sam's second grader, Erika, to her college pen pal, Caro. Erika's let-

FIGURE 6–20: Example of Positive Interactional Writing

Dutton
Take good care of yourself
I love you very much

ter shows the importance of interactional writing, even for very young children. Their writing often comes alive when they have a real audience. Caro had told Erika she had a pet and then asked Erika when her birthday was and what she liked to do. Figure 6–21 shows Erika's response to Caro's questions, as well as the front and back of the envelope she made to put Caro's letter in. Notice how she addressed the envelope to "Caro" at Fresno Pacific College. The back is a friendship message: "You are my friend."

A final example of interactional writing comes from a letter that was written by a seventh grader during the Gulf War (see Figure 6–22). The children at the school decided to write to all the servicemen who were sent

FIGURE 6–21: Example of Interactional Writing by Erika

I like animals I don't know when my birthday will be and what I like to play is my Barbies.

off to the war. Since Cesar's English was not yet fluent, he decided to write to a Spanish-speaking soldier. His letter is eloquent and very moving.

Personal Writing

Writing that serves the personal function primarily focuses on the interests and feelings of the writer. Our earlier example of Ana's writing (see Figure 6–16) is an example of personal writing. She is confidently telling who she is and what she can do. She can do many things and is <preparada para primero.>

Second grader Berta (see Figure 6–23) provides another example of writing that serves the personal function. She tells how she feels when she swings. This piece also serves a heuristic function, since she explains why swinging makes her happy.

Queridos Soldados.

Espero que cuando reciban esta carta les de la alegría que me va a dar a mí cuando yo sepa que ya la recibieron.

Miren nosotros sabemos que no es nada facil andar en la guerra porque no se sabe lo que va a pasar, pueden perder la vida y sin saber en que momento.

Al haberse ido a la guerra ustedes nos demuestran que son hombres valientes y que se arriesgan a perder la vida sin importarles nada, lo unico que les importa es pelear por la nacion y defenderla sin temor a perder sus vidas.

Yo y todos nosotros estamos orgullosos de todos ustedes porque ustedes estan lejos de sus familias y sus amigos pero sin embargo ustedes no se vencen.

Al pelear ustedes por la nacion nosotros sentimos que estan peleando por nosotros porque nosotros venimos aqui a progresar y si ustedes no hubieran ido en realidad no sabemos que pasaria.

Esperamos que se cuiden mucho y que regresen con vida y con mucha felicidad para que puedan otra vez mirar sus seres queridos.

Yo se que van a regresar victoriosos y con una sonrisa en su cara.

" Sinceramente César

FIGURE 6–22, Part 1: Example of Interactional Writing by César

Dear Soldiers.

I hope that when you receive this letter, it makes you as happy as it is going to make me when I know that you have received it.

Look, we know that it is not at all easy to be in the war because one doesn't know what is going to happen; you can lose your life and not know when.

By having gone to war, you show us that you are brave men and that you risk losing your life as if it weren't important; the only thing that is important to you is to fight for your country and to defend it without fearing to lose your life.

I and all of us are proud of all of you because you are far from your families and your friends, but nevertheless you will not be conquered.

As you fight for the nation, we feel that you are fighting for us because we came here to improve (our lives), and if you had not gone, really, we don't know what would happen.

We hope that you take good care of yourselves and that you return alive and happy so that you can again see your loved ones.

I know that you are going to return victorious and with smiles on your faces.

Sincerely,

César

FIGURE 6–22, Part 2: Example of Interactional Writing by César

Heuristic Writing

When writing is used for a heuristic function, the writer is using language to learn and discover. Much heuristic writing explains the *why* of some phenomenon. The writing from another second grader, Naomi, serves as a heuristic (see Figure 6–24). She describes what happens when the rain stops and a rainbow comes out. Though her letters are not clearly formed or neat, she does a good job of organizing her ideas.

A final example of writing that serves a heuristic function comes from second grader, José (see Figure 6–25). After Carolina took her class on a field trip on a train, José wrote about this first-in-a-lifetime experience. There are several erasures on the copy, which shows that José spent time reworking this piece. The trip had been an important experience, and he wanted to tell his readers why this was so.

Representational Writing

Heuristic writing is an attempt to explore questions and to answer why certain things happen. Representational writing is similar, but it is less exploratory or questioning. Instead, it is used to report information. All year long Rhonda's kindergarten students had a lot to tell her, and by the end of

Amimease feliz Loscolopios

por que pienso que doiabolar

Al sielo como superman

idolar como el es superm

FIGURE 6–23: Example of Personal Writing by Berta

The swings make me happy because I think that I am going to fly up to the sky like superman Flying like superman

---

the year they could use representational writing very well. A good example comes from Felipe (see Figure 6–26), who writes in his journal explaining where all his family members are this day.

Imaginative Writing
A story that bridges heuristic, representational, and the last of Halliday's functions, imaginative, is done by a fifth grader, Santiago. He had only

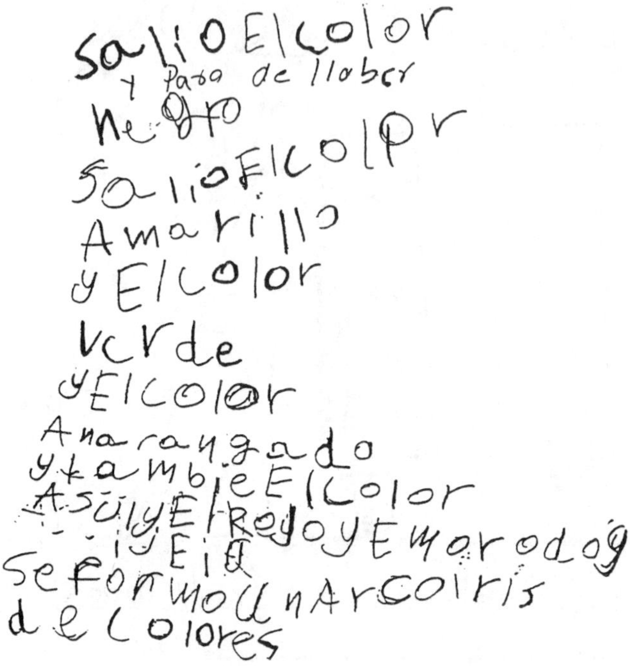

SaLiO El color
y paso de llober
he gro
SaLioElcolpr
Amarillo
y Elcolor
verde
yElcolor
Anarangado
ytambieElcolor
Asulyelrojoyemorodog
...iyEiQ
seformoUnArcoiris
de colores

FIGURE 6–24: Example of Heuristic Writing by Naomi

Color came out
and it stopped raining
black
Color came out
yellow
and the color
green
and the color
orange
and also the color
blue and red and purple
A rainbow of colors formed

---

been in the United States three months when he wrote this story. Because of the demonstrations his teacher Carol had provided by reading literature and his classmates had provided by publishing their own stories, Santiago decided to try to write his own piece. His previous schooling in Colombia had given him little experience with any kind of process writing, and this

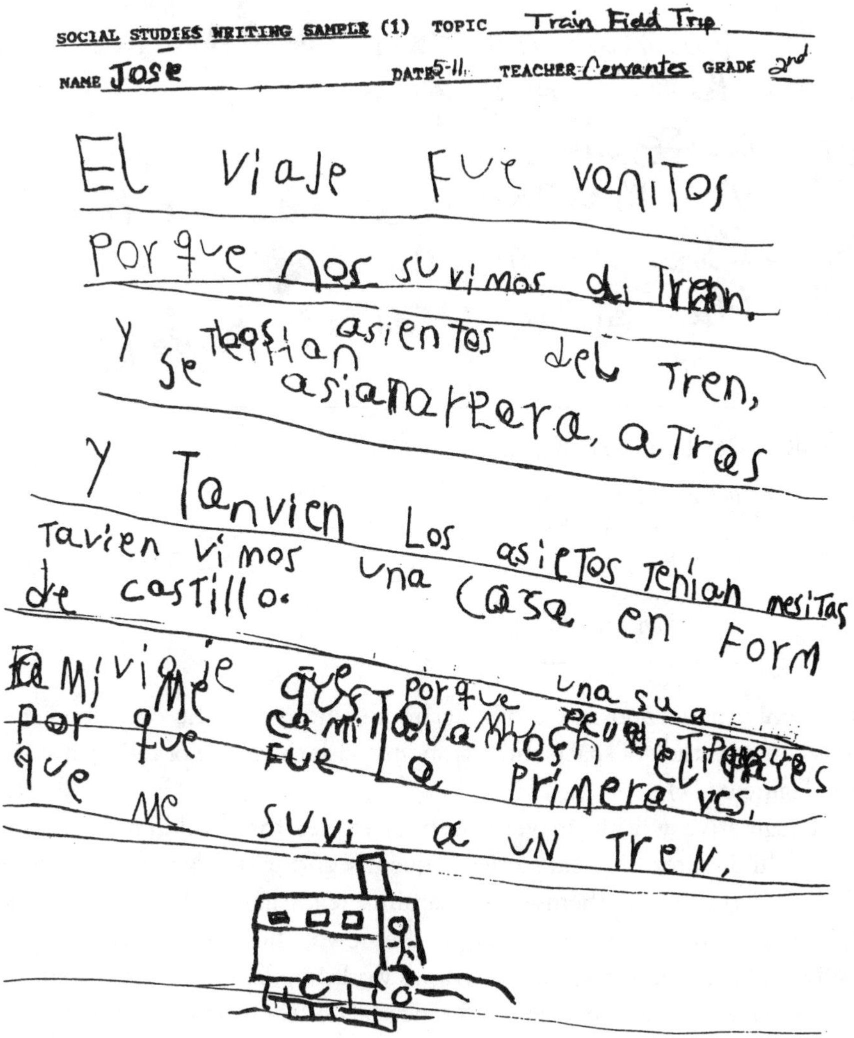

SOCIAL STUDIES WRITING SAMPLE (1) TOPIC Train Field Trip

NAME José   DATE 5-11   TEACHER Cervantes   GRADE 2nd

El viaje fue venitos
porque nos suvimos di tren.
Y se teosftian asientos del Tren,
asianarpera, atres
Y Tanvien Los asietos tenian nesitas
Tavien vimos una casa en Form
de castillo.
famiviaje megusto porque una sua
por que camivovamosh peruel paises
que fue fue la primera ves,
que me suvi a un tren.

FIGURE 6–25: Example of Heuristic Writing by José

The trip was beautiful.
because we got on the train.
and the seats on the train,
they (could) move back
and also the seats had little tables
also we saw a house shaped like a castle
I like the trip very much because it was
the first time I had been on a train.

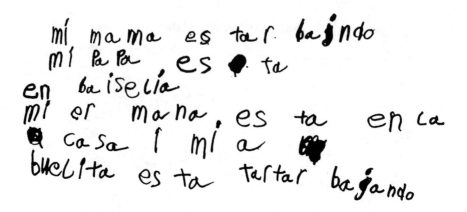

FIGURE 6–26: Example of Representational Writing by Felipe

My mom is working
My dad is in Visalia
My sister is at
home and my
grandmother is working

story, only his second in Carol's classroom, shows how he combined the class content study of space and astronomy with the genre of telling a story (see Figure 6–27).

Imaginative writing may be seen in stories that children make up. When children read or hear stories frequently during the day, they are more likely to write stories themselves. Carolina reads many books to her students and encourages them to read on their own, choosing from among the many books in the room. During writer's workshop, children write drafts of stories, have peer and teacher conferences about their writing, and publish books of their own, typing them in the computer lab with the help of the teacher or teacher's aide. Often that writing is clearly influenced by what they have read. Angélica chose to write *El sueño de ver a las ballenas* (*The Dream of Seeing the Whales*) (see Figure 6–28). Carolina and Angélica discussed together how the book was inspired by fairy tales the class had read earlier, as well as by stories they read during their study of whales including *El canto de las ballenas* (*The Song of the Whales*) (Sheldon, 1993), *Swimmy* (Lionni, 1963), *Big Al* (Clements, 1991), and *Humphrey the Lost Whale* (Tokuda & Hall, 1986). It is quite clear that Angélica drew on literature to write this lovely imaginative story.

A final example of imaginative writing is an unfinished piece by Isolina,

LAS noches

Nighttime

cuando yo era pequeño no me gustaba la noche porque no savia que era lo que alumbraba

When I was small I didn't like nighttime because I didn't know what lighted it.

y un dia me di cuente de que bian como animales en el cielo

and one day I realized that they were like animals in the sky

pero cuando fui creciendo me di cuento de que eron bonitos y me gustaban mucho mas

But when I was growing up I realized that they were pretty and I liked them much more

y que ser vian para alumbrar el camino en las noches para la jente de las fincas.

and that they served to light up the road at night for the people on the ranches.

y que caian meteoritos y mes gustaban.

and that meteors fell and I liked them.

FIGURE 6–27, Part 1: Example of Imaginative Writing by Santiago

le pregunte a mi papa
que era eso que avia ariba.

el me digo lo que era
desde que naci me gustan
las estrellas.

and I asked my father what that was that was up above.

and he told me what it was and since I was born I like the stars.

The End

FIGURE 6–27, Part 2: Example of Imaginative Writing by Santiago

(see Figure 6–29), the same girl who received the indignant note from her peer (Figure 6–29). Her teacher, Carolina, was very excited about the way Isolina was able to introduce the setting, to create the characters, and to build suspense. It was clear to Carolina that the reading and discussion in class had helped prepare Isolina for this kind of writing.

This second grader's story summarizes, in many ways, all that we have been talking about in these two chapters on writing. Isolina invents spellings for words she does not yet know. Already, most of her writing is conventional. Because she is encouraged to write and has read a lot, Isolina's story shows both imagination and risk taking. She uses sophisticated vocabulary like *abandonado* (abandoned) and *falleció* (died), words that would not be likely to appear on most controlled second-grade spelling lists. As her teacher has pointed out, Isolina understands and can use critical elements of a good story, including character, setting, and the presentation of a problem. The final version of Isolina's story will be edited so that all the spelling and punctuation will be conventional. Isolina recognizes the importance of producing conventional text since her audience extends beyond her teacher to her classmates. Because she

El Sueño
de Ver
A Las Ballenas

Escrito e Ilustrado
por
Angélica Martínez

The Dream of Seeing the Whales written and illustrated by Angélica Martínez.

Había una niña llamada Mónica. Soñaba con ver a las bellenas. Las quería ver porque era bonito ver a las ballenas orcas.

There was a girl named Mónica. She used to dream about seeing whales. She wanted to see them because it was beautiful to see orca whales.

Un día le iban a dar una sorpresa a Mónica.
-¿A dónde vamos a ir?- preguntó ella.
Su mamá le contestó:
-Es una sorpresa.
Le taparon los ojos para que no mirara el mar ni las ballenas.

One day they gave Mónica a surprise.
"Where are we going to go?" she asked.
Her mother answered:
"It's a surprise."
They blindfolded her so that she wouldn't look at the sea or the whales.

FIGURE 6–28, Part 1: Example of Imaginative Writing by Angélica

Cuando llegó al mar no pudo ver las ballenas porque no salieron. Se sintió triste porque no pudo mirar ninguna ballena.

When she arrived at the sea she couldn't see the whales because they didn't come out. She felt very sad because she couldn't see any whales.

-Vamos al apartamento. Allá te contaré lo que sé de las ballenas- dijo su mamá.

"Let's go to the apartment. There I will tell you what I know about whales," said her mother.

Mientras su mamá le contaba el cuento a Mónica de la ballena que se fue a San Francisco, Mónica se quedó dormida.

5

While her mother told Mónica the story of the whale that went to San Francisco, Mónica fell asleep.

El próximo día Mónica se levantó. Escuchó un sonido de ballenas. Por eso salió a ver y miró que estaban atrapando a las ballenas para comérselas.

6

The next day Mónica got up. She heard a sound of whales. Because of this she went to see and saw that they were trapping whales to eat them.

FIGURE 6–28, Part 2: Example of Imaginative Writing by Angélica

De repente, salió una hada detrás de una ballena y las desató. Las ballenas estaban felices porque ya no las iban a matar porque tenían una hada mágica.

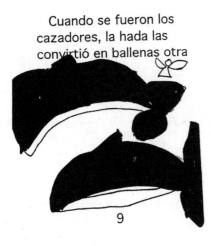

7

Suddenly, a fairy came out from behind one of the whales and let it loose. The whales were happy because now they were not going to kill them because they had a magic fairy.

Al día siguiente, los cazadores regresaron porque todavía las querían matar. Pero Mónica no iba a dejar que mataran a las ballenas. Mónica y la hada mágica espantaron a los cazadores convirtiendo a todas las ballenas en una ballena enorme.

8

The next day, the hunters returned because they still wanted to kill them. But Mónica wasn't going to let them kill the whales. Mónica and the magic fairy scared the hunters changing all the whales into one huge whale.

Cuando se fueron los cazadores, la hada las convirtió en ballenas otra

9

When the hunters went away, the fairy changed the whales again.

Las ballenas estaban cantándole una canción a Mónica.
Estaba feliz como las ballenas.

Fin

10

The whales were singing a song to Mónica. She was happy like the whales. The end

---

FIGURE 6–28, Part 3: Example of Imaginative Writing by Angélica

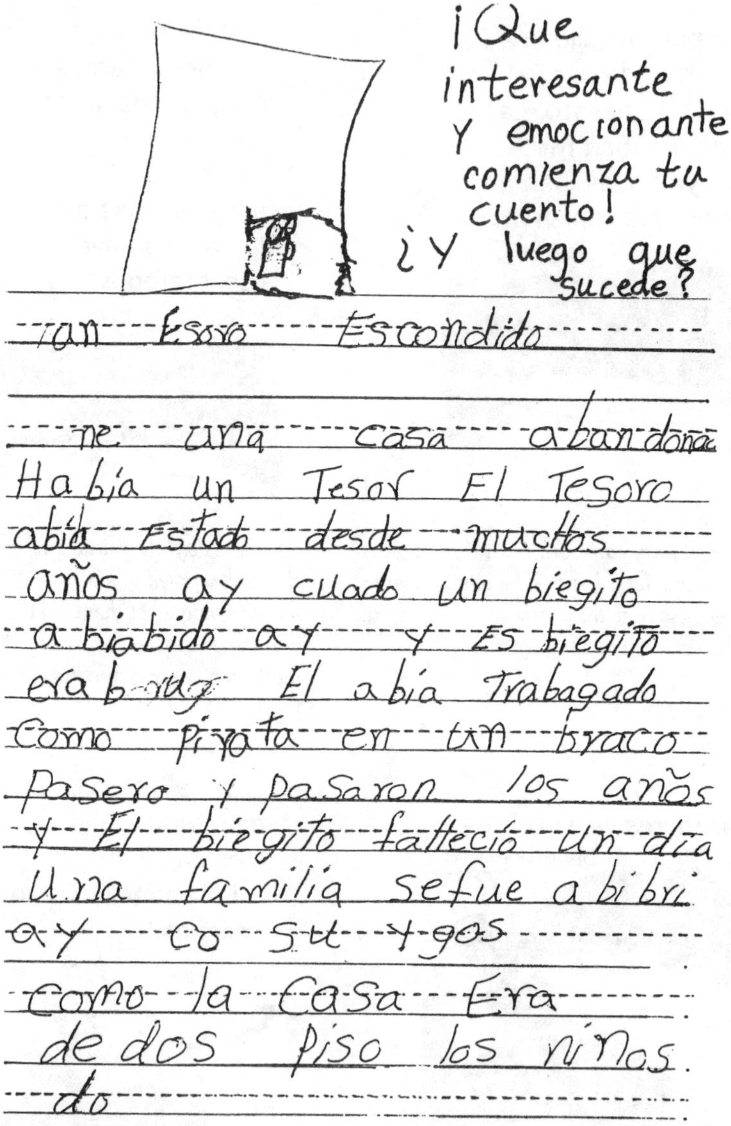

¡Que
interesante
y emocionante
comienza tu
cuento!
¿Y luego que
sucede?

an Esoro Escondido

ne una casa abandona
Había un Tesor El Tesoro
abía Estado desde muchos
años ay cuado un biegito
a biabido ay y Es biegito
era b_ug_ El abia Trabagado
como piyata en un byaco
Pasero y pasaron los años
y El biegito fallecio un dia
Una familia sefue abibri
ay co s_u_ y gos
como la Casa Era
de dos piso los niños
do

FIGURE 6–29: Example of Imaginative Writing by Isolina

A hidden treasure
In an abandoned house
There was a treasure. The treasure
had been there for many
years there when a little old man
had lived there and this little old man
was. . . . He had worked
as a pirate in a passenger ship
and the years went by
and the little old man died one day
a family went to live
there with their children
because the house was
a two story house the
children. . . .

writes in Spanish, she can also share her finished story with her family at home.

We began and ended this chapter with writing from Carolina's classroom. Carolina has organized a very effective writing program. She has studied how writing develops in both English and Spanish. This knowledge allows her to fully support all the children in her class as they write for a variety of purposes. In the next chapter, we look more closely at how good teachers like Carolina help all their students develop literacy by integrating reading and writing activities around relevant themes.

7
Putting Reading and Writing Together to Develop Biliterate and Bicultural Students

FRANCISCO

Ser bilingüe es como vivir en dos mundos. Uno puede hablar con personas en español y entrar en su mundo. Lo mismo pasa cuando hablas, escribes y lees en inglés. Ahora que empecé el programa de educación bilingüe, puedo ver qué tan valioso es ser bilingüe porque hay tantos niños que puedo ayudar en su primer idioma.

Translation

To be bilingual is like living between two worlds. One can speak to people in Spanish and enter into their world. The same thing happens when you speak, you write, and you read in English. Now that I have begun the bilingual education program, I can see how valuable it is to be bilingual because there are so many children that I can help in their first language.

Francisco, the author of the above quote, came to the United States from El Salvador when he was in the ninth grade. His mother, a migrant worker, brought Francisco and her other children to this country from their rural home one-by-one because she wanted a better life for them than was possible in their native country. By the time Francisco arrived, he was high school age. He was submersed in school where he was given classes in English as a second language. Like most students who come at the high school level, Francisco received no first language support.

Francisco is the first in his family to graduate from college, a feat that was not easy for a young man who knew no English when he arrived. In some ways he was lucky. Because he played soccer well, he got a scholarship to a small college where professors, and especially his coach, encouraged him and supported him. But still, there was a cost. It is only recently that he has begun to view himself as capable and his bilingualism as an asset. Because he struggled with English and academic success, he remained quiet in his college classes. When, as a senior, he did some observations in a bilingual classroom, he went into Sam's first-grade bilingual classroom. For the first time, Francisco saw how bilingual children in a bilingual classroom are able to participate fully. The students felt good about themselves as learners because they could use their first language strengths while they learned. Now, Francisco realizes that his bilingualism will allow him to help others so that they do not have to struggle as much as he did.

JANIE

It is important for me to be bilingual because it is a part of my culture that was nearly lost to me. I felt incomplete as a child and only as an adult have I been able to rediscover the part that I lost. Bilingual is who and what I am. I am proud of my culture and language. It adds a depth of richness to my life. I want to give that pride to others, especially children. I want them to know that they are special because they are bilingual, and they should not allow anyone to take their language away from them.

Janie is another student teacher who is finishing her final student teaching as a bilingual candidate. Her situation is similar to Francisco's in some ways, but different in others. Francisco started school in the United States in high school, and he continued to use Spanish at home. Janie, although born in Mexico, also entered school speaking Spanish, but she began in kindergarten at five years old when her family moved to the United States. Like Francisco, Janie received no Spanish support in school. She was submersed in English. She was discouraged from using Spanish; even her family believed the school and the teachers who assured everyone that the important thing was for Janie to become a fluent English speaker. As a result, although she spoke Spanish at home with her father, she visited Mexico only once as a child and did not learn to read or write in Spanish.

Another difference between Janie and Francisco is their cultural backgrounds. Janie has lived all her life as a Latina in a predominantly Anglo culture. Francisco grew up in a Latin culture with distinct traditions from those he encountered in the United States. When some family problems affected Janie in high school, she had a strong urge to reconnect with her culture and family in Mexico. She began to write to her grandmother in Spanish. Though her written Spanish was far from conventional, her grandmother welcomed this communication. As an adult Janie did return to Mexico with her husband and her three children, a visit of great importance to her.

Janie returned to college to become a teacher when her children were old enough to go to school. It was then that Janie went back to formally study Spanish. Even at that, she is more comfortable in English. In fact, she talks about how uncomfortable she felt as she began her college Spanish study, and how easy it was for her to become discouraged with her progress. Her writing in Spanish is improving, but she still is working towards full academic proficiency in her native language.

ANN

Para mí es importante ser bilingüe porque me gusta poder comunicarme con la gente que sabe español pero que no sabe inglés. No sólo me gusta poder estar en contacto con mis amigos de países donde hablan español, pero mis amigos de aquí también. Yo sé que no es fácil venir a un nuevo país y no saber el idioma. Por eso, como maestra, quiero poder ayudar a mis estudiantes que no hablan inglés. Sé que cuando apoyo su primer idioma podrán mejorar (o aprender) inglés mejor y no perder sus otras materias.

Translation:

For me it is important to be bilingual because I like to be able to communicate with people that know Spanish but don't know English. Not only do I like to be able to be in contact with my friends from countries where they speak Spanish, but my friends from here too. I know that it is not easy to come to a new country and not know the language. For this reason, as a teacher, I want to be able to help my students that do not speak English. I know that when I support their first language they will be able to improve (or learn) English better and not lose (get behind in) their other subjects.

The above quote comes from Ann, a bilingual teacher candidate who has had a different experience with Spanish. She is an Anglo student teacher who has lived in Mexico and also in Venezuela. She speaks Spanish almost natively and has lived in a family situation where bilingualism is supported and appreciated. She started school in Mexico, attended a bilingual school in the United States, and returned to Mexico and attended a Mexican school as a high school senior. These experiences allowed her to develop both conversational and academic proficiency in Spanish. In fact, Ann is, in many ways, a true example of a bilingual and bicultural person. She is comfortable in settings with her grandmothers, monolingual English speakers with traditions that are far removed from any Latin culture, and in settings—including parties and dances—where she is the only non-Latina present.

Our goal as bilingual educators must be to produce biliterate and bicultural citizens. In the first six chapters, we have explained approaches to teaching reading and writing that can help bilingual students succeed. In this chapter, we bring ideas about reading and writing together to show how bilingual teachers like Francisco, Janie, and Ann can lead their students toward biliteracy and biculturalism.

We begin by presenting a theoretical framework for conceptualizing a curriculum in which reading and writing development forms the cornerstone for academic success. Then we describe three thematic units that not only support Spanish/English bilingual students in Spanish, but also lead them into literacy in their second language, English. In addition, we will emphasize the importance of themes that validate biculturalism and a multicultural world view.

Collier's Model of Language Acquisition for School

Collier (1995) has developed a model of language acquisition for school that is relevant to bilingual students and teachers. In this model (see Figure 7–1) Collier shows that language acquisition includes three elements: language development, cognitive development, and academic development. It is important for teachers to understand that their students must grow linguistically, cognitively, and academically for them to achieve English language proficiency.

FIGURE 7–1: Collier's Model of Language Acquisition for School

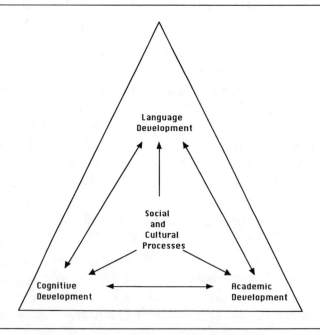

Development in all three of these areas is influenced by social and cultural processes. These sociocultural factors are at the heart of the model. They include individual variables such as anxiety and self-esteem, as well as larger social factors, like discrimination, whether overt or covert. For that reason, even if the school provides opportunities for positive language, cognitive, and academic development, social and cultural influences must also be examined because they have such strong positive or negative influences on students' language acquisition and academic performance.

A closer look at Francisco's educational experiences helps illustrates the components of Collier's model. Francisco came to the United States with a high level of Spanish proficiency. At his rural school he was a diligent student and learned to read and write in Spanish. Nevertheless, the school's resources were limited, and his teachers were not really able to help prepare him for schooling in the United States. English was not part of the curriculum at all.

When Francisco came to the United States as a freshman in high school, he was suddenly thrust into a completely new sociocultural setting. He was not prepared for the large urban high school he attended, where neither teachers nor most other students had any understanding of his background. There were some students from El Salvador, but most Latinos in the high school were from Mexico, and many of his teachers assumed he was Mexican. No first language support was available in content area subjects such as math, science, or social studies. Consequently, Francisco was placed in ESL and noncollege preparatory classes. These classes were taught by caring, but overworked teachers who had come to accept low expectations for their students.

Because he felt his English was inadequate and feared being teased or laughed at, Francisco seldom spoke up in class. Little was demanded of him, and as he reflected later on his secondary experience, he realized he was never asked to read a whole book or write more than single words in English. Most class periods were spent filling in worksheets. While he learned basic conversational English, his cognitive and academic potential was certainly not developed. Although Francisco did not experience great academic success, he received fairly good grades in his classes because he completed the assignments. At the same time, he did get support from his family, and he enjoyed playing on the school soccer team where most of his teammates spoke Spanish.

Francisco was accepted into college and given a soccer scholarship. However, he was not as well prepared academically as his college classmates. He felt completely lost as professors gave assignments. He remembers being incredulous as one teacher assigned several books for the semester and expected her students to complete one book in a week! He had never read an entire book in English, and knew the request was impossible for him. His grades his first semester were a not unexpected disaster, and Francisco felt hopeless and decided to quit school.

However, Francisco's Hispanic soccer coach intervened. He not only encouraged Francisco not to give up, but went to his home and talked to his mother, telling her how important it was for Francisco to continue. The encouragement of his family and coach were both important sociocultural influences. Francisco could understand his mother's strong desire for him to complete school and could sense his coach's belief in him. Both of these influences helped Francisco take a completely new look at himself and his future. From that point on he spent hours in the library challenging himself to fully develop his own cognitive, academic, and linguistic potential. His first two years of college were a continuous struggle to get off academic probation.

Francisco also found additional support. During his junior year, he befriended an Anglo girl who had lived in Mexico and the two of them began to date. This relationship helped him enter into an additional world of native English speakers and their culture. Of course, his girlfriend and her parents, college professors, also provided him with some academic and language support that reinforced his cognitive abilities.

Francisco now is a competent bilingual. He is biliterate, and because of his relationship with his girlfriend, he has had the opportunity to become bicultural too. As he begins to teach, he sees what he wants to do to help his Spanish-speaking students become successful. He wants them to maintain their first language, understand and be proud of their cultural heritage, and also succeed in the culture in which they live. To do that his students must develop literacy in Spanish and must also acquire English. The students need to feel supported by the school and community around them to develop linguistically, cognitively, and academically.

As Francisco does his student teaching, we want him to see a literacy curriculum that is consistent with our best knowledge of practices that promote full literacy development. In Chapter One we suggested that effective teachers organize around themes. We described the animal themes that four different bilingual teachers developed. Below we describe in detail three more thematic units that we believe are examples of the kind of curriculum that will help Spanish-speaking children in our schools become both biliterate and bicultural. These descriptions are composites drawn from practices we have observed in classrooms of effective bilingual teachers.

Todos somos iguales . . . Todos somos diferentes (We are all alike . . . We are all different)

Lorena teaches a combination first-second grade bilingual class in an inner city school with a great deal of cultural and linguistic diversity. Some of her students have lived in the city all their lives, others have moved to this school from small, surrounding rural towns, and still others have come directly from Mexico or Central America. Her students arrive with varying academic backgrounds. While most come to her speaking little or no English, others, though Hispanic, appear to speak more English than Spanish. Curriculum guidelines call for students to look at themselves and their surroundings, so Lorena decides to organize her curriculum around the theme, "We are all alike. We are all different."

To begin to have her students think about these ideas, Lorena first reads to them in Spanish, *Canción de todos los niños del mundo* (*Song of All the Children of the World*) (Ada, 1993), a big book that shows pictures of children from all over the world and tells how children, though different in some superficial ways, are all really the same. Drawing on the questions from Hansen (1989) mentioned in Chapter 2 (see Figure 7–2), she then asks them, <¿Qué recuerdan?> (What do you remember?), and records what the children say on a big piece of butcher paper. The children notice and comment upon how different the schools in China and Libya look, as well as how the children in Lesotho have a soccer ball just like theirs.

The discussion from her students leads Lorena to read another book, *Todos somos iguales: todos somos diferentes* (*We Are All Alike . . . We Are All Different?*) (Cheltenham, 1994). This book was originally written in English by a kindergarten class and then published by Scholastic. Lorena's children are fascinated by the idea that kindergartners wrote this book, and they enjoy seeing the pictures of the children. Lorena then has the students discuss different sections of the book that compare how people look the same and different, how families are the same and different, how places to live are the same and different, and how what children like to eat and the games they play are the same and different. She then asks the children to look at the people around them, and tell how they are the same or different. Roberto says, <Unos tienen ojos oscuros y otros claros.> (Some people

(según Jane Hansen, 1989)

1. ¿Qué recuerdas (recuerdan) de lo que leíste (leyeron)?
2. ¿Qué mas te gustaría (les gustaría) conocer?
3. ¿A qué te (les) recuerda lo que leíste (leyeron)?
4. ¿Qué otras cosas has (han) leído que te (les) recuerden esto que leíste (leyeron)?

Translation:

COMPREHENSION QUESTIONS

(according to Jane Hansen, 1989)

1. What do you remember?
2. What else would you like to know?
3. What else does it remind you of?
4. What other things have you read that remind you of this?

FIGURE 7–2: Hansen Questions

have dark eyes and some light.). Marta says, <Unos son más claros y otros más oscuros de la piel.> (Some have lighter and some darker skin.). Esteben offers, <Unos tiene el pelo liso y otros tiene el pelo chino.> (Some have straight hair and others have curly hair.). After some discussion, Lorena asks the children to draw a picture of someone and write how this classmate is alike or different from the child doing the writing.

Juanita, who is usually quite silent in class, draws a picture she does not like, but clearly writes down her ideas in quite sophisticated Spanish (see Figure 7–3).

While doing this activity, the children remember a book they read earlier in the year, *Espejito, ¡mira!* (*A Little Mirror! Look!*) (Avalos, 1991). This book features a built-in mirror and talks about the eyes, nose, hair, and face children see when they look in the mirror. Lorena makes a mental note to herself to read that book to the children again the next day during rug time and to revisit several of the poems she and the children have read about looking in the mirror and seeing oneself.

To finish her language arts time for the day, Lorena brings out the big book, *We Are All Alike . . . We Are All Different* (Cheltenham, 1991) for her English Language Development (ELD) lesson. After reading the book in Eng-

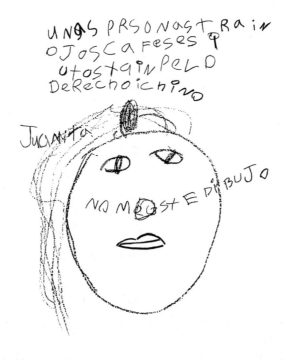

UNaS PRSONaST RaiN
OJosCa FeSes 9
utostqiN PeLO
DeRechoichiNo

JuaNita

NO MBaSt E DibuJO

FIGURE 7–3: Juanita's Writing

Some people have brown eyes
Others have straight hair and curly
Juanita
I don't like this picture

---

lish, the teacher writes "How are we alike? How are we different?" on a piece
of butcher paper and asks the students to look and think about ways their
classmates look alike and ways they look different. After brainstorming together, the teacher makes a list of the things the children say (see Figure 7–4).

Then the children take little squares of paper and write their names on
them. They put their name squares next to the words on this list that best
describe them. When they are finished, the class counts together in English
how many squares are in each category.

The next day Lorena begins Spanish language arts by reading the big
book, *Espejito, ¡mira!* with the children. The children laugh together as
they follow the text instructions while looking in the mirror in the book:
<denme una guiñada> (give me a wink); <pellizquen sus mejillas> (pinch
your cheeks); <toquen su cabello> (touch your hair); <arrugen la nariz>

brown eyes

black eyes

blue eyes

long hair

short hair

curly hair

straight hair

glasses

no glasses

FIGURE 7–4: Brainstorming List

(wrinkle your nose). She also reads them the big book, *Mis cinco sentidos* (*My Five Senses*) (Miller, 1994), and the children discuss how they all have those five senses.

Then the children read together two familiar poems which Lorena has copied on chart paper and has hanging on the wall. Both are about children looking in a mirror and appreciating their individuality. In the first, *Imagínate* (*Imagine*) (Mirtín, 1993), a child studies her face in verses that follow a pattern, <Yo veo mi cara que tiene dos ojos. Imagínate, mi cara con dos ojos.> (I see my face that has two eyes. Imagine! My face with two eyes.) (p. 46). In the second, *Yo* (*I*) (Ferre, 1993), a child asserts her individuality as she gazes into a mirror and repeats verses such as, <Ésta es mi cara, mi pelo; éste es mi cuerpo y mi voz.> (This is my face, my hair; this is my body and my voice.) (p. 64).

Lorena reminds the children that they are all special and asks them if they remember the book they read yesterday, *Todos somos iguales: todos somos diferentes* (Cheltenham, 1994). Several children tell her, <Sí, maestra. Lo leímos en español y también en inglés.> (Yes, teacher. We read it in Spanish and also in English.). Lorena tells them that today she is going to read them a story <de una jirafa que no estaba contenta con su propia cola> (about a giraffe who was not happy with his own tail). After reading *Los seis deseos de la jirafa* (*The Six Wishes of the Giraffe*) (Ada, 1989), Lorena asks the children, <Cuál parte les gustó más?> (Which part did you like best?). After some discussion, the children decide to make their own big book about a different animal who doesn't like some part of his body. They decide to do a story about <un elefante que no le gusta su trompa>

(an elephant who doesn't like his trunk). The students brainstorm the different things that the elephant might wish for to replace his trunk. Then they put these ideas in order to create a story. Lorena divides the class into groups, and each group illustrates and writes one page of their elephant tale.

That afternoon during English time, Lorena reads *Here Are My Hands* (Martin and Archanbault, 1985) with the children. She has put the words on a chart and shows the children the pictures in the book. As they read the words together, the children do corresponding hand motions. For example, when they read, "Here are my hands for catching and throwing," the children motion in pairs as if they are throwing and catching a ball. Lorena then asks the children if they remember what other things the children were doing in *Espejito, ¡mira!*, which they had read in the morning. She asks them if they can say *gruñir, pellizcar, tocar,* and *arrugar* in English. The children then use the basic pattern, "Here are my ———— for ————ing" to go with *wink, pinch, touch,* and *wrinkle.*

On the following day, Lorena begins Spanish language arts by reminding the children of *Los seis deseos de la jirafa* and the book about the elephant's trunk that they will continue to work on. Then she introduces a new story <de un niño que es diferente pero no puede cambiarse como la jirafa> (about a little boy who is different but can not change himself like the giraffe). She reads *El niño que tenía dos ojos* (*The Boy Who Had Two Eyes*) (Sánchez and Pacheco, 1988), the story of a child born with two eyes on a planet with one-eyed people. The one-eyed people have eyes that can see through things and see at huge distances. While the two-eyed child cannot see like that, he can see something no one else can: color. He becomes famous for this ability. After reading this story, Lorena asks the children, <¿Qué opinan?> (What do you think?). Felipe responds by telling how <El niño estaba triste al principio, pero cuando pudo ver el color, se puso muy contento.> (The boy was sad at first, but when he could see color he became very happy.). María says, <Yo estaba triste cuando no podía ver bien y lo llevaron a los doctores.> (I was sad when he couldn't see well and they took him to the doctors.).

Lorena continues with this theme of appreciating differences over the next several weeks. She reads several books to the children for discussion including *La niña sin nombre* (*The Girl Without a Name*) (Sanchez and Pacheco, 1988), about a girl lost in a foreign land who cannot speak the language or be understood, and *El amigo nuevo* (*The New Friend*) (D'Atri, 1993), the story of a new boy who moves into the neighborhood from

Japan. She then asks the children to compare those two stories. After this discussion, Lorena reads the Spanish text of a bilingual book, *Somos un arco iris: We Are a Rainbow* (Tabor, 1995), in which the narrator tells how his old home in Mexico is different from his new home in the United States and how it is important for all people to try to understand one another and appreciate one another.

Lorena uses the English text of *Somos un arco iris: We Are a Rainbow*, during her ELD time as well as two books by Morris, *Hats, Hats, Hats* and *Houses and Homes* (Morris, 1989, 1992). The books by Morris are full of beautiful photographs of people and places around the world. The limited text of these books supports the theme of appreciating differences. Near the end of the unit, Lorena brings in the book *People* (Spier, 1980), which, like *We Are All Alike . . . We Are All Different*, describes the many ways people all over the world are the same and different. She also reads the Spanish version of this book, *Gente* (Spier, 1993), during Spanish language arts time. After reading *Gente*, the children list all the different ways people are the same and different, as discussed in the book, including ideas such as <tenemos todo tipo de formas y tamaños> (we have all kinds of shapes and sizes), <somos de distintos colores> (we are of different colors), <algunos somos buenos y otros no> (some of us are good and others are not), <jugamos diferentes juegos> (we play different games), <vivimos en casas diferentes> (we live in different kinds of houses), <celebramos fiestas diferentes> (we celebrate different holidays), <comemos comida diferente> (we eat different food), <tenemos religiones diferentes> (we have different religions), <unos somos ricos y otros pobres> (some of us are rich and some are poor), and <hablamos idiomas diferentes> (we speak different languages).

For the culminating celebration of the theme, the children take one of the aspects described in *We Are All Alike . . . We Are All Different* or in *People* and make their own bilingual books about how people are alike and different. Lorena reads two big books about families to give the children some ideas. First, she reads *Con mi familia* (*With My Family*) (Romero, 1996), in which a little girl tells about the different ways her family shows love; the other book, *Con cariño* (*With Affection*)(Morris, 1990), is about families from all over the world.

The students then write and illustrate their own books. María's book, for example, tells how <todo el mundo come> (everyone eats), and then lists different things people eat: <unos comen carne y otros comen pescado> (some eat meat and others eat fish) and <unos comen espaguetis y

otros comen chow mein> (some eat spaghetti and others eat chow mein). Roberto's tells how <todos viven en una casa> (everyone lives in a house), <unas casas son grandes y otras son pequeñas> (some houses are big and others are small), and <unas son de madera y otras son de adobe> (some are of wood and some of adobe). Perhaps the most important result of Lorena's theme is how the children begin to accept differences in one another. When one child begins to tease another for looking different or doing something different, someone in the class usually reminds his or her class-mates using the refrain from the Cheltenham book, <Recuerden, todos so-mos diferentes y todos somos iguales también.> (Remember, we are all different and we are all alike too.). The literature Lorena uses for this theme is listed in Table 7–1.

Poetry

Silvio is a new third-fourth combination bilingual teacher in a rural school. Most of his students' families are associated in some way with agriculture, as either laborers in the fields or supervisors. Silvio understands his students and their families well because he was a migrant child. When he was young, a teacher encouraged him and that encouragement helped him to struggle to get through college and become a teacher so that he, in turn, could inspire children.

One of his key concerns as a teacher is that some of his colleagues at the school do not seem to expect much of the students who come to school speaking Spanish. The curriculum that most of these students get in both English and Spanish is simplified, fragmented, and unrelated to their interests or to the reality of their daily lives. Silvio's class consists of students with different backgrounds. Some have been in this school or nearby schools since kindergarten. Most of them speak Spanish and some English, but have little interest in reading and writing in either language. Several other students are new to his classroom from Mexico and El Salvador, and speak only Spanish. He also has two students from Oaxaca, Mexico, who speak Mixteco and a little Spanish, but very little English.

One of Silvio's first decisions is to get his students reading and writing in both Spanish and English, beginning with texts that are not too long or overwhelming. Since a local poetry festival is coming up, he chooses to start a unit on poetry. He pulls together a series of resources of poetry in Spanish to begin with and then reads some different pieces of poetry to his

Ada, Alma Flor. *Canción de todos los niños del mundo.* Boston: Houghton Mifflin Company (1993).

Ada, Alma Flor. *Los seis deseos de la jirafa.* Carmel: Hampton-Brown (1989).

Avalos, Cecilia. *Espejito, ¡mira!* Cleveland: Modern Curriculum Press (1991).

Cheltenham, Elementary School. *Todos somos iguales . . . todos somos diferentes.* New York: Scholastic (1994).

Cheltenham, Elementary School. *We are all alike . . . We are all different.* New York: Scholastic (1991).

D'Atri, Adriana. *El amigo nuevo, Nuestro Barrio.* Orlando: Harcourt Brace Jovanovich (1993).

Ferre, Ela. Yo. *Juegos y sueños: HBJ estrellas de literatura.* Orlando: Harcourt Brace Jovanovich (1993).

Martin, Bill Jr., and Archanbault, John. *Here are my hands.* New York: Henry Holt and Co. (1985).

Miller, Margaret. *Mis cinco sentidos.* Carmel: Hampton-Brown (1994).

Mirtín, Teresa Clerc. Imagínate. *Yo soy yo.* Boston: Houghton Mifflin Company (1993).

Morris, Ann. *Con cariño.* Carmel: Hampton-Brown (1990).

Morris, Ann. *Hats, hats, hats.* New York: Lothrop, Lee & Shepard Books (1989).

Morris, Ann. *Houses and homes.* New York: Lothrop, Lee and Shepard Books (1992).

Romero, Olga. *Con mi familia.* Carmel: Hampton-Brown (1996).

Sánchez, J.L. García, and Pacheco, M.A. *El niño que tenía dos ojos.* (Azaola, M., ed., *Los derechos del niños.*) Madrid: Altea (1988).

Sanchez, J.L. García, and Pacheco, M.A. *La niña sin nombre.* (Azaola, M., ed., *Los derechos del niño.*) Madrid: Altea (1988).

Spier, Peter. *Gente.* Barcelona: Editorial Lumen (1993).

Spier, Peter. *People.* New York: The Trumpet Club (1980).

Tabor, Nancy María Grande. *Somos un arco iris: We are a rainbow.* Watertown: Charlesbridge Publishing (1995).

TABLE 7–1: Literature for We Are All Alike, We Are All Different Unit

students asking them to <pensar en qué se parecen y en qué se diferencian los poemas> (think about how the poems are the same and different). He reads some rather sophisticated poetry from Fernando del Paso (1990) and Pablo Neruda (1987), some very short poems from alphabet poetry books (Broeck, 1983; Sempere, 1987), and some traditional playful poetry by Alma Flor Ada (1992).

After reading each poem, Silvio asks his students what their impressions are and lists their ideas on chart paper. By the time Silvio has finished reading some ten different poems, the chart has many different thoughts and questions about the poetry, including <tiene rima> (it rhymes), <me hace sentir confundido> (it makes me feel confused), <me gusta porque es alegre> (I like it because it is happy), <algunos poemas no tienen rima> (some poems don't rhyme), <¿una canción puede ser un poema también?> (can a song be a poem too?), <algunos poemas son difíciles para entender> (some poems are difficult to understand), <¿por qué escribe poesía un poeta?> (why does a poet write poetry?), <algunos poemas tienen palabras extrañas> (some poems have unusual words).

Silvio and the students look at their chart and talk about their observations and questions. Silvio brings up the poetry festival. This leads to a discussion of how they might prepare for it. Together they decide how they should study poetry together as a class. First, they should read lots of poems in Spanish. Then each student will memorize some poems and practice them in small groups to present to the class and maybe present at the festival.

In addition to reading the poetry of published authors, the students wonder if they can write some poetry of their own during their writing time each day. They decide that after they have read lots of poetry, they will be ready to think about writing their own. In addition, they talk about writing bilingual poems in both Spanish and English, and also writing poetry only in English.

Silvio's students begin the year with poetry and revisit poetry throughout the year. As the year progresses, Silvio draws on resources such as *Días y días de poesía* (*Days and Days of Poetry*) (Ada, 1991), for seasonal poetry ideas. He also reads different poetry books from the Mexican series *Reloj de Versos* (*Rhyming Clocks*) (Bartolomé, 1991; Cross, 1992; Forcada, 1992; Sabines, 1990). For English and bilingual poetry he draws on resources such as *A Chorus of Cultures: Developing Literacy Through Multicultural Poetry* (Ada, et al., 1993), as well as on local poets, and his school library media specialist. Poetry is an excellent way for Silvio's

Ada, Alma Flor. *Caballito Blanco y otras poesías favoritas, Días y días de poesía.* Carmel: Hampton-Brown Books (1992).

Ada, Alma Flor. *Canción de todos los niños del mundo.* Boston: Houghton Mifflin Company (1993).

Ada, Alma Flor. *Cinco pollitos y otras poesías favoritas, Días y días de poesía.* Carmel: Hampton-Brown Books (1992).

Ada, Alma Flor. *Días y días de poesía.* Carmel: Hampton-Brown Books (1991).

Ada, Alma Flor. *El cuento del gato y otras poesías favoritas, Días y días de poesía.* Carmel: Hampton-Brown Books (1992).

Ada, Alma Flor, Harris, Violet, and Hopkins, Lee Bennett. *A chorus of cultures: Developing literacy through multicultural poetry.* Carmel: Hampton-Brown Books (1993).

Barrera, R. (Ed.). Alborada. *Yo Soy Yo.* Boston: Houghton Mifflin (1993).

Bartolomé, Efraín. *Mínima animalia, Reloj de versos.* México, D.F.: CIDCLI (1991).

Bracho, Coral. *Jardín del mar, Reloj de versos.* México, D.F.: CIDCLI (1993).

Broeck, Fabricio Vanden. *ABC animales, Colección Piñata.* México, D.F.: Editorial Patria (1983).

Cabrera, Miguel. *Chiquilín.* Caracas, Venezuela: Conceptos. s.f.

Cross, Elsa. *El himno de las ranas, Reloj de versos.* México, D.F.: CIDCLI (1992).

Del Paso, Fernando. *De la A a la Z por un poeta.* México, D.F.: Grupo Editorial Diana (1990).

TABLE 7–2, Part 1: Silvio's Poetry Unit

students to develop literacy in both Spanish and English. Table 7–2 lists the literature Silvio used for this unit.

La importancia de la agricultura (The Importance of Agriculture)

Silvio sees the excitement of his students as they work with both familiar rhymes and new poetry, but he wants to extend their reading and writing into content areas too. Some of his students are not yet proficient readers and writers in Spanish or English. Others read and write quite well. Silvio needs to provide literacy experiences that will interest and involve students with very different academic backgrounds and different language

Dubin, Susana Dultzín. *Sonidos y ritmos*. Boston: Houghton Mifflin Company (1984).

Forcada, Alberto. *Despertar, Reloj de versos*. México, D.F.: CIDCLI (1992).

Gallego, Margaret A., Hinojosa-Smith, Rolando, Kohen, Clarita, Medrano, Hilda, Solis, Juan, and Thonis, Eleanor. *Tú y yo, HBJ Estrellas de la literatura*. Orlando: Harcourt Brace Jovanovich (1993).

Garza, Carmen Lomas. *Cuadros de familia*. San Francisco: Children's Book Press (1990).

Macías, Elva. *La ronda de la luna, El sueño del dragón*. México, D.F.: Ediciones Corunda (1994).

Nazoa, Aquiles. *Fábula de la ratoncita presumida*. Caracas: Ediciones Ekaré-Banco del Libro (1985).

Neruda, Pablo. *El libro de las preguntas*. Vol. Editorial Andrés Bello. Santiago de Chile (1987).

Parra, Nicanor. *Sinfonía de Cuna, En Cuento*. México, D.F.: CIDCLI (1992).

Peña, Luis de la. *Cosecha de versos y refranes, Literatura Infantil*. México, D.F.: CONAFE (1989).

Ramírez, Elisa. *Adivinazas indígenas, Colección Piñata*. México, D.F.: Editorial Patria (1984).

Sabines, Jaime. *La luna, Reloj de versos*. México, D.F.: CIDCLI (1990).

Sempere, Vicky. *ABC*. Caracas, Venezuela: Ediciones Ekaré-Banco del Libro (1987).

TABLE 7–2, Part 2: Silvio's Poetry Unit

proficiency levels. He realizes that an excellent way for his students to develop academic competence and become truly biliterate is by teaching content through a theme that draws on student background and experiences.

The small community where he lives and teaches depends heavily on agriculture. Many of his students are presently from migrant families, or were at one time migrant children, moving from town to town with the crops. Certainly, all the students in his class understand the importance of the land and of growing crops, including those whose parents are foremen or land owners. He wants all of his students to realize the importance of the work that many of their parents are involved in. Silvio decides to have his students explore the question, <¿Por qué es importante la agricultura?>

(Why is agriculture important?). He knows that his students' background experiences will help them as they read both literature and content texts on this topic.

Because the students began the year with poetry, it seems natural to Silvio to move into the agriculture theme through poetry. He begins the unit with several folk poems, riddles, and proverbs (Ada, 1991; Dubin, 1984; Garza, 1990; Peña, 1989; Ramírez, 1984). The ideas in these short, accessible texts capture the students' interest.

Then Silvio reads a stanza from the poem *Son del pueblo trabajador* (*Sound of the Working People*):

Cuando sale el sol	When the sun rises
las tierras de mi tierra	the earth of my land
cultivo yo,	I cultivate
cuando sale el sol,	when the sun rises
que soy el campesino	I am the fieldworker
trabajador,	laborer
cuando sale el sol.	when the sun rises.
(Ada, 1991, p. 41)	

Silvio asks the students to jot down the thoughts or memories this poem brings to mind. They share their ideas in pairs and then make a class list.

Silvio passes out a copy of the stanza for students to take home and read to their parents. He encourages the students to discuss the poem with their family, to find out what ideas it raises for them. He suggests that they write down their parents' impressions and come prepared to share their results in class the next day. Silvio uses this information to create a second list. Then the class compares the two sets of responses to the poem and discusses some of the reasons for similarities and differences. In some cases, the parents have a stronger response because their work experience is more immediate, while the children's impressions have come secondhand as they hear their parents talk about their days in the fields. In other cases, the responses are similar because the children have worked alongside their parents.

In November, during harvest time, Silvio chooses songs and poetry about the harvest of corn, the historic staple for the people of Mexico and Central America. The whole class memorizes *El maíz* (*Corn*) (Ada, 1992), a traditional poem that describes mature corn on the stalk, *Día de gracias* (*Thanksgiving Day*) (Ada, 1992), and *Día feliz* (*Happy Day*) (Ada, 1991), poems which describe traditional celebration meals in Spanish-speaking homes. They also sing together *Pizcamos mazorcas* (*Picking Ears of Corn*) (Ada, 1991).

During English language arts time, the students enjoy learning "Opening Corn," (Ada, et al., 1993), a poem about an ear of corn. The poem draws on the senses with lines like "sounds like pulling down a zipper," "smells like onions," "feels like the road has bumps," and "looks like a witch's yellow white hair." (p. 95) The students brainstorm other comparisons that would describe corn. Then they try making up similar poems about pumpkins and onions.

From poetry Silvio turns the students to riddles beginning with the following one for corn:

Allá en el llano	There in the plain
está uno sin sombrero.	is one without a hat.
Tiene barbas, tiene dientes	He has a beard, he has teeth
y no es un caballero.	and he is not a horseman.
(Gallego, et al., 1993, p. 29).	

After reading and guessing several different riddles, the students write their own riddles in pairs and read them aloud for the class to guess. This activity also spills over into English language arts time, and the students often use the same topics in English that they first wrote and talked about in their native language.

To further extend the agriculture theme, Silvio reads two stories, *El chivo en la huerta* (*The Goat in the Garden*) (Kratky, 1989) and *La marrana dormida* (*The Sleeping Pig*) (Seale and Tafolla, 1993). Both of these stories are about animals that are in a field of crops where they should not be. The stories describe the attempts of other animals to get them out. In the end, an insect is the hero in each story. These similarities offer Silvio the opportunity to encourage his students to compare and contrast the stories. In addition, since the animals in the stories use mainly their sounds to try to get the pests out of the crops, poetry and stories using other animal sounds such as *Sonidos y ritmos* (*Sounds and Rhythms*) (Dubin, 1984), *Pepín y el abuelo* (*Pepín and the Grandfather*) (Perera, 1993), *Alborada* (*Dawn*) (Barrera, 1993), *El coquí* (*El Coquí Puerto Rican Tree Frog*) (Ada, 1992), and *Concierto* (*Concert*) (Ada, 1992) offer the students further play with the sounds of language as well as additional opportunities for reading and writing.

Next, Silvio reads the big book, *Granjas* (*Farms*) (Madrigal, 1992), to the class. The students are fascinated by the description of *la granja de hortalizas* (vegetable farm), *la granja lechera* (dairy), *la granja triguera* (wheat farm), and *la granja de naranjas* (orange farm). It is a natural step here for Silvio to ask the third of Hansen's questions <¿A qué les recuerda lo que leí?> (What does what I read remind you of?). The students excitedly share their own and their parents' experiences on the different types of farms, and one proudly tells how his own father often tells him what the book said, <La agricultura es la actividad más importante del mundo.> (Agriculture is the most important activity in the world.) (p. 6).

After this discussion, Silvio explains that the class is going to do different inquiry projects on the topic of *La agricultura y su importancia* (Agriculture and Its Importance), and he asks the students <Qué más quieren saber ustedes sobre la agricultura?> (What else would you like to know about agriculture?). The students write questions in groups and then share their questions as Silvio writes them on a large piece of butcher paper. Some students want to know about what kinds of things make the plants on a farm grow better. Some want to know why pineapples and mangos from their countries will not grow in this area. Others want to know why farm laborers earn so little money, and how much it costs to run a farm. Others want to know more about irrigation, and still others want to know what is necessary to raise farm animals properly. The class decides to form groups to investigate these topics. Each group will write a report to share with the class, and the reports will be combined to create a class book on agriculture.

To get the information that they need to explore their questions, the students decide to use different resources. They plan to interview people in their families and the community, to call or write the local farm bureau for speakers and information, and to look at resource books they have in their classroom including reference books such as *La vida de las plantas* (*The Life of Plants*) (Costa-Pau, 1993), *Plantas* (*Plants*) and *Animales* (*Animals*) (Sealey, 1979), *Experimenta con las plantas* (*Experiment with Plants*) (Watts and Parsons, 1993), *Los secretos de las plantas* (*The Secrets of the Plants*) (Burnie, 1990), *Quiero conocer la vida de las plantas* (*I Want to Know About the Life of Plants*) (Marcus, 1987), and *Quiero conocer la vida de los animales* (*I Want to Know About the Life of Animals*) (Marcus, 1987).

Two of Silvio's students who came to his class directly from Mexico had very little previous schooling. The limited texts of the poetry, riddles, and the two stories about animals in a field are accessible to them, especially when the class reads them together or when they have opportunities to read with a buddy. However, Silvio also wants these students to do other reading, so he provides them with books about farms and agriculture that have more limited text to use as they explore their questions. These include books such as *El rancho* (*The Ranch*) (Almada, 1994), *Chiles* (Kratky, 1995),

El campo (*The Country*) (Rius and Parramon, 1987), *Mi primera visita a la granja* (*My First Visit to the Farm*) (Parramón and Sales, 1990), *Las plantas* (*Plants*) (Walker, 1995), *De la semilla a la fruta* (*From the Seed to the Fruit*) (Zenzes, 1987).

To supplement the content books, during literature study time Silvio brings in different kinds of literature that support the agriculture theme. He shows the students a series of books written by children in Mexico that reflect their indigenous cultures and languages. All the books are written bilingually in Spanish and the children's native languages and also are illustrated by the children. Although most of the books are about the rural life of the children, Silvio shows two in particular to his students. In *La milpa de Don Ricardo* (*The Corn Field of Don Ricardo*) (Mateos, 1992), the Nahua children tell, in their native language and in Spanish, the story of how Don Ricardo cultivates his corn field, and in *Don Juan, su familia y sus plantas* (*Don Juan, His Family and His Plants*) (Mateos, 1991), Otomi children tell, in their native language and in Spanish, about how one should care for and use their plants and animals. After Silvio shows his students the books, they get excited about writing illustrated bilingual books in Spanish and English for their inquiry about agriculture.

Another literature study that Silvio does with his students begins with a folktale that teaches the content concept of *cultivos alternados* (rotating crops). First, Silvio reads *Ton-tón el gigantón* (*Ton-tón, the Big Old Giant*) (Cumpiano, 1992), an Ecuadorian folktale about a giant who is tricked by a peasant woman when he demands all the produce of her land. First, she gives him the choice of taking what grows above the ground or below the ground. When he chooses what grows above, she plants potatoes. The next season when he chooses what grows below, she raises beans. Finally, when he wants half the field, she grows wheat and puts in stakes to make it impossible for him to harvest his half of the field. One of the conclusions of the story is that the growing of different crops in the field each year made the harvest better.

After reading and discussing this story with his class, Silvio invites his students to read another version of the story *El gigantón cabelludo* (*The Hairy Giant*) (Gondard, 1993) and then compare and contrast the two versions. After reading and discussing the two stories, the class also reads and discusses together a short content article on *Cultivos alternados* (Rotating Crops) (Gallego et al., 1993). This article gives them additional information about crop rotation.

Another folktale that the students read is *La gallinita, el gallo y el frijol* (*The Hen, the Rooster and the Bean*) (Kratky, 1989). In this cumulative tale, the hen tries to get water to help the rooster get rid of the bean that is caught in his throat. When she asks the river for water, the river asks for a flower. She goes, then, to the flower who demands thread to tie her vines. When the hen asks the girl for the thread, the girl requests a comb. This series of demands continues until the hen finally gets the needed water to dislodge the bean from the rooster's throat. The students relate this story to the traditional song "I Know an Old Lady Who Swallowed a Fly" that they had learned in English language arts, and the story, "The House that Jack Built," which also has a similar cumulative pattern. They decide to look at those stories again and try to find other cumulative stories like them.

As the inquiry continues, different topics bring up different readings. Since cotton is a common crop that is grown, one group of students decides to study how cotton is changed into cloth. To help all the students understand this process, Silvio reads *Las cosas cambian* (Bourne, 1992), the story of how cotton is converted into jeans. Since this book is also available in English, *Things Change* (Bourne, 1992), it is also an excellent book for reading during English language arts.

A literature book that Silvio reads to his students during English language arts that connects with the topic of growing cotton especially catches his students' attention. *Working Cotton* (Williams, 1992) tells of an African American family picking cotton in the central valley of California where Silvio teaches. After the children listen to the story, they begin to talk about how hard it is to work in the hot fields. Some of the children who have to move with the crops also talk about how they do not like to move.

This discussion encourages Silvio to bring out two books in Spanish about children of migrant families who move with the crops: *El camino de Amelia* (*Amelia's Road*) (Altman, 1993) and *Tomates California* (Seale and Ramírez, 1993). The students discuss the children in these stories. This leads to the topic of rights for farm workers and the hero of the farm workers, César Chávez. One of the students runs to the book corner and pulls out *César Chávez: Líder laboral* (*César Chávez, Labor Leader*) (Morris, 1994). Silvio tells them that they should read the book in small groups if they have not already read it, and that they will talk about the book as a whole class in the next few days.

During English language arts the next day, Silvio asks a group of students to copy a poem in English, "César Chávez, Farm Worker Organizer," onto large chart paper. The poem comes from *Latino Rainbow: Poems About Latino Americans* (Cumpián, 1994, p. 29). The children then discuss how lines like "Tractors have barns, animals have stalls, but the migrant worker has nowhere to lay his head" (p. 29) are related to stories like *El camino de Amelia* and *Tomates California*. The class then looks at *Earth Angels* (Buirski, 1994), a powerful book of photographs and short quotes from field workers about the difficulty of their lives, including the problems of child labor and pesticides. After some discussion, Silvio shows the students three other books that deal with farm workers and their children that he thinks might be interesting reading: *A Migrant Family* (Brimmer, 1992), *Lights on the River* (Thomas, 1994), and *Voices from the Fields* (Atkin, 1993).

The weeks that follow in Silvio's room are full of activity. Students read, share, and write about what they are learning. They decide that what they have learned about plants, animals, and agriculture, in general, is important to share with others in their school, and they plan a day when other classes will come into their room so that they can read the stories and reports they have written and explain what they have learned.

The students also want to share with their parents. They want their parents to know what they have learned, but they also want to show their parents their appreciation for the hard work their parents do. After much discussion, the students decide to make a big book entitled, *La importancia de la agricultura* (*The Importance of Agriculture*). Every group will contribute two pages to the book. One page will record what they learned in their inquiry and the other will include poems telling how they feel about being part of *la agricultura*. The students will read their pages of the book to their parents during the upcoming Christmas celebration, which will feature refreshments and a piñata. Table 7–3 lists the books Silvio used for this unit.

Silvio has accomplished his goal. His students are reading and writing. However, he has accomplished some other things that may be even more important. Through a curriculum that is relevant to the lives of his students, he has helped them appreciate what they and their families contribute to society. His students are becoming biliterate by reading both quality literature and content texts in Spanish and English, by discussing what they read, and by engaging in meaningful writing. The writing allows students to show what they have learned and how they have been touched by this empowering curriculum.

Ada, Alma Flor. *Caballito Blanco y otras poesías favoritas, Días y días de poesía*. Carmel: Hampton-Brown Books (1992).

Ada, Alma Flor. *Cinco pollitos y otras poesías favoritas, Días y días de poesía*. Carmel: Hampton-Brown Books (1992).

Ada, Alma Flor. *Días y días de poesía*. Carmel: Hampton-Brown Books (1991).

Ada, Alma Flor, Harris, Violet J., and Hopkins, Lee Bennett. *A chorus of cultures: Developing literacy through multicultural poetry*. Carmel: Hampton-Brown Books (1993).

Almada, Patricia. *El rancho, Literatura 2000*. Crystal Lake: Rigby (1994).

Altman, Linda Jacobs. *El camino de Amelia*. (Santacruz, Daniel, Trans.) New York: Lee & Low Books (1993).

Atkin, S. Beth. *Voices from the fields: Children of migrant farmworkers tell their stories*. Boston: Little, Brown and Company (1993).

Barrera, R., (ed.). Alborada. *Yo Soy Yo*. Boston: Houghton Mifflin (1993).

Bourne, Phyllis Montenegro. *Las cosas cambian*. Carmel: Hampton-Brown Books (1992).

Bourne, Phyllis Montenegro. *Things change*. Carmel: Hampton-Brown Books (1992).

Brimmer, L.D. *A migrant family*. Minneapolis: Lerner Publications Company (1992).

Buirski, Nancy. *Earth angels*. San Francisco: Pomegranate Artbooks (1994).

Burnie, David. *Los secretos de las plantas*. Madrid: ALTEA.

Costa-Pau, Rosa. *La vida de las plantas, Mundo invisible*. Bogotá: Editorial Norma (1993).

Cumpián, Carlos. *Latino rainbow: Poems about Latino Americans, many voices one song*. Chicago: Childrens Press (1994).

Cumpiano, Ina. *Ton-tón el gigantón*. Carmel: Hampton-Brown (1992).

Dubin, Susana Dultzín. *Sonidos y ritmos*. Boston: Houghton Mifflin Company (1984).

Gallego, Margaret, Hinojosa-Smith, Rolando, Kohen, Clarita, Medrano, Hilda, Solis, Juan, and Thonis, Eleanor. *Cultivos alternados, HBJ Estrellas de la literatura*. Orlando: Harcourt Brace Jovanovich (1993).

TABLE 7–3, Part 1: Literature from The Importance of Agriculture Unit

Gallego, Margaret, Hinojosa-Smith, Rolando, Kohen, Clarita, Medrano, Hilda, Solis, Juan, and Thonis, Eleanor. *Tú y yo, HBJ Estrellas de la literatura*. Orlando: Harcourt Brace Jovanovich (1993).

Garza, Carmen Lomas. *Cuadros de familia*. San Francisco: Children's Book Press (1990).

Gondard, Pierre. *El gigantón cabelludo, HBJ Estrellas de la literatura*. Orlando: Harcourt Brace Jovanovich (1993).

Kratky, Lada Josefa. *El chivo en la huerta*. Carmel: Hampton-Brown (1989).

Kratky, Lada Josefa. *Chiles, Pan y Canela*. Carmel: Hampton-Brown Books (1995).

Kratky, Lada Josefa. *La gallinita, el gallo y el frijol*. Carmel: Hampton-Brown (1989).

Madrigal, S. *Granjas*. Carmel: Hampton-Brown Books (1992).

Marcus, Elizabeth. *Quiero conocer la vida de las plantas, Quiero conocer*. México, D.F.: Sistemas Técnicos de Edición (1987).

Marcus, Elizabeth. *Quiero conocer la vida de los animales, Quiero conocer*. México, D.F.: SITESA (1987).

Mateos, Rocío López. *Don José, su familia y sus plantas*. México, D.F.: Instituto Nacional Indigenista (1991).

Mateos, Rocío López. *La milpa de Don Ricardo*. México, D.F.: Instituto Nacional Indigenista (1992).

Morris, Clara Sánchez de. *César Chávez: Líder laboral*. Cleveland: Modern Curriculum Press (1994).

Parramón, J.M., and Sales, G. *Mi primera visita a la granja, Mi primera visita*. Woodbury: Barron's (1990).

Peña, Luis de la. *Cosecha de versos y refranes, Literatura Infantil*. México, D.F.: CONAFE (1989).

Perera, Hilda. *Pepín y el abuelo*. Boston: Houghton Mifflin Company (1993).

Ramírez, Elisa. *Adivinazas indígenas, Colección Piñata*. México, D.F.: Editorial Patria (1984).

Rius, María, and Parramon, Josep María. *El campo, Un día en*. Woodbury: Barron's (1987).

Seale, Jan, and Tafolla, Carmen. La marrana dormida. *Yo Soy Yo.* (Barrera, Rosalinda, (ed.) Boston: Houghton Mifflin (1993).

TABLE 7–3, Part 2: Literature from The Importance of Agriculture Unit

Seale, Jan, and Ramírez, Alfonso. *Tomates, California*. Boston: Houghton Mifflin (1993).

Sealey, Leonard. *Animales, Colección Nuestro Mundo*. Barcelona: Editorial Juventud (1979).

Sealey, Leonard. *Plantas*. (Sealey, Leonard, ed., *Colección nuestro mundo*.) Barcelona: Editorial Juventud (1979).

Thomas, Jane Resh. *Lights on the river*. New York: Hyperion Books for Children (1994).

Walker, Colin. *Las plantas, Concept science en español*. Cleveland: Modern Curriculum Press (1995).

Watts, Claire, and Parsons, Alexandra. *Experimenta con las plantas*. (Rodríguez, Beatriz, Trans.) Madrid: CESMA (1993).

Williams, Sherley. *Working cotton*. Orlando: Harcourt Brace Jovanovich (1992).

Zenzes, Gertrudias. *De la semilla a la fruta*. México, D.F.: Fernández Editores (1987).

TABLE 7–3, Part 3: Literature from The Importance of Agriculture Unit

Conclusion

Our purpose in writing this book was to describe the reading and writing processes in Spanish, and to share with teachers ideas about how to best help Latino students develop literacy in their first language: Spanish. We planned to write a very short book that would cover the basics and serve as a quick reference. However, the book expanded as we attempted to include ideas from the rich research base in Spanish reading and writing. We also wanted to share the wealth of Spanish literature for young readers and writers that has been produced in recent years. Our book grew because the topic was so important and there was so much to be said.

We do not pretend that we have said all that needs to be said. We have tried, however, to share some of the key ideas that we think all Spanish/English bilingual teachers should consider. It is important to consider what the effective features of a quality Spanish reading and writing program might be. To decide what constitutes effective features, it is critical to understand the reading process. When one understands how readers construct meaning, it is possible to make informed choices about an appropriate reading program for emergent readers. The same kind of informed decision making is important for bilingual teachers in the area of writing. Only when teachers understand how spelling develops in Spanish and in English can they support their students as they move from invented spelling to conventional writing.

We develop literacy so that we can understand our world and share that understanding. In our final chapter we have given examples of how teachers have developed quality biliteracy programs by drawing on a wealth of literature and by organizing themes around topics of interest to their students. Teachers working in Spanish/English bilingual classrooms must not simply teach their students to read and write: they must teach them to think and act to build a better world. Biliterate people are going to be leaders in the next century, and only if we help our bilingual students understand how to make the world a better place can we say that our teaching has really been successful.

LITERATURE REFERENCES

Ada, Alma Flor. *Caballito Blanco y otras poesías favoritas, Días y días de poesía*. Carmel: Hampton-Brown Books (1992).

Ada, Alma Flor. *Canción de todos los niños del mundo*. Boston: Houghton Mifflin Company (1993).

Ada, Alma Flor. *Cinco pollitos y otras poesías favoritas, Días y días de poesía*. Carmel: Hampton-Brown Books (1992).

Ada, Alma Flor. *Días y días de poesía*. Carmel: Hampton-Brown Books (1991).

Ada, Alma Flor. *El cuento del gato y otras poesías favoritas, Días y días de poesía*. Carmel: Hampton-Brown Books (1992).

Ada, Alma Flor. *Los seis de la jirafa*. Carmel: Hampton-Brown (1989).

Ada, Alma Flor. *Olmo y la mariposa azul, HBJ Estrellas de la Literatura*. Orlando: Harcourt Brace Javanovich (1993).

Ada, Alma Flor. *Una semilla nada más*. Carmel: Hampton-Brown Books (1990).

Ada, Alma Flor, Harris, Violet J., and Hopkins, Lee Bennett. *A chorus of cultures: Developing literacy through multicultural poetry*. Carmel: Hampton-Brown Books (1993).

Allen, Marjorie, and Rotner, Shelley. *Cambios*. Carmel: Hampton-Brown Books (1991).

Almada, Patricia. *El rancho, Literatura 2000*. Crystal Lake: Rigby (1994).

Almada, Patricia. *Patas, Literatura 2000*. Crystal Lake: Rigby (1994).

Altman, Linda Jacobs. *El camino de Amelia*. (Santacruz, Daniel, Trans.) New York: Lee & Low Books (1993).

Alvarez, Carmen Espinosa Elenes de. Mi libro mágico. México, D.F.: Enrique Sainz Editores (1979).

Aron, Evelyn. *Cántame en español: Sing to me in Spanish*. Mexico, D.F.: Multidiseño Gráfico (1988).

Atkin, S. Beth. *Voices from the fields: Children of migrant farmworkers tell their stories.* Boston: Little, Brown and Company (1993).

Avalos, Cecilia. *Espejito, ¡mira!.* Cleveland: Modern Curriculum Press (1991).

Barberis. *¿De quién es este rabo?, Colección Duende.* Valladolid, Spain: Miñon (1974).

Barrera, Rosalinda, (ed.). Alborada. *Yo Soy Yo.* Boston: Houghton Mifflin (1993).

Barrett, Norman. *Cocodrilos y caimanes, Biblioteca Gráfica.* New York: Franklin Watts (1991).

Barrett, Norman. *Monos y simios, Biblioteca Gráfica.* New York: Franklin Watts (1991).

Barrett, Norman. *Serpientes, Biblioteca Gráfica.* New York: Franklin Watts (1990).

Bartolomé, Efraín. *Mínima animalia, Reloj de versos.* México, D.F.: CIDCLI (1991).

Beck, Jennifer. *Patas, Literatura 2000, Nivel 3.* Crystal Lake: Ribgy (1994).

Bolton, F., and Snowball, D. *Growing radishes and carrots.* New York: Scholastic Inc. (1985).

Bos, Burny, and De Beer, Hans. *Oli, el pequeño elefante.* Barcelona, Spain: Editorial Lumen (1989).

Bourne, Phyllis Montenegro. *Las cosas cambian.* Carmel: Hampton-Brown Books (1992).

Bourne, Phyllis Montenegro. *Things change.* Carmel: Hampton-Brown Books (1992).

Bracho, Coral. *Jardín del mar, Reloj de versos.* México, D.F.: CIDCLI (1993).

Bragado, Manuel. *Doña Carmen.* Boston: Houghton Mifflin (1993).

Brimmer, L.D. *A migrant family.* Minneapolis: Lerner Publications Company (1992).

Broeck, Fabricio Vanden. *ABC animales, Colección Piñata.* México, D.F.: Editorial Patria (1983).

Browne, Anthony. *Gorila.* (Esteva, Carmen, Trans., *A la orilla del viento.*) México, D.F.: Fondo de Cultura Económica (1991).

Browne, Anthony. *Zoológico.* (Esteva, Carmen, Trans., *A la orilla del viento.*) Mexcio, D.F.: Fondo de Cultura Económica (1993).

Brusca, María Cristina, and Wilson, Tona. *Tres amigos: Un cuento para contar.* Boston: Houghton Mifflin (1995).

Buirski, Nancy. *Earth angels.* San Francisco: Pomegranate Artbooks (1994).

Burnie, David. *Los secretos de las plantas.* Madrid: ALTEA (1990).

Cabrera, Miguel. *Chiquilín*. *Caracas*. Venezuela: Conceptos. s.f.

Cappellini, Mary. *¿Quién quiere helado?*, *Literatura 2000*. Crystal Lake: Rigby (1994).

Cappellini, Mary, and Almada, Patricia. *Literatura 2000*. Crystal Lake: Rigby (1994).

Carl, Eric. *La oruga muy hambrienta*. New York: Philomel Books (1989).

Carl, Eric. *The very hungry caterpillar*. Cleveland: The World Publishing Company (1969).

Cervantes, Jesús. *Voy a la escuela*. Carmel: Hampton-Brown Books (1996).

Charpenel, Mauricio. *El ranchito*, *Pan y Canela*, *Colección* A. Carmel: Hampton-Brown Books (1995).

Cheltenham, Elementary School. *Todos somos iguales . . . todos somos diferentes*. New York: Scholastic (1994).

Cheltenham, Elementary School. *We are all alike . . . We are all different*. New York: Scholastic (1991).

Cherry, Lynne. *La ceiba majestuosa: Un cuento del bosque lluvioso de las Amazonas*. Boston: Houghton Mifflin (1996).

Clements, Andrew. *Big Al*. New York: Scholastic (1991).

Cole, Joanna. *El autobús mágico: Planta una semilla*. New York: Scholastic (1995).

Comerlati, Mara. *Conoce nuestros mamíferos*. Caracas, Venezuela: Ediciones Ekaré Banco del Libro (1983).

Costa-Pau, Rosa. *La vida de las plantas, Mundo invisible*. Bogotá: Editorial Norma (1993).

Cowcher, Helen. *El bosque tropical*. New York: Scholastic (1992).

Cowley, J. *Los animales de Don Vicencio*. Auckland, New Zealand: Shortland (1987).

Cristini, Ermanno, and Puricelli, Luigi. *En el bosque*. New York: Scholastic (1983).

Cross, Elsa. *El himno de las ranas, Reloj de versos*. México, D.F.: CIDCLI (1992).

Cumpián, Carlos. *Latino rainbow: Poems about Latino Americans, many voices one song*. Chicago: Childrens Press (1994).

Cumpiano, Ina. *Pan, pan, gran pan*. Carmel: Hampton-Brown Books (1990).

Cumpiano, Ina. *Ton-tón el gigantón*. Carmel: Hampton-Brown Books (1992).

Cutting, Brian, and Cutting, Jillian. *Semillas y más semillas*. (Andujar, Gloria, Trans., Pye, Wendy, ed., *Sunshine science series*.) Bothell: Wright Group (1995).

Darlington, Arnold. *Diviértete con una lupa, El niño quiere saber.* Barcelona: Ediciones Toray (1984).

D'Atri, Adriana. *El amigo nuevo, Nuestro barrio.* Orlando: Harcourt Brace Jovanovich (1993).

Del Paso, Fernando. *De la A a la Z por un poeta.* México, D.F.: Grupo Editorial Diana (1990).

Detwiler, Darius, and Rizo-Patrón, Marina. *Libro del ABC.* Boston: Houghton Mifflin (1993).

Dobbs, Siobhan. *El tigre Carlitos.* (Barrera, Rosalinda, Crawford, Alan, Sabrina Mims, Joan, and Dávila de Silva, Aurelia, eds., *Celebremos la literatura.*) Boston: Houghton Mifflin (1993).

Drew, David. *Pistas de animales, Informazing!* Crystal Lake: Rigby (1993).

Dubin, Susana Dultzín. *Sonidos y ritmos.* Boston: Houghton Mifflin (1984).

Ediciones Litexsa Venezolana, (ed.). *Aprender a contar.* Caracas, Venezuela: Cromotip (1987).

Ehlert, Lois. *Growing vegetable soup.* San Diego: Harcourt Brace & Company (1987).

Fernández, Laura. *Pío, pío. Yo soy yo.* (Barrera, Rosalinda; Crawford, Alan; Mims, Joan Sabrina; and de Silva, Aurelia Davila, eds.) Boston: Houghton Mifflin (1993).

Ferre, Ela. Yo. *Juegos y sueños: HBJ Estrellas de la literatura.* Orlando: Harcourt Brace Jovanovich (1993).

Flores, Guillermo Solano. *Pon una semilla a germinar, Niño científico.* México, D.F.: Editorial Trillas (1985).

Forcada, Alberto. *Despertar, Reloj de versos.* México, D.F.: CIDCLI (1992).

Fowler, Allan. *Podría ser un mamífero.* (Marcuse, Aída E., Trans., *Mis primeros libros de ciencia.*) Chicago: Childrens Press (1991).

Gallego, Margaret, Hinojosa-Smith, Rolando, Kohen, Clarita, Medrano, Hilda, Solis, Juan, and Thonis, Eleanor. *Cultivos alternados, HBJ Estrellas de la literatura.* Orlando: Harcourt Brace Jovanovich (1993).

Gallego, Margaret, Hinojosa-Smith, Rolando, Kohen, Clarita, Medrano, Hilda, Solis, Juan, and Thonis, Eleanor. *Tú y yo, HBJ Estrellas de la literatura.* Orlando: Harcourt Brace Jovanovich (1993).

Garza, Carmen Lomas. *Cuadros de familia.* San Francisco: Children's Book Press (1990).

Garza-Williams, Liz. *Papi y yo, Pan y Canela, Colección A.* Carmel: Hampton-Brown Books (1995).

Ginzo, Courel. (Baker, W., and Haslam, A., eds.) *Make It Work!* Madrid: Ediciones SM (1993).

Gondard, Pierre. *El gigantón cabelludo, HBJ Estrellas de la literatura*. Orlando: Harcourt Brace Jovanovich (1993).

Goodall, Jane. *La familia del chimpancé*. México, D.F.: SITESA (1991).

Granowsky, Alvin. *Los animales del mundo*. (Johnson, C., ed., *Especies del mundo en peligro de extinción*.) Lexington: Schoolhouse Press (1986).

Heller, Ruth. *Chickens aren't the only ones*. New York: Scholastic (1981).

Heller, Ruth. *Las gallinas no son las únicas*. México, D.F.: Grijalbo (1990).

Hofer, Angelika, and Ziesler, Günter. *La familia del león*. México, D.F.: SITESA (1992).

Ingpen, Robert, and Dunkle, Margaret. *Conservación*. México, D.F.: Editorial Origen S.A. (1991).

Jeunesse, Gallimard, and de Bourgoing, Pascale. *The egg*. First Discovery Books. New York: Scholastic (1992).

Jordan, Helene J. *Cómo crece una semilla*. (Fiol, María A., Trans., *Harper Arco Iris*.) New York: Harper Collins (1996).

Knowles, Rick, and Morse, Kitty. *Lyric language*. Carlsbad: Penton Overseas, Inc. (1992).

Kratky, Lada Josefa. *Animals and their babies*. Carmel: Hampton-Brown Books (1991).

Kratky, Lada Josefa. *Chiles, Pan y Canela*. Carmel: Hampton-Brown Books (1995).

Kratky, Lada Josefa. *El chivo en la huerta*. Carmel: Hampton-Brown Books (1989).

Kratky, Lada Josefa. *En mi escuela, Pan y Canela, Colección A*. Carmel: Hampton-Brown Books (1995).

Kratky, Lada Josefa. *La gallinita, el gallo y el frijol*. Carmel: Hampton-Brown Books (1989).

Kratky, Lada Josefa. *Los animales y sus crías, ¡Qué maravilla!* Carmel: Hampton-Brown Books (1991).

Kratky, Lada Josefa. *Orejas, Pan y Canela, Colección B*. Carmel: Hampton-Brown Books (1995).

Kratky, Lada Josefa. *Pan y Canela, Pan y Canela*. Carmel: Hampton-Brown Books (1995).

Kratky, Lada Josefa. *Pinta, pinta, Gregorita*. Carmel: Hampton-Brown Books (1990).

Kratky, Lada Josefa. *Uno, dos, tres y cuatro, Pan y Canela, Colección* A. Carmel: Hampton-Brown Books (1995).

Kratky, Lada Josefa. *Veo, Veo Colas, Pan y Canela, Colección* A. Carmel: Hampton-Brown Books (1995).

Krauss, R. *The carrot seed*. New York: Scholastic, Inc. (1945).

Krauss, R. *La semilla de zanahoria*. (Palacios, A., Trans.) New York: Scholastic, Inc. (1945, 1978 trans.).

Kuchalla, Susan. *¿Cómo son los animales bebés?, ¿Cómo son?* México, D.F.: SITESA (1987).

Lavie, Arlette. *Aprender a contar*. Venezuela: Ediciones Litexsa Venezolana (1987).

Lionni, Leo. *Frederick*. New York: Knopf (1973).

Lionni, Leo. *Swimmy*. New York: Knopf (1963).

Lionni, Leo. *Tili y el muro, Listos ¡Ya!* Orlando: Harcourt Brace Jovanovich (1993).

Long, Sheron. *¿Cuál es el mío?, Pan y Canela, Colección* B. Carmel: Hampton-Brown Books (1995).

Macías, Elva. *Laronda de la luna, El sueño del dragón*. México, D.F.: Ediciones Corunda (1994).

Madrigal, S. *Granjas*. Carmel: Hampton-Brown Books (1992).

Marcus, Elizabeth. *Quiero conocer la vida de las plantas, Quiero conocer*. México, D.F.: Sistemas Técnicos de Edición (1987).

Marcus, Elizabeth. *Quiero conocer la vida de los animales, Quiero conocer*. México, D.F.: SITESA (1987).

Martin, Bill Jr., and Archanbault, John. *Here are my hands*. New York: Henry Holt and Co. (1985).

Marzollo, Jean. *I'm a seed*. New York: Scholastic (1996).

Mateos, Rocío López. *Don José, su familia y sus plantas*. México, D.F.: Instituto Nacional Indigenista (1991).

Mateos, Rocío López. *La milpa de Don Ricardo*. México, D.F.: Instituto Nacional Indigenista (1992).

McMillan, Bruce. *Growing colors*. New York: William Morrow & Co. (1988).

Miller, Margaret. *Mis cinco sentidos*. Carmel: Hampton-Brown Books (1994).

Mirtín, Teresa Clerc. *Imagínate. Yo soy yo*. Boston: Houghton Mifflin Company (1993).

Moore, Jo Ellen, and Evans, Joy. *Las plantas*. (Ficklin, Dora, and Wolfe, Liz, Trans.) Monterey: Evan-moor Corp (1992).

Mora, Pat. *¿Qué dice el desierto?* Boston: Houghton Mifflin (1993).

Morris, Ann. *Con cariño.* Carmel: Hampton-Brown Books (1990).

Morris, Ann. *Hats, hats, hats.* New York: Lothrop, Lee & Shepard Books (1989).

Morris, Ann. *Houses and homes.* New York: Lothrop, Lee & Shepard Books (1992).

Morris, Clara Sánchez de. *César Chávez: Líder laboral.* Cleveland: Modern Curriculm Press (1994).

Murphy, Barnes. *Un jardín en tu dormitorio, El niño quiere saber.* Barcelona: Ediciones Torray (1983).

Nazoa, Aquiles. *Fábula de la ratoncita presumida.* Caracas: Ediciones Ekaré-Banco del Libro (1985).

Neruda, Pablo. *El libro de las preguntas.* Vol. Editorial Andrés Bello. Santiago de Chile (1987).

Paqueforet, Marcus. *A comer, mi bebé, Libros del Rincón.* México, D.F.: Hachette Latinoamérica/SEP (1993).

Paqueforet, Marcus. *A dormir, mi bebé, Libros del Rincón.* México, D.F.: Hachette Latinoamérica/SEP (1993).

Paqueforet, Marcus. *A pasear, mi bebé, Libros del Rincón.* México, D.F.: Hachette Latinoamérica/SEP (1993).

Paqueforet, Marcus. *Un cariñito, mi bebé, Libros del Rincón.* México, D.F.: Hachette Latinoamérica/SEP (1993).

Parra, Nicanor. *Sinfonía de cuna, en cuencto.* México, D.F.: CIDCLI (1992).

Parkes, Brenda, and Smith, Judith. *El patito feo.* Crystal Lake: Rigby (1989 Spanish trans.).

Parkes, Brenda. *¿Quién está en la choza?* (Flores, Barbara, Trans.) Crystal Lake: Rigby (1990).

Parramón, J.M., and Sales, G. *Mi primera visita a la granja, Mi primera visita.* Woodbury: Barron's (1990).

Peña, Luis de la. *Cosecha de versos y refranes, Literatura Infantil.* México, D.F.: CONAFE (1989).

Perera, Hilda. *Pepín y el abuelo.* Boston: Houghton Mifflin (1993).

Pratt, Kristin Joy. *Un paseo por el bosque lluvioso.* Nevada City: Dawn Publications (1993).

Ramírez, Elisa. *Adivinazas indígenas, Colección Piñata.* México, D.F.: Editorial Patria (1984).

Rius, María, and Parramon, Josep María. *El campo.* Woodbury: Barron's (1987).

Romero, Olga. *Con mi familia*. Carmel: Hampton-Brown Books (1996).

Sabines, Jaime. *La luna, Reloj de versos*. México, D.F.: CIDCLI (1990).

Sánchez, J.L. García, and Pacheco, M.A. *El niño que tenía dos ojos*. (Azaola, Miguel, ed., *Los derechos del niño*.) Madrid: Altea (1988).

Sanchez, J.L. García, and Pacheco, M.A. *La niña sin nombre*. (Azaola, Miguel, ed., *Los derechos del niño*.) Madrid: Altea (1988).

Saville, Malcolm. *Explorando el bosque, El niño quiere saber*. Barcelona: Ediciones Toray (1982).

Scholastic. *Los panes del mundo*. Supplement to *Scholastic News*. New York: Scholastic (1993).

Seale, Jan, and Tafolla, Carmen. *La marrana dormida. Yo Soy Yo*. (Barrera, Rosalinda, ed.) Boston: Houghton Mifflin (1993).

Seale, Jan, and Ramírez, Alfonso. *Tomates, California*. Boston: Houghton Mifflin (1993).

Sealey, Leonard. *Animales*. (Sealey, Leonard, ed., *Colección nuestro mundo*.) Barcelona: Editorial Juventud (1979).

Sealey, Leonard. *Plantas*. (Sealey, Leonard, ed., *Colección nuestro mundo*.) Barcelona: Editorial Juventud (1979).

Sempere, Vicky. *ABC*. Caracas, Venezuela: Ediciones Ekaré-Banco del Libro (1987).

Sheldon, Dyan. *El canto de las ballenas*. (Rivera, Nelson, Trans.) Caracas, Venezuela: Ediciones Ekaré-Banco del Libro (1993).

Somme, Lauritz, and Kalas, Sybille. *La familia del pingüino*. México, D.F.: SITESA (1991).

Spier, Peter. *Gente*. Barcelona: Editorial Lumen (1993).

Spier, Peter. *People*. New York: The Trumpet Club (1980).

Tabor, Nancy María Grande. *Somos un arco iris: We are a rainbow*. Watertown: Charlesbridge Publishing (1995).

Taylor, Kim, and Burton, Jane. *Frog, See how they grow!* London: Dorling Kindersley (1991).

Taylor, Kim, and Burton, Jane. *Ranitas, Mira cómo crecen*. México, D.F.: SITESA (1992).

Thomas, Jane Resh. *Lights on the river*. New York: Hyperion Books for Children (1994).

Tokuda, Wendy, and Hall, Richard. *Humphrey the lost whale*. Torrance: Heian International (1986).

Torres, Edna. *El desierto.* (Fonseca, Rodolfo, ed., *Educación ambiental.*) México, D.F.: CONAFE (1994).

Urbina, Joaquín. *La culebra verde.* Caracas, Venezuela: Gráficas Armitano.

Walker, Colin. *Las plantas, Concept science en español.* Cleveland: Modern Curriculum Press (1995).

Walker, Colin. *Las semillas crecen.* (Andujar, Gloria, Trans., Pye, Wendy, ed., *Sunshine science series.*) Bothell: Wright Group (1995).

Walker, Colin. *Plantas y semillas.* (Andujar, Gloria, Trans., Pye, Wendy, ed., *Sunshine science series.*) Bothell: Wright Group (1995).

Watts, Claire, and Parsons, Alexandra. *Experimenta con las plantas.* (Rodríguez, Beatriz, Trans.) Madrid: CESMA (1993).

Watts, Barrie. *Duck, See how they grow!* London: Dorling Kindersley (1991).

Watts, Barrie. *Patitos, Mira cómo crecen.* México, D.F.: SITESA (1992).

Wexo, John Bonnett. Los animales en extinción. *Zoobooks* (1981).

Williams, Sherley. *Working cotton.* Orlando: Harcourt Brace Jovanovich (1992).

Willow, Diane, and Jacques, Laura. *Dentro de la selva tropical.* Watertown: Charlesbridge Publishing (1993).

Wright, Alexandra. *¿Les echaremos de menos?* Watertown: Charlesbridge Publishing (1993).

Zak, Monica. *Salven mi selva.* México, D.F.: Sistemas Técnicos de Edición (1989).

Zawisza, Tita. *Conoce a nuestros insectos.* Caracas, Venezuela: Ediciones Ekaré-Banco del Libro (1982).

Zenzes, Gertrudias. *De la semilla a la fruta.* México, D.F.: Fernández Editores (1987).

Professional References

Ada, Alma Flor. Creative reading: A relevant methodology for language minority children. *NABE '87. Theory, research, and application: Selected papers.* (Malavé, L.M., ed.) Buffalo: State University of New York (1988).

Ada, Alma Flor, and Olave, María del Pilar. *Hagamos Caminos.* Reading: Addison-Wesley (1986).

Adams, Marilyn. *Beginning to Read: Thinking and learning about print.* Cambridge: MIT Press (1990).

Alvarez, Carmen Espinosa Elenes de. *Mi libro mágico.* México, D.F.: Enrique Sainz Editores (1979).

Anderson, Richard, Hiebert, Elfrida, Scott, Judith, and Wilkinson, Ian. *Becoming a nation of readers: The report of the commission on reading.* Champaign: Center for the Study of Reading (1985).

Barrera, Rosalinda. Reading in Spanish: Insights from children's miscues. *Learning to read in different languages.* (Hudelson, S., ed.) Washington, D.C.: Center for Applied Linguistics (1981).

Barrera, Rosalinda, and Crawford, Alan. *Vamos, Programa de lectura en español de Houghton Mifflin.* Boston: Houghton Mifflin (1987).

Bellenger, Lionel. *Los métodos de lectura.* Barcelona: Oikos-Tau (1979).

Braslavsky, Berta. *La escuela puede.* Buenos Aires: Aique (1992).

Braslavsky, Berta. *La querella de los métodos en la enseñanza de la lectura.* Buenos Aires: Kapelusz (1962).

Brown, Hazel, and Brian Cambourne. *Read and retell.* Portsmouth: Heinemann (1987).

Buchanan, Ethel. *Spelling for whole language classrooms.* Winnipeg: Whole Language Consultants, Ltd. (1989).

California Reading Task Force. Every child a reader. Sacramento: California Department of Education (1995).

Calkins, Lucy. *The art of teaching writing*. Portsmouth: Heinemann (1986).

Calkins, Lucy. *Living between the lines*. Portsmouth: Heinemann (1991).

Castedo, Mirta Luisa. Construcción de lectores y escritores. *Lectura y vida 16*, (3) 5–25 (1995).

Cervantes, Carolina. The support of Spanish language literature in reading, writing, and second language acquisition. Unpublished manuscript (1992).

Chall, Jean. *Learning to read: The great debate*. New York: McGraw Hill (1967).

Chomsky, Carol. Reading, writing, and phonology. *Harvard Education Review 40*, (2) 287–309 (1970).

Clark, Irene. *Zoo-phonics in español*. Groveland: Zoo-phonics. (1994).

Collier, Virgina P. Acquiring a second language for school. *Directions in Language and Education*. Washington, D.C.: National Clearninghouse for Bilingual Education NCBE (1995).

Crowell, Caryl G. Documenting the strengths of bilingual readers. *Primary Voices K–6 3*, (4) 32–37 (1995).

Cummings, D.W. *American English spelling*. Baltimore: Johns Hopkins University Press (1988).

Dubois, Mará Eugenia. Algunas interrogantes sobre comprensión de la lectura. *Lectura y Vida 4*, 14–19 (1984).

Dubois, María Eugenia. Lectura, escritura y formación docente. *Lectura y Vida 16*, (2) 5–12 (1995).

Edelsky, C. Bilingual children's writing: Fact and fiction. *Richness in writing: Empowering ESL students*. (Johnson, D., and Roen, D., ed.) New York: Longman, 165–176 (1989).

Edelsky, C. *Writing in a bilingual program: Había una vez*. Norwood: Ablex (1986).

Ferreiro, Emilia. Diversidad y proceso de alfabetización: De la celebración a la toma de conciencia. *Lectura y Vida 15*, (3) 5–14 (1994).

Ferreiro, Emilia, and Teberosky, Ana. *Literacy before schooling*. (Castro, K.G., Trans.) Portsmouth: Heinemann (1982).

Ferreiro, Emilia, and Teberosky, Ana. *Los sistemas de escritura en el desarrollo del niño*. México: Signi Ventiuno Editores (1979).

Flesch, Rudolph. *Why Johnny can't read*. New York: Harper and Row (1955).

Flesch, Rudolph. *Why Johnny still can't read*. New York: Harper and Row (1981).

Freeman, Yvonne S. Celebremos la literatura: Is it possible with a Spanish reading program? In *Report card on basal readers: Part II*. (Shannon, P., and Goodman, K.S., ed.) 115–128. Katonah: Richard C. Owen (1993).

Freeman, Yvonne S. The contemporary Spanish basal in the United States. Doctoral dissertation, University of Arizona, Tucson (1987).

Freeman, Yvonne S. The contemporary Spanish basal reader in the United States: How does it reflect current knowledge of the reading process?" *NABE Journal 13*, (1) 59–74 (1988).

Freeman, Yvonne S. Do Spanish methods and materials reflect current understanding of the reading process? *The Reading Teacher 41*, (7) 654–664 (1988).

Freeman, Yvonne S. Métodos de lectura en español: ¿Reflejan nuestro conocimiento actual del proceso de lectura? *Lectura y Vida 9*, (3) 20–28 (1988).

Freeman, Yvonne S., Goodman, Yetta M., and Serra, Marisela B. Revalorización del estudiante bilingüe mediante un programa de lectura basado en literatura auténtica. *Lectura y Vida 16*, (1) 13–24 (1995).

Freeman, Yvonne S., and Whitesell, Lynn. What preschoolers already know about print. *Educational Horizons 64*, (1) 22–25 (1985).

Freire, Paulo. *Pedagoía del oprimido*. México, D.F.: Siglo Veintiuno Editores (1970).

Freire, Paulo, and Macedo, Donaldo. *Literacy: Reading the word and the world*. South Hadley: Bergin and Garvey (1987).

Goldenberg, Claude, and Gallimore, R. Local knowledge, research knowledge, and educational change: A case study of early Spanish reading improvement. *Educational Researcher 20*, (8) 2–14 (1991).

Goodman, Kenneth. Cues and miscues in reading: A linguistic study. *Elementary English 42*, (6) 635–642 (1965).

Goodman, Kenneth. *El lenguaje integral, Serie de la palabra*. Buenos Aires: Aique (1995).

Goodman, Kenneth. *Lenguaje integral*. (Osuna, Adelina Arellano, Trans.) Mérida: Editorial Venezolana (1989).

Goodman, Kenneth. *On reading*. Portsmouth: Heinemann (1996).

Goodman, Kenneth. *Phonics phacts*. Portsmouth: Heinemann (1993).

Goodman, Kenneth. Reading: A psycholinguistic guessing game. *Journal of the Reading Specialist* May 126–135 (1967).

Goodman, Kenneth. Revaluing readers and reading. *Revaluing troubled readers*, Tucson: University of Arizona, Office of Language and Literacy, 1-11. (1986b).

Goodman, Kenneth. Unity in reading. *Becoming readers in a complex society: Eighty-third yearbook of the National Society for the Study of Education*. (Purves, A., and Niles, O., eds.) Chicago: University of Chicago Press 79–114 (1984).

Goodman, Kenneth. *What's whole in whole language*. Portsmouth: Heinemann (1986a).

Goodman, Kenneth, Goodman, Yetta, and Hood, Wendy, (eds.). *The whole language evaluation book*. Portsmouth: Heinemann (1989).

Goodman, Kenneth, Smith, E.B., Meredith, R., and Goodman, Yetta. *Language and thinking in school: A whole language curriculum*. 3rd ed. Katonah: Richard C. Owen (1987).

Goodman, Yetta, (ed.). *How children construct literacy*. Newark: International Reading Association (1990).

Goodman, Yetta, and Goodman, Kenneth. Vygotsky in a whole language perspective. *Vygotsky and education: Instructional implications and applications of sociohistorical psychology*. (Moll, L., ed.) Cambridge: Cambridge University Press 223–250 (1990).

Goodman, Yetta, and Marek, Ann. *Retrospective miscue analysis: Revaluing readers and reading*. Katonah: Richard C. Owen (1996).

Goodman, Yetta, Watson, Dorothy, and Burke, Carolyn. *Reading strategies: Focus on comprehension*. Katonah: Richard C. Owen (1996).

Goodman, Yetta, and Wilde, Sandra, (eds.). *Literacy events in a community of young writers*. New York: Teachers College Press (1992).

Graves, Donald. *Writing: Teachers and children at work*. Portsmouth: Heinemann (1983).

Halliday, Michael A.K. *Learning how to mean*. London: Edward Arnold (1975).

Hansen, Jane. Comprehension questions to make reading and writing connections. *Graduate seminar in literacy*. Fresno, CA (1989).

Hansen, Jane. *When writers read*. Portsmouth: Heinemann (1987).

Harste, Jerome. Reflection. Connection. In conference booklet, Whole Language Umbrella Conference. Niagara Falls, NY (1992).

Heldt, Antonio Barbosa. *Cómo han aprendido a leer y a escribir los mexicanos*. México, D.F.: Editorial Pax-Mexico (1971).

Hendrix, Charles. *Cómo enseñar a leer por el método global*. Buenos Aires: Editorial Kapelusz (1952).

Honig, Bill. *How should we teach our children to read?* Thousand Oaks: Corwin Press (1996).

Hooked on phonics. Gateway Educational Products, USA (1984).

Hudelson, Sarah. An investigation of the oral reading behaviors of native Spanish speakers reading in Spanish. *Learning to read in different languages.* (Hudelson, S., ed.) Washington, D.C.: Center for Applied Linguistics (1981).

Hudelson, Sarah. *Write on: Children writing in ESL.* Englewood Cliffs: Prentice Hall Regents (1989).

Juel, Connie. *Learning to read and write in one elementary school.* New York: Springer-Verlag (1994).

Marek, Ann. Using evaluation as an instructional strategy for adult readers. In *The whole language evaluation book.* (Goodman, K., Goodman, Y., and Hood, W., eds.) Portsmouth: Heinemann, 157–164 (1989).

Moreno, María Stella Serrano. La enseñanza-aprendizaje de la lectura. Universidad de los Andes (1982).

Myer, Karen. *Estrellita: Accelerated beginning Spanish reading* [videotape]. Oxnard: Estrellita (1995).

Pellicer, Félix. *Didáctica de la lengua española.* Madrid: Magisterio Español (1969).

Pérez, Bertha, and Torres-Guzman, María. *Learning in two worlds: An integrated Spanish-English biliteracy approach.* New York: Longman (1992).

Pinker, Steven. *The language instinct: How the mind creates language.* New York: William Morrow and Company (1994).

Ramsey, Marathon Montrose, and Spaulding, Robert K. *A textbook of modern Spanish.* New York: Holt, Rinehart and Winston (1963).

Read, C. Preschool children's knowledge of English phonology. *Harvard Education Review 41*, (1) 1–34 (1971).

Rigg, Pat, and Enright, D. Scott. *Children and ESL: Integrating perspectives.* Washington, D.C.: Teachers of English to Speakers of Other Languages (1986).

Rodríguez, María Elena. Hablar . . . en la escuela: ¿Para qué? . . . ¿Cómo? *Lectura y vida 16*, (3) 31–40 (1995).

Roper/Schneider, H. Spelling, word recognition, and phonemic awareness among first grade children. University of Texas (1984).

Rosenblatt, Louise. *The reader, the text, the poem: The transactional theory of the literary work.* Carbondale: Southern Illinois University Press (1978).

Sequeida, Julia, and Seymour, Guillermo. El razonamiento estratégico como factor de desarrollo de la expresión escrita y de la comprensión de lectura. *Lectura y Vida 16*, (2) 13–20 (1995).

Silabario Larense. Caracas: Editorial Larense (1994).

Silabario obelisco. Caracas: Editorial Larense (1994).

Simon, T. *Pédagogic expérimentale*. Paris: Armand Colin (1924).

Smith, Frank. *Reading without nonsense*, (2). New York: Teachers College Press (1985).

Smith, Frank. *Understanding reading*. New York: Holt, Rinehart and Winston (1971).

Solé i Gallart, Isabel. El placer de leer. *Lectura y vida 16*, (3) 25–30 (1995).

Thonis, Eleanor. *Literacy for America's Spanish-speaking children*. Newark, Delaware: International Reading Association (1976).

Watson, Dorothy, (ed.). *Ideas and insights: Language arts in the elementary school*. Urbana: National Council of Teachers of English (1987).

Watson, Dorothy. Whole language: Why bother? *The Reading Teacher 47*, (8) 600–607 (1994).

Weaver, Constance. *Reading process and practice: From socio-psycholinguistics to whole language*. 2nd ed. Portsmouth: Heinemann (1994).

Wilde, Sandra. *You kan red this! Spelling and punctuation for whole language classrooms, K–6*. Portsmouth: Heinemann (1992).

INDEX